Xara® Xtreme 5: The Official Guide

id Bouton

Mc
Graw
Hill

New York   Chicago   San Francisco   Lisbon
London   Madrid   Mexico City   Milan   New Delhi
San Juan   Seoul   Singapore   Sydney   Toronto

Library of Congress Cataloging-in-Publication Data

McGraw-Hill books are available at special quantity discounts to use as premiums and sales promotions, or for use in corporate training programs. To contact a representative, please c-mail us at bulksales@mcgraw-hill.com.

Xara® Xtreme 5: The Official Guide

1234567890   DOC DOC   019

ISBN   978-0-07-162559-3
MHID   0-07-162559-3

Sponsoring Editor	Roger Stewart
Editorial Supervisor	Jody McKenzie
Project Manager	Smita Rajan, Glyph International
Acquisitions Coordinators	Joya Anthony
Technical Editor	Mara Zebest
Copy Editor	Malinda McCain
Proofreader	Carole Shields
Indexer	Jack Lewis
Production Supervisor	Jim Kussow
Composition	Glyph International
Illustration	Glyph International and Gary Bouton
Art Director, Cover	Jeff Weeks

This book is dedicated to my father, Jack Orvin Bouton,
who bought me my first set of pencils.

About the Author

Gary David Bouton has been illustrating professionally for over 30 years; he became an author of graphics software documentation in 1992 and this is his 25th book. A user of Xara since 1995, Gary is a firm believer in the convergence of art tools and the synergy of combining digital and traditional artistic concepts and ideas.

Gary has received four international awards in desktop publishing and illustration, and he teaches what he practices, through books ranging from the *Inside Adobe Photoshop* series, to video editing and CGI, modeling and rendering, vector drawing, and creating web content. Gary and his wife Barbara host The Pixel Dust Forum at theboutons.com, a haven for artists and anyone who appreciates art. The site also offers support for this and Gary's past books and contains several repositories for downloading free content (and some *non-free* creations at the store).

About the Technical Editor

Mara Zebest is a graphic artist who uses her knowledge and skills in both volunteer and commercial work. Mara has taught classes on Adobe and Microsoft programs for a local school district and has been a guest instructor at a nearby community college. She has experience working in a graphics marketing department, which has also afforded her printing production experience. Mara has been a contributing author and technical editor for numerous books covering a multitude of Adobe and Microsoft products.

Contents at a Glance

Contents

Foreword

When designers and artists today need to express an idea, it is no longer the familiar pencil and brush we turn to. A creative synergy made up of traditional and new media types is the Gold Standard, a combination of illustrations, photographs, text, and even animation can be found in the final work. So naturally we are obliged to turn to Program A, and then Program B, and so on to realize a completed vision.

To accommodate the designers' desire to avoid switching applications every minute to complete their graphical ideas, many applications today extend their features with each new version. A popular photo editing program has grown from a shop into a warehouse, with new features and tools that address fields other than photography. Each new release of the leading vector drawing package adds desktop publishing tools and templates, and desktop publishing programs adopt photo correction tools.

In addition to extending a program's features, this method of coping with user needs obliges artists to reacquaint themselves with the interface and heightens a learning curve that is often already too steep. While it is true that good graphic design requires the mastery of many skills, it only makes sense to combine the tools required by those skills into single, flexible program. Why should people be forced to buy and learn three or more separate applications to create one document?

I wanted to build a sleek, integrated multifunction Swiss Army knife for document creation and not an ungainly "3 separate apps in one" invention. Xara Xtreme takes the convergence of media types in visual communications to the obvious and logical conclusion. With Xara Xtreme, you have a single creative application that fuses the best of vector graphics, photo editing, website building, animation, and page layout features into one powerful, fully integrated software program. With Xara Xtreme you work in one consistent environment and use tools that serve several functions in a truly intuitive fashion, which gives you the results you desire very quickly.

Gary Bouton has followed the history of Xara from its beginning, in 1995, through to the very latest version. He has seen the program evolve from being a very fast drawing program, sold by Corel, to being the versatile, all-around graphics program it is today.

Gary has authored and co-authored more than 25 books from a variety of publishers, covering a range of media disciplines. But regardless of the topic, all of his books have something in common. They not only teach readers how to use graphics software—understanding the settings and tools and commands—but they teach readers how to express themselves artistically.

Gary is not only a capable and confident writer, he is also a talented and versatile artist. To really show off the capabilities of the software and to inspire others, you need to be an artist as well as a great writer. As you can see from the scores of tutorials he's created throughout this book, Gary knows how to get the most out of the program. His examples, along with the gallery of Xara artists from around the world included in the book, will inspire you and show just how much Xara Xtreme is capable of.

Give it a try! In this wired and competitive visual world, you'll want to take your ideas to the extreme. Let our workspace and this wonderful book unleash your creative imagination right now!

Charles Moir
Principle Designer of Xara Xtreme
Founder, The Xara Group

Acknowledgments

This book would not be a book without the fine, seasoned, brilliant programmers at The Xara Group. I'd like to thank:

- **Charles Moir, CEO and founder of The Xara Group** For his invaluable assistance and advice, usually at a moment's notice, verifying specific steps and the inner workings of various tools in this new version of Xtreme.

- **Bhavesh Bhavan, Neil Howe, and the rest of the terrific folks at The Xara Group** They went the extra mile and answered technical questions, in PlainSpeak, as they were busting to meet their own deadlines for the release of Version 5.

- **Kate Moir and Nova Fisher** For burning the midnight oil getting the first Xara GrandMaster Awards in order.

- **Daniel Will-Harris, Gary Priester, and Chris Dickman** For agreeing to the Herculean task of helping judge the GrandMaster Awards, when there were *scores* of world-class compositions we had to narrow down to six.

Other gifted individuals also helped to make this book what it is, and happily I'm still friends with them! Thanks to:

- **Matt Wagner** My agent, for helping me find the right publisher for this book. It has been a 10-year pipe dream of which Matt has shared the past three.

- **Roger Stewart** For really believing in this title. From the word "go," Roger saw that Xara Xtreme is an important program, and he has been nothing less than 200% supportive of our effort to make this application irresistible in the hands of those who have a deep desire to express themselves graphically.

- **Nick Curtis** Typographer Extraordinaire and all-around Good Guy, for giving McGraw-Hill Professional and The Xara Group permission to distribute special editions of several of his most popular typefaces.

- **Mara Zebest** Who has put up with technical editing my books for longer than I can remember. Thanks, Mara!

- **Barbara Bouton** My wife and partner, without whose unflagging devotion and creative support during these marathon stretches, writing books would probably leave me wandering out in our yard with a divining rod and an aluminum foil hat.

- **Nicky Elliott-Producer at Monkey Pants Media in Australia** For helping us secure permissions to use Bang Shang A Lang's media in this book. Also, for allowing us to feature BSL's music video. Visit www.monkeypants.com.au if you can't physically make it to Oz, mate.

- **Bruce Carter and Mark Mulligan, Head Bangers** For graciously allowing us to use the band's media in Chapter 11.
- **Special thanks to Jody McKenzie, Jim Kussow, Malinda McCain, Smita Rajan, and the rest of the fine people at McGraw-Hill** For making this book everything I anticipated and much more than I dreamed of.

Introduction

Guiding Yourself to Artistic Accomplishments

You have probably heard at least once in your life the difference between *knowledge* and *wisdom*. Knowledge resides in a vacuum; you need to take its lid off and wave the container around a few times before the contents settle into wisdom.

This has similarly been my experience writing documentation about computer software. I believe that some facts are good, but facts need to be *contextualized*—they need to germinate—before they can become a part of a solution to a goal set before you.

Xara Xtreme 5: The Official Guide would not be a guide at all if it did not *lead* you someplace. For example (a poor example), you come to a dead end when the instructions for using a tool consist only of:

1. To draw a circle, choose Tool, hold CTRL, and then drag.

We would be in a lot of trouble if the instructions for operating a chain saw were this presumptuous.

Circles are *fine* to draw, but seldom do they represent a *complete* artistic idea. In Xtreme, complex, visually interesting compositions often begin with simple shapes, so a tutorial needs to reflect this. As a complete idea—and a complete tutorial in which drawing a circle is *in context*— let us try drawing a crescent moon.

1. Create a circle by holding CTRL while dragging with the Ellipse Tool.

2. Using the Selector Tool, drag the circle above and to the left of the circle's original position on the page. Before releasing the mouse button, tap the right mouse button to drop a copy of the circle above the original.

3. Press CTRL-A to select all, and then press CTRL-2 to subtract the copy of the circle from the original (or choose Arrange | Combine Shapes | Subtract Shapes).

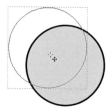

| 1. CTRL and drag with Ellipse Tool. | 2. Drag with Selector Tool, right-click, and then release both mouse buttons. | 3. Select both circles and then press CTRL-2 to subtract. |

That is really as hard as it gets with the tutorials in this book; you are guided toward a goal, you can modify the goal to suit scores of personal art needs, and the end goal is as simple or as ambitious as the situation calls for. The Xara Xtreme interface provides no mysteries but only things you have not discovered yet. The intention of this book is to work the element of discovery into a creative *process*: you pick up the knowledge of how a tool or feature works, you discover several purposes for the tool, and finally you take your newfound wisdom and apply it—to realize an idea on paper. The thing we call *skill* lies outside of *The Official Guide's* curriculum: skill comes with time and practice. If you take the time, this book provides you with the *other* stuff, so your footing is sound in a new application, your bearings are based first on knowledge and eventually on instinct, and sooner than you know it, WYIIWYG: *What you imagine is what you get.*

What You Need to Bring to the Party

In a word, you will get the most out of Xara Xtreme if you bring along the right *attitude*. If you are serious, somber, and intent on conquering a new application, you will defeat the purpose of learning to work with a design program. Work can be *fun*—Leonardo DaVinci was an extremely light and fun guy (or so Mona said)—and getting into the *spirit* of self-expression is an essential.

■ By design, Xara Xtreme is laid out so it is almost transparent to the user. This should be your personal goal while learning Xtreme. You will know you have arrived at a new creative stratum when you are drawing something and are concentrating on your work rather than on the tool you are using. Most of Xara's Toolbox tools serve more than one function, depending on your mouse gestures and any keyboard modifiers you are pressing. Therefore, after you have taken time to develop skill, you will feel as though the Xtreme workspace is something *different* from a standard computer program interface. It is responsive, *truly* intuitive to use, and gives you the feedback artists need when they use physical media. If you find yourself becoming immersed in Xara Xtreme, do not freak. You are simply in your element, doing what it is that brings an idea to life.

▓ You will find more than you imagine in Xtreme if you allow for some yin and yang to occur. That is, you command Xtreme to perform certain calculations, but also leave yourself open to letting the application's features influence your work and your ideas. You will quickly discover new purposes for tools; the TalkGraphics forums have new posts almost daily about something strange and wonderful an Xtreme user has discovered. Xara Xtreme is as extensible as your own curiosity allows it to be.

▓ Get excited about all the unrealized possibilities you have before you with Xara Xtreme. It is not just an artist's prerogative to have a passion about waking up each morning and contemplating all the great new stuff you will accomplish; it is a personal responsibility. I have been working with Xara for over a decade (taking breaks once in a while) and do not feel I have plumbed its depths. Do not see this as intimidating, but rather as a source for *excitement*. You have wrapped presents under the tree every day.

The Structure of The Official Guide

A new version of a program is always a challenge to document, to address the needs of first-time users plus current users who have upgraded. The content of *The Official Guide*, therefore, is structured to get you up and running in the first few chapters, and then the book branches out to cover new, specific areas of Version 5. If you are new to vector drawing, Chapter 1 is an excellent place to begin; by Chapter 5—which shows you how to create and apply object fills—you will have enough details tucked away to go exploring some of the how-tos described in chapters dedicated to a single artistic area. Chapter 13, for example, shows you how to draw elements into photographs whose presence is undetectable from the photo. Chapter 11 flattens the learning curve for creating a multi-page website—complete with links to video and web widgets that will make your first website look like you have been doing this for years.

Although books are analog devices, the truly useful aspect of them that has survived the ages is that you can bookmark a place a lot faster than in a web browser. Learn exactly what it is you want to learn today, lend your learning experience some quality time (shut the door to your study after soundproofing it), and I think you will be exceptionally satisfied with what you will see you can create.

How to Download the Tutorial Files

About the tutorial files: You can download all the files you'll need to complete the tutorials in this book—and some bonus content here and there—at www.mhprofessional.com/computingdownload and at theboutons.com, a mirror site for files. At the beginning of each chapter, you'll see a Downloads icon. Download Chapter 04.zip, for example, before you begin Chapter 4's exercises; extract the files to a location that you can easily find on your hard disk. Then, when a step calls for you to load "Zebra acquires non-voting stock.xar" (or any native Xara file—the author's just being silly here), you do so in your copy of Xara Xtreme.

Similarly, several typefaces are included with the example files; you should install these fonts before beginning a tutorial that calls for the fonts. Bitmaps are also part of the tutorials; in Xara Xtreme, you import a copy of these bitmaps by pressing CTRL-ALT-I or choosing File | Import.

Photographic Retouching

The PDF Bonus Chapter "Photographic Retouching"—and the tutorial files—show you how to alter bitmap images. If you want to resize only the important part of a photo, Xara Xtreme 5 now features Content-Aware Photo Resizing.

Live Effects work on both vector and bitmap images to correct and stylize photography. The Panorama Maker is an easy-to-use, scripted feature that intelligently stitches a series of photos together. The Bonus Chapter also shows you how to retouch a significant object out of a photograph—using vector shapes.

Download and dig in! It's our gift to our readers and everyone who loves flawlessly enhanced photography.

www.mhprofessional.com/computingdownload

mirror site:

www.theboutons.com

1

Up and Running with Xara Xtreme

After you've launched Xara Xtreme and closed the Tips box, you're presented with a new blank document. The interface might look sparser than other graphics applications, but tremendous design power is there—it's simply not in the way so you can concentrate on your work.

This chapter provides an orientation to where the features are located, how to access and use tools and other features. Also, if you are just starting out with vector drawing, you'll learn about shapes, how to create something visually meaningful and interesting, and in general how vector artwork differs from bitmap paintings and photos.

 You can uncheck the Show Tips On StartUp if you don't want to see the Tips box each time you launch Xara Xtreme. If you want to see the box in the future, you can access it from the Help I Tip Of The Day menu; the toggle box to turn it on can be reactivated here.

 Download and extract the contents of Chapter01.zip, which contains everything you need to work through this chapter's tutorial steps.

Understanding Today's Drawing Programs

When your goal is to explore what can be done with an application, it makes sense to understand an application's target *purpose*. Today's design programs can be roughly divided into two categories: *raster* (more commonly called *pixel* and *bitmap*) paint-type programs and *vector* drawing programs. Xara Xtreme belongs to the category of vector drawing programs, as do its competitors, CorelDraw and Adobe Illustrator. However, most vector drawing applications can also handle bitmap imports and even generate bitmap images, so the dividing line has become somewhat smudged. More designers are familiar with bitmap paint programs than with vector drawing programs, and the following sections describe the differences. As you work through this book, you proceed with a concrete understanding of how to get the most out of what Xara Xtreme does.

Bitmaps and Vectors

Bitmap-based design work is relatively simple to understand when compared to vector drawing: A bitmap is a "canvas," divided into cells to which you apply color by using a brush or other tool. The cell, the basic unit of color in a bitmap, is called a *pixel*, a placeholder for color, which has an undefined size until an artist contextualizes a bitmap drawing by using real-world units. Bitmaps are measured in resolution, a fractional expression called pixels per inch. *Dots per inch* is slang we use; it actually refers to print resolution, but the two terms are used synonymously. Although bitmap programs enable artists to change the size of a bitmap image, this usually leads to some blurriness or other type of visual distortion. This is because all bitmap images are *resolution-dependent*, unlike vector drawings. The visual content of a bitmap-based image is a "done deal" with respect to resolution the moment you create a new document, such as a digital photo or painting. You cannot ask a bitmap application to intelligently change the resolution of a bitmap image any more than you can ask a digital camera to go back and add detail to a photo you're unhappy with. Enlarging a bitmap always introduces some loss of focus and duplicated pixels without adding visual data.

Understanding the Unique Characteristics of Vector Artwork

Although paint programs might be fairly intuitive to use, they do not own the category of digital design media, largely because of the resolution dependence of bitmap images.

Vector drawing tools bring with them a host of design advantages over bitmap-based artwork:

- **Vector artwork can scale without distortion** Drawing programs do not use the canvas and pixel sort of math that bitmap programs do. The building blocks of vector artwork are *paths* and the *attributes* you assign to paths, most commonly *outline width* and *shape fill*. Vector artwork is resolution-*in*dependent;

the components of your design work are pure geometry (math), not based on page size or any other constraint. When, for example, you design something that eventually needs to be twice the size that you originally drew it, and you command Xara to scale the design up to 200%, the *geometry of your design remains intact* and only the design's *scale* on the page changes. Whether you print to a postage-stamp size or to the side of a camper van, you can use the same file for printing. The design details are shown exactly the same because the program is able to perform the mathematical calculations on the equations when resizing the lines and shapes you create. Happily, all *you* need to do is build the path lines and the application does the math for you.

- **Objects are not affixed to a canvas**   Part of the flexibility in designing vector artwork is that a new page is not only blank, but it's also a vacuum; shapes you create always float. If you have experience with bitmap-based programs such as Photoshop or Painter, an analogy is that vector programs surround shapes with transparency. However, shapes are independent of one another; they can be moved, scaled, and rotated ad infinitum, and they have a front-to-back order not only on the page but also on any number of layers you choose to create.

- **You edit to correct, with no need to erase**   Although a physical pencil usually has an eraser on its other end, you don't erase shapes, parts of shapes, or anything else when you've made a mistake. In fact, Xara doesn't have an eraser tool as most bitmap editing programs have. When you make a mistake designing a shape, you press CTRL-Z to perform Edit | Undo, you use the Shape Editor Tool and the Selector Tool to refine a nearly perfect shape, or you delete the shape or the points and line segments that make up unwanted parts of the shape.

Xara will generate bitmaps on-the-fly, so sharing a JPEG rendering of Xara artwork with a friend is quite easy.

Draw Once with Vectors, Use Many Times

A good question to ask yourself is when a bitmap paint program is appropriate for design work, and when you'd be wiser to turn to

Xara for a project. If you anticipate that the design you submit will never need significant revisions and will only be used at one set of dimensions—such as a photo you retouch—you might be safe to use a bitmap editing program. bitmap program. However, one of the beauties of designing with vectors is that your efforts never result in a set piece; you can scale individual shapes larger or smaller, move shapes (and groups of shapes), in general, and perform significant alterations to the composition of objects in seconds with vector designs.

Figure 1-1 demonstrates a perennial problem with bitmap-based designs, in this example, a detailed illustration of a watermelon. Clearly, a bitmap paint program was the wrong choice of applications when the recipient returns and wants a

Original bitmap

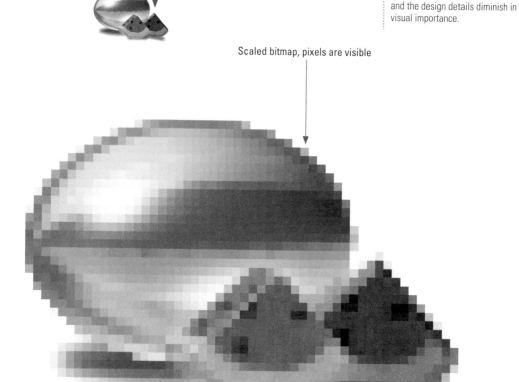

FIGURE 1-1 Bitmap designs have a finite number of pixels. To make the design larger, pixels are added, and the design details diminish in visual importance.

Scaled bitmap, pixels are visible

T-shirt sized version of the artwork. Once a bitmap has been painted or captured as a digital photograph, no program on Earth can intelligently *add* details automatically; it can only create new pixels based on an evaluation of the color pixels that already exist in the picture. Sophisticated design applications such as Xara can perform some blending and color averaging when making bitmap blow-ups, but because they are resolution-dependent, you'll never see more visual detail or quality. At best, the blown-up photo looks blurry, and at worst, the pixels that make up the details of the design become more prominent than the image itself.

On the other hand, the same watermelon illustration, drawn in Xara Xtreme, contains all the design details the artist cared to add. As a vector-type drawing, the watermelon slices can be individually moved, rotated, duplicated to serve 2–100 picnickers, and most importantly, scaled up (or down) with no loss of detail. Figure 1-2 shows examples of scaling, rotating, and reworking the composition and a wireframe view to show

FIGURE 1-2 Draw a shape and get a return investment on your labors.

Separate objects

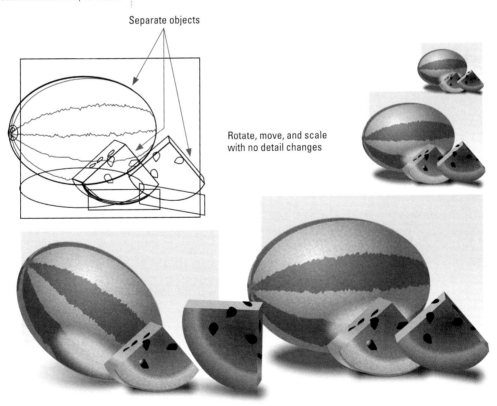

Rotate, move, and scale
with no detail changes

you exactly how few shapes were needed to create the drawing. Often, it is the fill and outline property you apply to shapes that gives a design visual robustness, and not always the intricacy of path you draw.

Exploring the Xara Interface

The following sections get you up to speed with the features in Xara Xtreme. You'll see a relationship between creating a shape with a tool and *assigning* an effect or other property to the shape; the interface is shown in Figure 1-3.

Most tools in Xara Xtreme serve more than one use. You use keyboard modifiers (CTRL and SHIFT, most often) in combination with dragging a tool on the page to change the action you perform. You also have the pop-up context menu you can access when using a tool; right-clicking provides you with several invaluable options.

The Items in the Interface

As in most design programs, your Xara tools are located in the Xara Xtreme Toolbar. A *control bar* is the name of the general category of interface elements that can dock or be floated, including the Toolbar.

To float a control bar, position your cursor toward the edge of the bar and then drag into the workspace—the area where the page and the pasteboard are. To dock a floating bar, drag it by the top to the position you intend it to dock—you'll see a dotted line preview of the bar when you're undocking or docking it. When the preview dotted line becomes thick, this is your signal to release the mouse button so the bar docks or floats.

Other control bars in Xara provide information about object location, areas where you can manually set positions and path outline width and provide additional settings for tools based on which tool is currently chosen. One of the most important bars in Xara contains the galleries; they're referred to as palettes in other applications and store all the resources you'll need for filling and stroking paths, plus a Designs gallery, invaluable for quickly accessing the drawings you may have installed

Infobar (contextual)   Standard bar   Galleries control bar   Drawing page   Pasteboard outside page

Pages

Toolbar

Color Editor

Color picker (eyedropper)

Set "no color"

Color line with Color gallery Standard Palette swatches loaded

Status line   A gallery (palette)

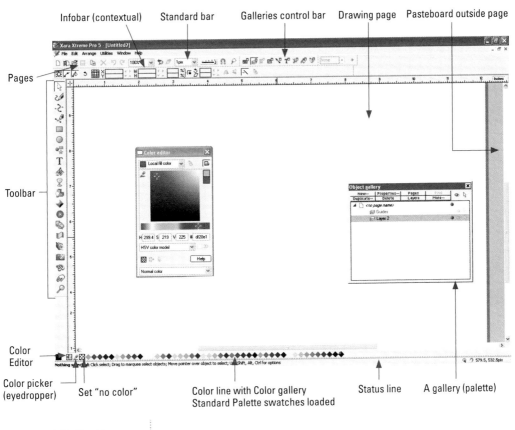

FIGURE 1-3 The Xara Xtreme interface

from the CD. Galleries are also great for cataloguing your own collections of your artwork.

■ **Galleries**   Toggle the various galleries on and off by clicking an icon on the Galleries control bar. A gallery appears and disappears at the last position where it floats in the interface. You will probably want to access the Object gallery most often, for adding layers and locating and moving objects.

The Object gallery not only lists all shapes on a page but also generates 16x16 pixel thumbnails representing individual shapes. If you are zoomed so close to the page that some objects are out of view, click on an object's mini-thumbnail and Xara zooms and pans you to the shape you've clicked.

■ **Pages**   Xara is capable of creating multi-page documents, perfect for desktop publishing documents. To create a new page (within the same document), click the Insert A New Blank Page After The Current Page icon on the Standard Toolbar, and you're moved to the blank new page onscreen. Xara multi-page documents are presented as a continuous-feed arrangement, easy to navigate by pressing PageUp and PageDown (or by dragging the middle mouse button to pan). To delete the current page, click Edit | Pages | Delete Current Page. If you are more comfortable with the desktop publishing metaphor of facing pages onscreen, you can press CTRL-SHIFT-O (Utilities | Options) and check Double Page Spread on the Page Size tab.

■ **Tools**   Many of the drawing tools serve multiple functions. For example, you can draw *and* edit by using the Shape Editor Tool. The Toolbar is covered in more detail in the following section. From top to bottom, the Toolbar is organized with tools for creating shapes, special effects and dynamic relations such as Contours and Blends, tools for dynamically editing an imported photo or other bitmap artwork, and the Push and Zoom Tools.

■ **The Color Line**   By default, the Xara color line is populated with the Standard Palette library of swatches. You show or hide color libraries via the Color gallery; you right-click a folder and then choose Show In Color Line. A permanent library cannot be directly added to or changed, and you know the swatches on the color line are from a library by their diamond shape. *Local* colors—colors specific to a document that you add to the color line—appear there by naming a color through the Color editor and the Color gallery. You can save your own colors to the color line by naming colors (covered in Chapter 5) and then saving a Xara file as a template via File | Save Template. To apply a solid color swatch to a shape, left-click a swatch when the object is selected, or drag a swatch and drop it onto a shape. You SHIFT-click a swatch to assign that swatch as a selected object's outline color; if a shape has no outline width, Xara applies a default width of one pixel when you SHIFT-click a swatch. When you drop a swatch onto a shape, you're in the

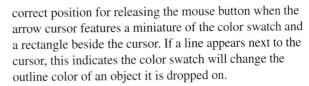

correct position for releasing the mouse button when the arrow cursor features a miniature of the color swatch and a rectangle beside the cursor. If a line appears next to the cursor, this indicates the color swatch will change the outline color of an object it is dropped on.

- **Set 'no color'**   Vector shapes are pure geometry—they have no true appearance onscreen or when printed unless you assign the object a fill color (or texture), an outline width and color, or both. If you left-click over the Set 'no color' box, the selected shape's interior then has no color; in effect, it's transparent—although Xara has a Transparency Tool for creating *degrees* of transparency. SHIFT-click the Set 'no color' box to remove the color outline of a selected object; if you watch the Set Line Width box on the Standard Toolbar while doing this, note that the width becomes None—no outline color equals no outline.

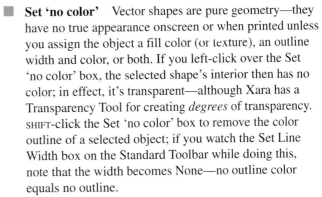

- **The Color picker**   This tool, located to the left of the Set 'no color' box, functions like an eyedropper tool does in other design programs. To use it, first have a source shape with a color (or an imported bitmap) and then create a shape. With the shape selected, click and *hold* the Color picker; then drag to the object or image from which you want to sample and apply the color to the selected shape. If you keep the mouse button held after the cursor is over the target object or image, a pop-up appears with information about the color components of the targeted color. Using the Color picker is a terrific way to fill shapes with the same color if you haven't named a color that would be available as a swatch on the color line.

- **The Color editor**   When you want to mix a new color to use, you click the Color editor icon to the left of the Set 'no color' box, or press CTRL-E. A good idea is to extend this palette by clicking the Advanced options button in upper-right corner of the editor box; doing so shows the color models and provides a drop-down option list to allow for making a tint/shade/or link to another color. It's intuitive to use, it has its own Color picker, and you can change the color of a selected shape just by dragging the sliders.

- **Galleries and the Galleries Control Bar**   By default, you have all the Galleries (resources for projects) you'll need in these palette-style boxes. You click on a Gallery button to open the gallery, click a second time to toggle it closed. Alternatively, every Gallery has a close box in the upper-right corner.

- **Infobar**   This control bar is contextual; options change as you change tools and/or tasks. If you seek an option with a specific tool, look to the Infobar first. The right-click pop-up menu also provides contextual options, and CTRL, ALT, and SHIFT are modifier keys when you draw and edit paths.

- **Standard bar**   By default, this control bar rests above the Infobar. The options and settings it provides do not change as you change tools. Look to the Standard bar when you want to create a new document, save one, change the zoom level of the page, change from high-quality preview to wireframe (view quality), change the point size of object outlines, and enable/disable snapping a shape to another shape.

- **Status line**   This strip at the bottom of the interface provides moment-to-moment data about your cursor position onscreen, what is currently selected, the layer upon which you're working, type of object selected, and other useful information. There is also a Live Drag button at right that toggles on and off to provide an onscreen preview of edits and movements of shapes *before* you release the mouse button, and a snapping indicator that changes shape when a shape is in position to snap to a different shape or a guide.

Understanding the Elements of a Shape

Chapter 3 provides extensive documentation on working with the three path-drawing tools in Xara: the Shape Editor, the Pen, and the Freehand and Brush Tools. However, it's very natural to go tearing into an exciting program before reading all the documentation, and you might have created a path without a basic understanding of how paths work, how they become shapes, and how to edit them. And where's the darned Eraser Tool?! Some explanation of vector paths is in order here.

Vector shapes have no visible characteristics until you fill one or apply an outline width. Vectors are math formulae that indicate a position in space and a direction. When a vector course changes, design programs use control points to mark the point of change. A curve passes through these control points, and the control points have properties. The control points have a *smooth* property when a curve passes through it without an abrupt change in course—the direction lines binding the control handles to the control point are in 180 degree opposition to each other. However, when a designer wants a sharp change in path course, a *cusp* property is assigned to the control point. The line between two control points (sometimes called a path's *segment*) can be straight (a line) or curved. When a line is curved, the curve usually begins and ends with control points along the path and two handles that lie off the path, called *(control) point handles*. Point handles are used to set the *tension* (the severity of the curve coming out of the control point) and the *bias* (how much the curve leans toward one or the other bounding control point). Although the description sounds daunting, control handles are easy and intuitive to use with visual feedback.

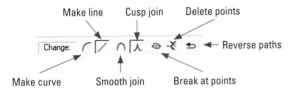

Make line   Cusp join   Delete points

Change:

Make curve   Smooth join   Break at points   Reverse paths

The primary tool for editing lines and shapes in Xara Xtreme is the Shape Editor Tool; occasionally, for certain edits, the Selector Tool can be used. However, in addition to moving control points and point handles, you'll want other options when you're just beginning a vector drawing program. Only when the Shape Editor Tool is chosen and a shape is selected do you see all of the Shape Editor's extended functions on the Infobar.

When a control point is selected, it appears as a hollow red node. Both the selected control point and its neighboring points display control handles if the segments are curved. Unselected control points are displayed as black dots. With the Shape Editor Tool (and the Selector Tool if you CTRL-click to select points when the Show Object Edit Handles button is toggled on from the Infobar), you can move multiple control points for quick adjustments to a path (press the SHIFT key to select more than one control point). Unlike Illustrator, Xara allows only closed paths to be filled.

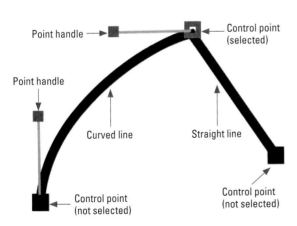

Point handle   Control point (selected)

Point handle

Curved line   Straight line

Control point (not selected)   Control point (not selected)

Checking Out the Toolbar

Much of the power in Xara Xtreme comes from the direct manipulation of objects—and the direct creation of objects. Therefore, a good place to begin tapping into the power is by perusing the tools used to make objects, located on the Toolbar, with options displayed on the Infobar at the top of the drawing window.

Figure 1-4 shows the tools, what they're called, and the shortcut keys for them.

Xara Xtreme Pro has a choice in Utilities to Customize key shortcuts. If you own the Pro version, use this utility to map keys to shortcuts you find personally easy to remember, or to the shortcuts you've memorized from other programs.

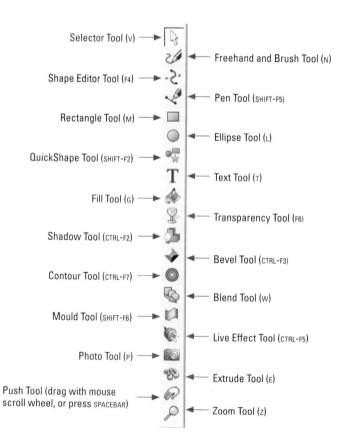

Selector Tool (v)
Freehand and Brush Tool (n)
Shape Editor Tool (f4)
Pen Tool (shift-f5)
Rectangle Tool (m)
Ellipse Tool (l)
QuickShape Tool (shift-f2)
Text Tool (t)
Fill Tool (g)
Transparency Tool (f6)
Shadow Tool (ctrl-f2)
Bevel Tool (ctrl-f3)
Contour Tool (ctrl-f7)
Blend Tool (w)
Mould Tool (shift-f6)
Live Effect Tool (ctrl-f5)
Photo Tool (p)
Extrude Tool (e)
Push Tool (drag with mouse scroll wheel, or press spacebar)
Zoom Tool (z)

Figure 1-4 The Xara Xtreme Toolbar

Exploring the Cool Stuff

Many individuals who have seen examples of the outstanding graphics created by experienced artists:

1. Understand that Xara Xtreme packs a phenomenal amount of design power into a deceptively simple interface.

2. Download the trial version and "play with the really cool stuff!"

Breaking with computer manual tradition, the following sections guide you through some of the astounding capabilities found in Xara Xtreme. In a short series of steps, you'll be producing *results*, which is always the end goal of learning a new program. Learning something more significant than how to press CTRL-S in the first chapter is fun and a refreshing departure.

The Fill Tool and Gradients

Fills for objects by default are solid colors; however, you can use the Fill Tool in Xara to apply gradients, fractals (for quickly adding visual complexity to simple outline shapes), and bitmaps you import or access from the Fill gallery. Try out the following steps:

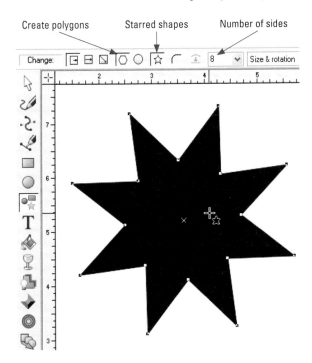

1. To create an interesting closed shape to fill, choose the QuickShape Tool, click the Create Polygons and the Starred Shapes buttons on the Infobar, and then choose 8 from the Number Of Sides drop-down on the Infobar. Drag a shape.

2. Choose the Fill Tool.

3. By default, a linear gradient is created with the Fill Tool when you drag on an object, and the gradient travels from white at the start point to current active color for the end color where you release the mouse button. Decide on the direction for your linear gradient and then click and drag.

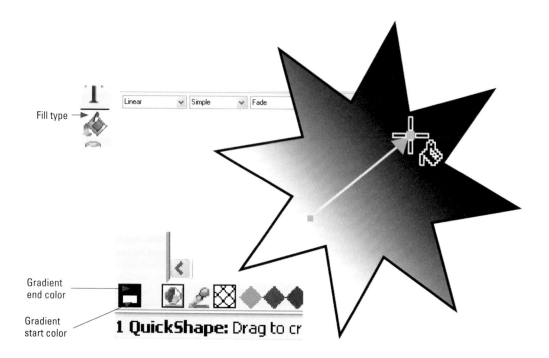

4. To change the direction of the linear gradient, click the end point, and then drag it around. Similarly, you might also want to click the start point handle and drag it around. The gradient handles can be located *outside* of the object; doing so decreases the amount of a gradient color within view.

5. To change the color of the start point, click on the start point: when the control handle is highlighted, you're good to go. Now click any color swatch on the color line to change the color or mix a new color in the Color editor.

6. Click the other gradient control handle (the end point); click a different color on the color line. You've just created a custom gradient.

7. Gradient-type fills can be customized by adding colors; you can have three, four, or more colors making transitions to one another. Try this: Position the Fill Tool cursor over the gradient line onscreen. When the crosshair cursor displays a little hand, you're in position to

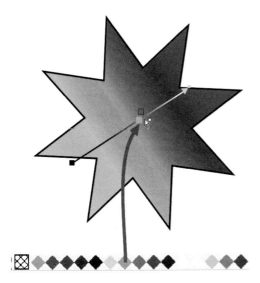

add another gradient point on the line to add an additional color—double-click to insert a position for an intermediate color.

8. Decide on a color on the color line. Click the color swatch while the new intermediate point is highlighted.

You can now reposition the new color across the gradient to emphasis or decrease its relation to the start or end colors. Use the Fill Tool or the Selector Tool (with the Show Fill Edit Handles button toggled on from the Infobar)—to hover over the color handle on the direction line. When you cursor turns into a cross hair with a tiny four-headed arrow (move) icon, you can drag to reposition the color handle.

Work with Transparency

Transparency works in flat and several gradient and fractal styles; you choose the style from the Infobar when one or more objects are selected and the tool is chosen. The Transparency Tool can operate very much like the Fill Tool—interactively, you drag on an object to set start and end opacity. You also have a number of blending modes (Transparency-type drop-down list) for transparency; the default is called Mix, but the Infobar includes other modes such as Stained Glass and Bleach.

The following example uses a vector art background and a bitmap PNG image; bitmaps can be assigned transparency exactly like vector shapes.

Open Haunted studio apartment.xar now, and let's see how to make the ghost bitmap image visually integrate with its bachelor's pad using transparency:

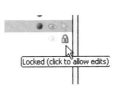

1. The document is all set up for you to import the Standard ghost.png bitmap. Look at the Object gallery now—click the button; see that the top layer is chosen to host the ghost and that the vector background is visible but locked. You can press CTRL-ALT-I to import (File | Import), and you can also minimize the Xara window and simply drag bitmap files into the page in the window.

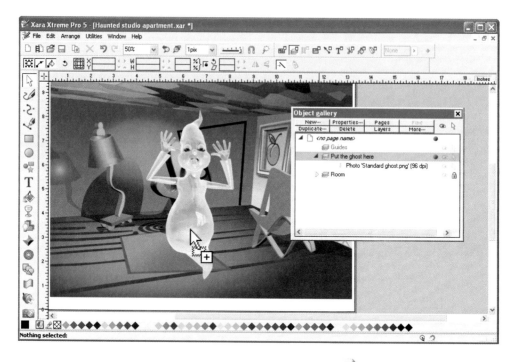

Standard
ghost.png

2. With the Selector Tool chosen, position the ghost in the
center of the scene. You can also scale him by dragging
on a corner selection bounds handle or make him fat or
skinny by dragging on a center selection bounds handle.

3. With the ghost selected, choose the Transparency Tool.

4. Drag, beginning at where his neck was when he was
alive, down to where his knees used to be.

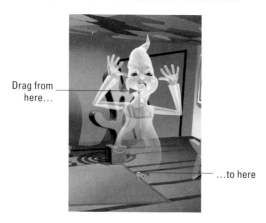

Drag from
here...

...to here

5. Experiment now by changing the position of the start and end points to the transparency. If you drag the start point (0% transparency) upward, more of the ghost will vanish. If you drag the end point upward, the transparency graduation becomes more mild. When the end point is off the bitmap, the end point never reaches total transparency.

Hold CTRL to constrain the direction of a transparency—and also a gradient fill—to 45 degree increments. You can modify this angle constraint in Options (CTRL-SHIFT-O). Also, if you've already made a gradient direction line that is a little off one of the constraint points, you can straighten it by holding CTRL and dragging on the point. It'll snap to the closest angle.

6. Let's say you don't want the bottom of the ghost to be completely transparent. You could locate the end point far away from the bottom of the bitmap, but also try this: Click the bottom (end point) for the transparency to select it. Drag the Transparency slider on the Infobar from its current state of 100% to, let's say 70%. You control the amount of transparency at the start and end points by selecting them and then using the slider on the Infobar to fine-tune the degree of transparency you seek. You can also type in the amount in the field next to the slider and then press ENTER.

7. Finally, take the Transparency type out for a spin. Choose Bleach mode (bleach works well on sheets) from the Transparency type drop-down list and you'll see that the ghost has lost most of his green color.

Keep the document open. You'll use it in the following sections.

Make Instant Shadows

The Shadow Tool, like most of the features in Xara, is interactive. You choose the "lightbulb in front of an 'L'" icon on the Toolbar, and then click on an object to add the shadow while setting an initial shadow direction. Then you use the Infobar options to set the amount of blurriness and density. You can even change the *type* of shadow once an object has a shadow.

The default shadow type is a Wall shadow (a *drop-shadow*), which is terrific for fancy desktop publishing and web graphics, but it visually puts an object into a 2D state, as though the object is flat. For this ghost composition, the little ex-fellow needs to be in the scene, not on top of it, so this is a job for the Floor shadow mode (*cast*, as opposed to *drop* shadow) of the Shadow effect. Here's how to make the ghost cast a *verrrrrry* scary shadow into the background:

1. The Shadow Tool can select an object, so the ghost doesn't need to be selected right now; choose the Shadow Tool and then click and drag down and right on the ghost to set the default Wall Shadow type and the direction of the shadow relative to the object.

2. Click the Floor Shadow button on the Infobar.

3. Increase the Shadow transparency (density) of the shadow to about 40% and then set the Shadow blur to about 25 pixels (measured as the radius from the edge of the shadow).

4. Now, click on the shadow, not the ghost, with the Shadow Tool. Look at the status line to confirm what is selected. Drag the shadow around until the shadow is cast on the wall and the furniture and ignore the folk tales that ghosts don't cast shadows.

5. You can change the color of the shadow. With the shadow selected, experiment by clicking on a dark green swatch on the color line. Figure 1-5 is your spirit guide for the preceding steps.

Floor shadow   Shadow blur   Shadow transparency

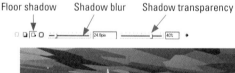

FIGURE 1-5 Use the Shadow Tool to quickly create dramatic and accurate floor and wall shadows.

1 shadow on layer Put the ghost here: Move pointer over object to shadow

Painless and Professional 3D with the Extrude Tool

Right inside of Xara is a little piece of 3D wonderland in the form of the Extrude Tool. This tool can be used to project a 2D shape (or group of shapes) backward along an imaginary depth plane, and you can interactively rotate the 3D object to produce captivating imagery in mere seconds.

The best shape to begin with, to get the best results with the Extrude Tool, is of an object that is fairly planar in the real world. A brick, a cookie cutter, almost any shape that extends in a direction without changing shape can be simulated by using the Extrude Tool.

Extrude examples.xar is for your examination. Just take the shapes apart to better see how to build things such as a trophy and a mailbox.

The suitcase.xar file consists of a set of grouped objects. With the exception of the handle, a real suitcase is fairly flat, which makes it ideal for re-creating via extruding. Let's play virtual bellhop now:

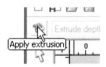

1. Open suitcase.xar in Xara.

2. Choose the Extrude Tool, click the suitcase object, and then click the Apply Extrusion button on the Infobar. Doing this produces the effect, but the depth, direction, and other parameters aren't set yet. Alternatively, you can simply drag on any shape with the Extrude Tool to apply an extrusion in a random direction and a random depth. Doing this is fun, but doesn't produce predictable results.

3. Place your cursor over the front face of the 3D object; your cursor should feature a tiny four-headed arrow (move) tool. When you drag now, the pivot point for the suitcase is the cursor, and by dragging in various directions you'll be able to rotate the suitcase—to pose it for the most interesting view—with very little effort.

4. Don't concern yourself when rotating the suitcase that the lighting isn't where you need it. Lighting is accomplished by clicking the Show Lights (lightbulb) icon in the Infobar. Click the icon now.

5. Make sure before you drag that your cursor is directly on one of the 3D arrows; your cursor changes to a tiny light bulb when you're directly over one. Now drag the bulb to move it around the center of the suitcase. You cannot drag it away from or toward the object—if you need more light, read on.

6. To adjust the properties of a light, double-click on a light to open the Color editor. The top drop-down list shows Light 1 color, Light 2 color, and so on. Choose one of the lights (by default, 2 and 3 are not as bright or as pure in color as Light 1), and then change its color to something closer to white. Most all edits in Xara are live, so use your visual feedback to tell when a light is adjusted correctly.

7. If you'd like an unusual suitcase, you can change the Bevel type style of the extrude to make the extruded side chiseled or wavy. Experiment with different styles on the Infobar drop-down list. The default is Rounded; you can also achieve neat effects by dragging the Bevel size slider to the right of the styles drop-down. For example, a rectangle with rounded corners, a deep extrude property, rounded edges, and a high bevel size, appears to bring the front and back faces of the object toward the middle. The result is something that looks like a cough drop or a Scandinavian hassock. Figure 1-6 shows the key controls for the Extrude Tool.

FIGURE 1-6 Use the Extrude Tool to project a path in a parallel line toward the distance.

Bevel type
(style of edge)   Show lights   Corners

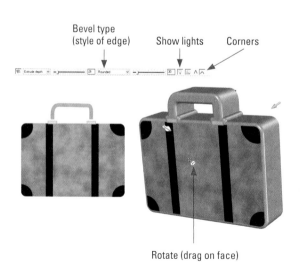

Rotate (drag on face)

8. Finally, there is both a manual and a precise way to set the depth of an extruded shape. To do so manually, display the object so you can see the side, the depth of the shape. Then position your cursor on the side of the shape, and when the cursor turns into a two-headed (instead of a four-headed) arrow, drag to change the object's depth. Or you can use the Extrude depth slider to the right of the Extrusion parameter field when the object (not a light) is chosen (by default, it is chosen) to precisely increase and decrease the object's depth, the distance between the front and the back of the paths.

Drag side to set depth

Hey, you're doing okay for getting through only the first chapter! This is but the surface you've scratched, so when you're itching to learn more:

1. Place your thumb and index finger over the right page. Your *right* thumb and index finger works best.

2. Pretend you're clicking Next Page, drag the page 180 degrees to the left, and read on.

2

Options and Customizing Xara Xtreme

The programmers at The Xara Group are so smart that they *didn't* build an edition targeted at an ideal individual. The interface is very flexible so you can set up your copy of Xara just the way you want it. This chapter is all about customizing Xara; you'll see how to build a control bar for your most-used tools, and how to import and create your own color swatches. Whatever way you prefer to work, you'll soon have the workspace set up with preferences that make the best sense for you.

 Download and extract the contents of Chapter02.zip, which contains everything you need to work through this chapter's tutorial steps.

Make Menu Items into Workspace Buttons

You can perform two types of customizing in Xara Xtreme:

- **Change the environment**   These changes can consist of putting buttons on control bars (including the Toolbar), *removing* buttons from their standard place on control bars, making a custom control bar. In general, any UI changes you make with the Window | Control Bars command are saved to the system Registry, and you're ill-advised to attempt to edit the Registry directly. There are one or two exceptions: mouse-click behavior is a global setting, for example, but it's accessed through the Options palette.

- **Store changes in a template**   You can specify ruler measurements, page sizes, colors shown on the color line, and many other document-centric properties in the Options palette.

Dragging a button off of a control bar *Deletes* the button; it doesn't float in the workspace or anything. The change is made to the Registry and to restore the button, you'll need to access the Control Bars dialog box again.

The Options palette holds many preferences, particularly those you want to change from day to day. Instead of remembering the keyboard shortcut CTRL-SHIFT-O, it makes sense to put Options as a button on the Toolbar, as follows:

1. Choose Window | Control Bars.

2. Scroll to the bottom of the list and then check Button Palette. The Button Palette appears; you might want to consider checking Floating in the Use Large Buttons For area of the Control Bars box. Larger buttons are easier to locate, particularly with a large screen resolution.

3. The Options button has an orange wrench head as its icon (if you hover your cursor, the tool tips can help you identify buttons). Hold ALT, and then drag the Options button to the Toolbar.

Hold ALT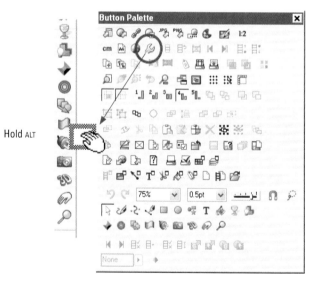

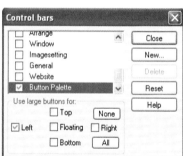

4. That's all there is to it, but don't close the Control Bar box yet; you'll want to do more customizing in the following section.

Don't click ALT and drag default buttons from control bars listed in the Control Bars box other than Button Palette. Doing this actually moves the buttons from their control bar to the new location. Then in the future when you want to dock a control bar, a desired button might be missing and the only way to restore it is to use the Reset button, which restores all changes you've made to *all* control bars.

 You can rearrange buttons even if the Control Bars box is closed. For example, if the Options button isn't exactly where you'd like it on the Toolbar, hold ALT and then drag the button up or down.

Build Your Own Control Bar

Technically, the Toolbar is a control bar, and it is part of the standard set of control bars in Xara that you can dock and undock and hide via the Control Bars box.

 To undock the Toolbar, you need to position the cursor precisely at the divider screen element (the "thumb") and then drag the Toolbar into the drawing window. The Toolbar reorients to landscape; you can then resize and reorient it by dragging a corner of the floating palette. To dock the Toolbar, drag it over the vertical window edge and then release the mouse button after the outline preview shows the proposed location for it.

Let's suppose you want to design your own Toolbar, showing only the buttons you most often use. You could modify the default Toolbar, but doing this creates a permanent change you might not want. Instead, you can build your *own* Toolbar and then hide the default one:

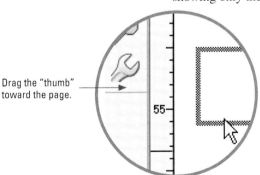

Drag the "thumb" toward the page.

1. Open the Controls Bars box if it's not open and click New.

2. Name the New control bar in the following dialog box and click OK. A very small control bar with no buttons appears, floating in the workspace.

3. Put a check next to the Button Palette on the Control Bars list if it's not currently onscreen.

4. Hold ALT and drag the buttons you want from the Button Palette to your custom Toolbar. Anything on the palette can be added; you don't need to restrict yourself to tools. For example, Fit Text To Curve is a good operation,

and you can access it more quickly on a floating Toolbar than through the Arrange menu.

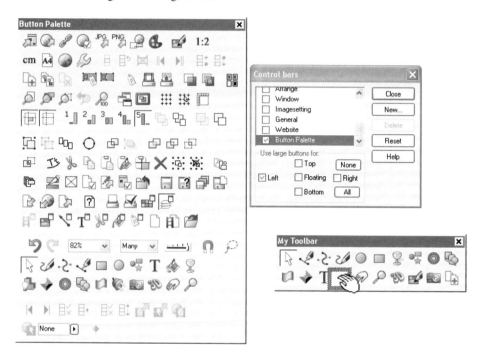

5. You can uncheck the Toolbar entry on the Control Bars box now, and close the box. You now have a floating control bar (which you can dock and undock at the top, right, or bottom of the interface), easy to position close to where you are working.

Keep the control bars and the Button Palette onscreen for the following section; an invaluable customization is coming up.

Adding a Control Bar to Your Workspace

You'll find several operations—such as subtracting a top shape from a bottom shape—indispensable for editing shapes. You can access them via the Arrange menu and by keyboard shortcuts, but it's much more convenient to put the Arrange Control bar above the Standard bar. To do this:

1. Scroll down the palette list in the Control Bars box until you locate Arrange.

2. Put a check in the box.

3. If necessary for your work preferences, drag the Arrange control bar left or right by its thumb (the vertical or horizontal line after the last button), or even drag it below the Standard bar to dock it there.

You now have a wealth of operations in plain and easy sight that you can perform with a shape.

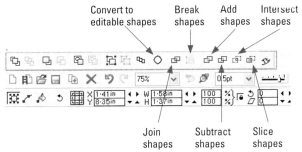

Creating One-Stop Zoom Resources

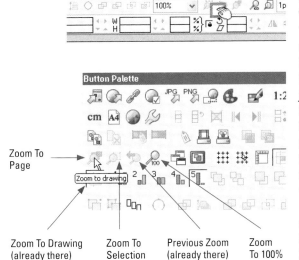

To designers, zooming and panning are like toll booths to the creative highway; you have to come to a stop before you continue on an important journey. Although choosing the Zoom Tool reveals several preset buttons on the Infobar, only two of them are on the Standard bar—the bar that's always onscreen. Having the whole set of zoom presets always visible is very fast and convenient.

On the Button Palette, hold down ALT and drag the zoom preset buttons you *don't* have on the Standard bar to a position next to the two that are there (Zoom To Drawing and Previous Zoom).

Collecting, Adding, and Organizing Color Swatches

If you don't care for the swatches that appear by default on the color line, now is the time to exercise your personal tastes and perform a little more customizing (and learn some good stuff along the way). Colors as displayed on the color line are local to a document.

- You add colors locally to the color line by using the Color Editor or the Color gallery.

- You add color collections to the Color gallery by copying a valid PAL or ACO file to the Xara Palettes folder.

- You can edit the color line (local colors) in Xara, but you cannot edit global color palettes that reside in the Palettes folder on your hard disk.

 XPal, created by fellow Xaraist Brian Etherington, is a free program in which you can generate PAL files to add to the Xara Palettes folder. Download it at www.smokingun.co.uk/sg/freestuff .htm.

Show a Color Library on the Color Line

If you have a PANTONE color swatch you need to match for a client in an illustration, or have a Web Safe color you need to use, it's very simple to display either of these libraries on the color line:

- To add a library to the color line, click the Color gallery on the Galleries control bar. Right-click over the library you need, and then choose Show In Color Line from the pop-up (context) menu.

- To remove a library from the color line, right-click over the collection in question on the Color gallery and then click Show In Color Line to remove its check mark and toggle the gallery off.

- If a friend or coworker named colors in an Adobe Illustrator document (with the AI file extension), you can add these colors to the color line by dragging the AI file into a Xara drawing page while Xara is not maximized (don't drag color files onto the color line; it doesn't work this way). Unlike ACO and PAL color files, an Illustrator file shows named colors and not RGB values when you hover your cursor over the color line. Because Xtreme version 5 supports color matching between Xara documents, you'll get an attention box asking if you want to match colors. Click Match and, depending on the number of named colors, they will appear in a moment or two.

The ACO and PAL files in the zip archive can be copied to your Xara Palettes folder so these author-created palettes will be available for you to use in any document in the future.

Naming and Importing Colors

PAL and ACO files are shown both in the Color gallery and on the color line tagged only by their RGB values, without user-friendly names such as Dusty Rose or Midnight Blue. Fortunately, you can *manually* name and save a color, and you can import a Xara document that contains named colors—and save the document as a template for using a color set on the color line any time you like. Put color palette.xar in a convenient location (the Desktop is good), and follow these steps for importing and saving a nicely arranged, properly named designer set of color swatches:

1. Launch Xara Xtreme and then click the Minimize/Restore button so you can drag a document into the drawing window.

2. Choose Options before proceeding; use the CTRL-SHIFT-O shortcut or (even shorter) click the Options button you learned how to add to the Toolbar earlier in this chapter.

3. Click View, and then *un*check Delete Unused Colors When Saving And Loading. The color line can become overly crowded if you save all colors whether they're used in your drawings or not. However, you need to uncheck this box when you're creating and saving colors. Click OK to close the Options box.

4. Drag color palette.xar file into the window (or alternately, choose File | Open and navigate to the file). Several things have happened. You don't need to have a drawing in a Xara document to import named colors; the drawing of the palette is for you to examine in your spare time to see how it was designed. You can press

CTRL-A (select all) and then press BACKSPACE or DELETE to remove the illustration from the document now. You can also simply open the document (CTRL-O) and the colors will appear on the color line.

5. Check out the color line. Click the Color gallery; as shown in Figure 2-1, all the colors are named in the color palette.xar folder. If you hover your cursor over the color line, the names of the colors appear as tool tips.

6. Before saving this document, if you disapprove of any of the swatches, click an unappealing one in the Color gallery and then click Delete at the top of the Color gallery.

7. Choose File | Save Template. In the Save Template dialog box, name the file, and (optionally) check the Use As Default Template box. If you do this, every time you launch Xara and every time you press CTRL-N or choose File | New, your template document and its saved colors open as a new file.

FIGURE 2-1 When you take the time to name colors, they can be imported.

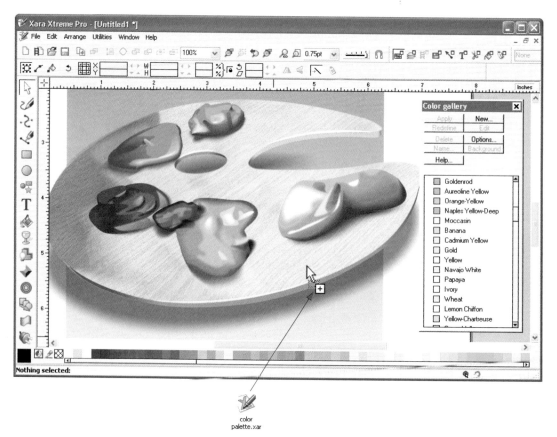

color
palette.xar

Similarly, let's say you want to mix up your own colors, name them, and save them to a template where they are featured on the color line. Here's how to do this:

1. Start a new document. This will serve as your color line template.

2. Import any colors you want to use frequently, using any of the methods described in the previous section for showing on the color line.

3. Click the Color Editor button at the bottom left of the interface.

4. Click the Show Advanced Options button at top right to extend the Editor until you can see all its features.

New Named Color   Advanced options

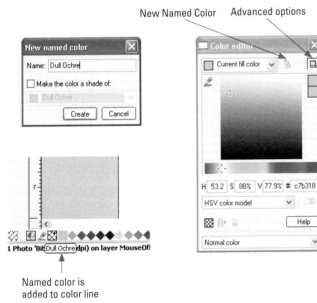

Named color is
added to color line

5. Mix up a color. The HSV color model is the easiest in which to define colors, but you can also choose Grayscale, RGB, or CMYK from the drop-down list below the color field.

6. Click the New Named Color Tag button on the Color Editor.

7. In the New Named Color dialog box, type a name for your color; you can edit the name in the future by right-clicking it on the color line or using the Rename button in the Color gallery. Press the Create button or press ENTER.

Exploring (and Exercising) Your Options

Configuring the control bars is a good first step; now let's turn to Options. The Options box contains several tabs that relate to properties: the size of the drawing page, the proximity of objects to snap-to points, how groups of objects behave when you apply transparency, and more. The following sections explain and offer suggestions for making drawing elements and tools *behave* the way you need them to.

The General Tab

This area of Options is where you can set most of the interface preferences and behaviors for objects you manipulate.

- **Recent file list size**
  The maximum number of files that will appear on the File | Open recent menu is 20. There's no reason not to choose the maximum value.

- **Current layer always visible and editable**
  This option applies when you're creating a drawing that's on several working layers. When checked, a layer automatically becomes editable when you click its name on the Object gallery. If the layer is locked, this option allows the layer to automatically become unlocked without the need to click a check box.

Make properties persistent

Group object transparency option

How many files listed under File | Open Recent menu

Preferences for selecting multiple objects

Nudge distance

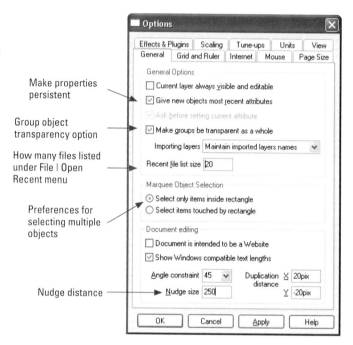

- **Give new objects most recent attributes**   Using this option is a matter of personal preference. If you want all the text you type to be the same justification, point size, and typeface, check this box. On the other hand, if you intend to create a variety of shapes, all with unique colors, you might not want this option.

You can also save layers, font styles, and other preferences to a template. For example, if you want to begin a new document based on a template with Garamond 14 pt, center justification, as the default font, you choose the Type Tool, set these parameters on the Infobar, and then save the document by using File | Save Template. Similarly, you can create a template that has three or four layers to start with, or begin documents with orange shapes with 4-pt green outlines. You specify these attributes—you don't need to actually create a shape with these attributes—and then save the document as a template.

■ **Make groups be transparent as a whole**   By default, object transparency is set on an object-to-object basis. However, if you need to create a group of shapes that all have the same amount of transparency, checking this option overrides object transparency and treats grouped objects as having a single transparency value.

■ **Importing layers**   When you drag a Xara file from the Designs gallery or from a drive window into a new document, you have the choice of bringing in new visual data all to the same layer—Import Layers Into The Active Layer (which can create a messy composition if the file has a lot of objects on different layers) or Import Layers Into New Layers (creating somewhat less of an object management chore)—or to import the file with its layers in their original structure (Maintain Imported Layers Names). You might be best served by choosing Maintain Imported Layers Names.

■ **Marquee object selection**   Your choice here is most relevant to how you have worked in another drawing application. If you're new to vector drawing, choosing Select Items Touched By Rectangle is a quick way to select objects. However, if you want to be explicit with mouse motions and marquee selecting (diagonally drag while you hold the mouse button to "lasso" a page area to select objects), select Only Items Inside Rectangle offers precision control.

Xtreme also supports "scribble selection," and this works regardless of your Options settings. To quickly select anything your cursor touches, hold ALT and then drag your cursor back and forth over shapes as though you're scribbling something.

■ **Document editing**   The Document Is Intended To Be A Website and Show Windows Compatible Text Lengths options relate to the Website creation capabilities of Xara, thoroughly documented in Chapter 11. Briefly, the Website option treats links on HTML pages as links to *groups* of objects and not, for example, to only the text on a button in a group of objects. If you're only designing for print, this option is not relevant to your work. The Windows-Compatible Text-Length option is also for Web documents and not for print. Very few Web browsers display text point size or line length as the author intended; lines of text can run long, break in awkward places, or have incorrect spacing because Web text displays differently than operating system and application text. This option reconciles point size for text you enter for a document intended for the Web and adjusts line lengths to closely match text as it displays in Web browsers.

- **Angle constraint**   The degree of rotation set for objects you rotate when holding CTRL. A good, all-purpose amount is 45 degrees, but you might want a different constraint value for a specific assignment. Angle constraint also applies to the skewing operations you perform on objects.

- **Nudge size**   This controls the increment by which an object or an object element moves when you press the arrow keyboard keys. The value you type in this box is usually attributed to the measurement specified on the Units tab; however, if for example, Page units is set to pixels, you can still set a Nudge size to 1 inch by typing **1in** (no space) in the field.

Use keyboard combos to change the way nudge distances are performed. Hold CTRL and then press an arrow key to nudge 5 times the defined distance. Holding SHIFT multiplies the distance 10 times; CTRL-SHIFT nudges by 1/5th the defined distance; holding ALT nudges an object by one pixel; ALT-SHIFT plus an arrow key nudges by 10 pixels. Pixel distance by default is defined as 96 pixels to an inch.

- **Duplication distance**   A duplicate of an object (and objects) is identical in its structure to a clone of objects. Xara gives you three options for creating copies of shapes: CTRL-K (Edit | Clone) duplicates the selected shape directly on top of the original; while CTRL-D (Edit Duplicate) offers the advantage of offsetting the position of the copy in relation to its original. This field provides the distance of offset for the duplicate: X is the measure of left-to-right page distance. Positive values in this field place duplicates to the right of the currently selected shape, while positive values for Y are the vertical measure and travel upward regardless of the Grid and Ruler tab Coordinates settings. Therefore, if you want to build an array of identical objects traveling from page top left to bottom right, enter positive units in X and negative values in the Y field here.

The third way to create copies of shapes is to use the standard Windows convention of pressing CTRL-C and then CTRL-V. Unlike Cloning and Duplicating, copies inserted from the Clipboard land precisely in the center of the interface screen, not the drawing page.

Constraining Your Way to Making Pie Wedges

Pie wedges are useful in charts and also as Web elements. You can easily use all the features covered up to this section for manually creating multiple pie wedges; you change the math a little to result in the number of pieces you want to create. In the following steps, a six-piece pie is created. You need six isosceles triangle shapes to carve six pie wedges from a circle; the interior angle of an isosceles triangle is 60 degrees. Using Angle Constraint of 60 degrees, you create a triangle with the QuickShape Tool and point it at the center of a circle. Then use the Drop Copy technique to build the other five triangles, each perfectly aligned so you can intersect them with the underlying circle.

The *Drop Copy* technique is the most important part of the steps to follow; you'll often find yourself using it for fast, complex scene creation. With an object selected, you hold down the left mouse button and drag the object to a destination on the page where you want a duplicate. Before releasing the left mouse button, you tap the right mouse button so that both buttons are depressed briefly. Then you release both buttons and a duplicate is dropped under your cursor. Let's build a six-wedge design now:

1. Beginning with a new document, go to Options, and set the Angle Constraint on the General tab to 60 degrees.

2. Choose the Ellipse Tool, and then hold CTRL to constrain the proportions of the new object to a perfect circle. Drag and then release the mouse button when you have a circle of about 3 inches in diameter (it might be displayed on the Infobar as 288pix).

3. Fill the circle with a medium tone color—any color will do.

4. With the QuickShape Tool selected, set the number of sides to 3 on the Infobar.

5. Hold CTRL while you drag a triangle, constraining the direction of the triangle while you're creating it. Move the cursor up and down a little when you've arrived at a size for the triangle of more than half the width of

the circle. The Infobar will tell you when the triangle is rotated 90 degrees, with one angle pointing directly to the right of the page. You'll also visually see this; release the mouse button when you have a right-pointing triangle.

6. With the circle selected, click on it again with the Selector Tool to put it into rotate/skew transformation mode. Now you can clearly see the object's center marked with a tiny cross hair inside a circle.

7. If you don't have rulers visible, press CTRL-L to toggle the rulers on. Click in the horizontal ruler and drag down; similarly click in the vertical ruler and drag to the right to create guides over the circle to meet at this center point of the circle.

8. Drag the triangle until its right point lies on the intersection of the guides.

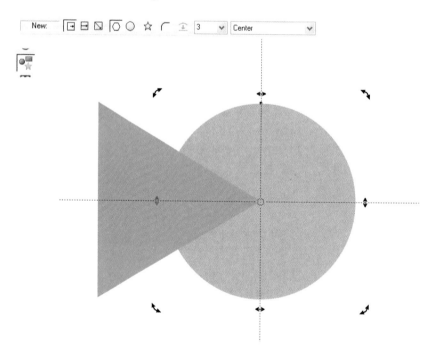

9. SHIFT-CLICK to select both objects and then click the Intersect Shapes button you put on the Standard bar earlier (or choose Arrange | Combine Shapes | Intersect Shapes). The triangle is now a pie wedge with a curved left side.

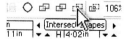

10. Click the selected pie wedge shape to display its center point. With the Selector Tool still active, drag the center of the triangle to lie on the intersection of the guides.

Drag to relocate
the object center

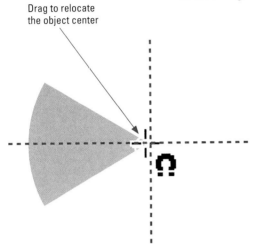

11. The pie wedge is in rotation mode. Hold CTRL and drag the upper-right double-headed rotation arrow marker down. Right-click and then release both buttons when the copy has snapped into the 60-degree rotation position.

12. Repeat step 11 four more times to complete the design. As you can see in Figure 2-2, making this complex composition is easy work, and the angle of constraint and shape combinations make the process smooth and predictable.

Use Nudge Distance for Pattern Creation

Nudging by using the keyboard arrow keys is not only useful for precise positioning of objects and to nudge objects out of the way when you're trying to view underlying shapes. It's also handy for building seamless tiling patterns. Suppose you want to create a seamless tiling pattern from a few shapes you've drawn. By using a nudge distance that matches the height and width of a background rectangle, you can clone and then nudge shapes so they wrap from top to bottom and left to right.

Previous copy

Hold down CTRL and
drag a corner handle

Right-click before
releasing left mouse
button to drop a copy

Copy

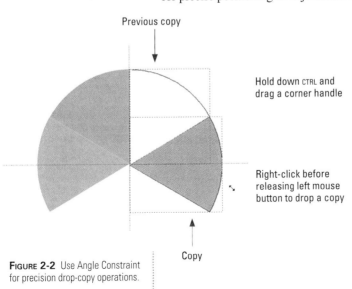

FIGURE 2-2 Use Angle Constraint for precision drop-copy operations.

Open seamless tile.xar; part of the work has been done for you. The background green pattern tiles seamlessly; it's your background for your assignment, and it's precisely 512 by 512 pixels. Follow these steps to create a seamless tiling pattern from the leaf shapes, or draw a shape or two of your own:

1. Move the large grouped flower anywhere until it falls off part of the edge of the underlying square; this is the key to making nudge distance work for you in pattern creation.

2. Open the Options box, and then type **512pix** in the Nudge Size field; close the Options box.

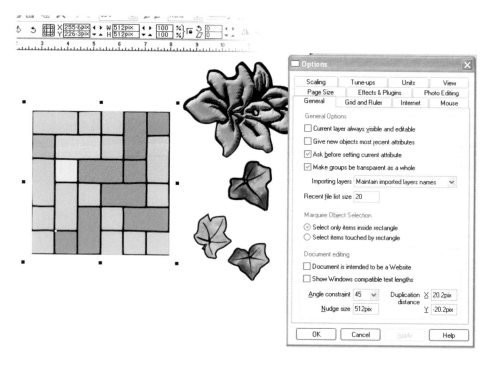

3. Press CTRL-K to put a copy of the large flower directly on top of the original.

4. Use your keyboard arrow keys to reposition the copy of the flower in the opposite direction from where it falls off the square. If it falls off the right side, nudge the copy one arrow-stroke left. If it falls off the top, offset the copy by nudging it to the bottom. Figure 2-3 shows where the duplicates lie in one of many possible pattern configurations.

If a copy of your shape or group of shapes falls off both the bottom and the right, for example, you will need three copies, not just one, to complete the wrap-around pattern effect. In this example, you need a copy to continue the pattern from the right to the left side, a copy to continue from the bottom to the top side, and then a copy to continue from top right to top left.

FIGURE 2-3 Nudge the distance of the background to make the foreground objects appear to tile seamlessly.

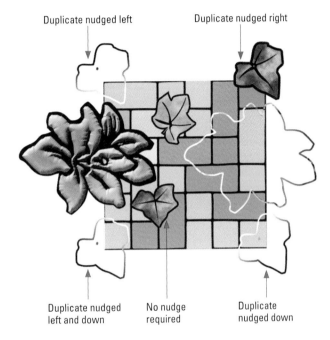

Duplicate nudged left

Duplicate nudged right

Duplicate nudged left and down

No nudge required

Duplicate nudged down

5. Press CTRL-A to select all, and then press Q to create a ClipView object. The leaf areas that fall outside the square are hidden from view and you have a seamless tiling pattern now.

6. With the ClipView object selected, press CTRL-SHIFT-C to open the Create Bitmap Options box. Click Create, and the box closes with a bitmap copy of the seamless tile you created. Now to test it out.

7. With the Freehand and Brush Tool (press N to choose it), draw a large, uneven blobby shape, releasing the mouse button at your start point; the little plus symbol on the cursor tells you when you're in position to close the shape.

8. Click the Fill Tool on the Toolbar. On the Infobar, choose Bitmap from the Fill Type drop-down list.

9. Toward the center of the Infobar is a Bitmap Name preview drop-down. Because the bitmap you created in step 6 is embedded in the Xara Xtreme document, it's on the list. Choose it; the shape fills (by default) with a single tile of your flower pattern.

10. Choose Repeating tile from the Fill Tiling drop-down list.

11. You'll see a center point above the bitmap fill, with two control handles extending from this point. Drag one of the outer points on the control handle outward to scale the repeating tile, and then try rotating the pattern by dragging the control point in any direction. Clearly, you have a *seamless* tile, and the steps for creating scores of your own.

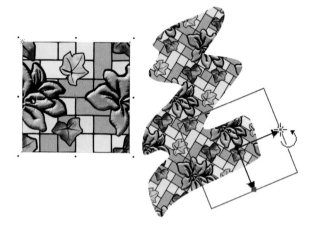

Units Options

Moving back to Options, the Units tab is important for working in a measurement that best suits the project at hand. You can set the Page units to inches, pixels, or European units such as metres; before you press Apply, you'll want to adjust the Nudge size and Duplication distance. If, for example, you specify feet when you previously had Nudge size set up for pixels, you'll receive an attention box about the page size limit (you can nudge an object by 200 pixels but not 200 feet). Font units are usually best set up as measured in points; publishers like to work in points and occasionally picas when evaluating column widths. However, if you need to do sign work, you'll want to use inches, feet, or some other common non-typographical unit to make certain the logo or other signage fits on the proposed physical sign. Page units have nothing to do with rulers; page units are reflected on the W and H suffixes on the Infobar when you select an object and are told the size and the position on the page.

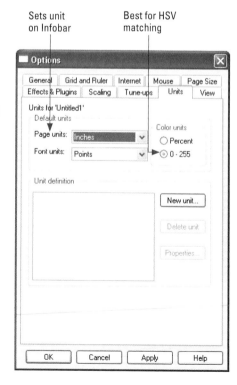

Sets unit on Infobar

Best for HSV matching

Do not confuse the new unit measurements with the Scaling tab's features. If you need to scale a page to miles for creating travel instructions, you use Scaling, *not* the Units tab in Options.

Increment Options

Xara provides two measurements for Color Units. If you work primarily for Web design or personal printing to an inkjet, you're wisest to click the 0–255 button here. The result is that when you use the Color Editor in RGB color mode, color components are displayed from 0 to 255, a standard more consistent with color definition in other applications. A specific color in Xara will be a snap to match in Photoshop, for example,. The exception is CMYK commercial printing mode. If you do a lot of press work, you'll want to use Percent Color Units. The color components of CMYK are usually measured in percentages (50% black, for example), so if you're destined for print, go with percentages.

To "zero" the rulers (that is, to make the origin of the rulers coincide with the top left of a drawing page), drag the cross-hair box at the junction of the horizontal and vertical rulers to the upper-left corner of the drawing page. If you want to start a new origin, you drag the origin box (this action produces temporary guides) to the point on the page where you need 0,0. Xara rulers work almost identically to desktop publishing applications.

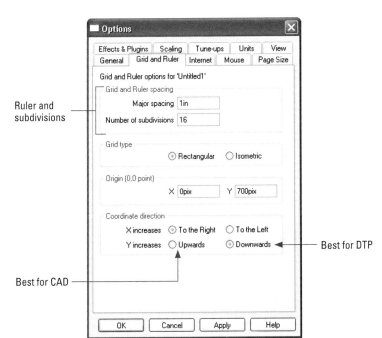

Ruler and subdivisions

Best for DTP

Best for CAD

Grid and Ruler Options

You have the best of all worlds when you use a combination of the Units and Grid and Ruler Options: you can have the Infobar report size and position of shapes, using inches, and have the rulers set up to pixels. At the top of the Grid and Ruler tab in Options is Grid And Ruler Spacing. If you type in values only, the units will default to the current units of measurement. However, if you know the abbreviation Xara uses (very standard: pix = pixels, in = inches, cm = centimeters and so on), you can type **100pix** in Major Spacing (just as an example) and **10** in Number Of Subdivisions, and these settings only affect the rulers, not the measurements on the Standard bar.

Coordinate direction applies to rulers and to the position and scale fields on the Standard bar. Although CAD and other technical work positions the page's zero point at the bottom left (moving positive values up and to the right), if you're into desktop publishing (DTP) and fine art, you will want to click the Y Increases Downwards button; your pages then measure as expected with a zero origin at top left.

You have two grid-type display options for a nonprinting grid: Rectangular and Isometric. You can easily display the grid by pressing the apostrophe key ' (the Show Grid command is also found under Window); pressing ' a second time toggles the grid off. The grid follows the spacing you've defined.

 To toggle snapping to the grid, the command is under Window. A faster method is to press DELETE on the number keypad.

Unlike a rectangular grid (which displays major spacing and subdivisions at right angles from one another), the isometric grid's spacing markers are offset at 30, 90, and 120 degrees, making a hexagonal matrix. If you do any architectural illustration work, the isometric grid is of invaluable help because you can use it to draw three-quarter views of building and objects with flattened (unrealistic) perspective. An isometric view *has* no vanishing point: parallel lines of a structure never converge in the distance as you'd expect when viewing photorealistic illustrations.

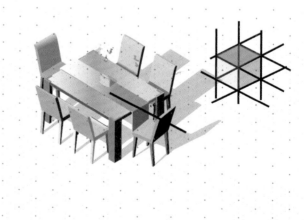

Mouse Characteristics

You can use both mouse buttons and a mouse's wheel to perform tasks and navigate a document in Xara. The Mouse tab in Options lets you set up behaviors the way you'd like to work.

By default, your mouse controls perform the following in Xara:

- **Left mouse button**   Selections, default behavior.
- **Right mouse button**   Brings up pop-up (context) menu when in drawing page and offers several options over color line, relevant to choosing outline, fill, and Contone colors (when a bitmap image is currently the selection). Also used with the left mouse button for the Drop Copy duplication gesture.
- **Mouse wheel**   Scrolling behaves as in most Windows applications, scrolling the window up and down. Lateral scrolling is available when the mouse supports this feature. Dragging (click and drag) with the wheel toggles to the Push Tool for convenient panning of the document window.

Context menu

Controls snapping sensitivity

Unless you use the mouse as a Southpaw, there's really no advantages to changing the left button's behavior (lefties can set the left button to Popup menu and the right to Normal click). However, Xara offers document zooming instead of scrolling with the scroll wheel, and this feature is one of the most *accurate* ones in graphics software: when you click Zoom In/Out in the Mouse Wheel Movement field, you zoom in and out *on the position of your cursor—not* on the center of the window. However, you can temporarily toggle to the zooming feature by holding down the CRTL key while using the scrolling wheel.

 Although the pop-up for right-button clicks provides some options when your cursor is over the color line, you might prefer to set the outline color by using a right-click. This preference is not set under Mouse, but instead in the View tab of Options, covered in the following section.

Other right-button options are as follows and are the same for left-button options:

- SHIFT-**click**   A good reason to set the right button to SHIFT-click is that this is the default mouse gesture for setting the outline color for a shape, quicker than accessing this command from the default pop-up menu. If a shape has no outline, a SHIFT-click over a color swatch adds the default outline width and the color you chose.

- ALT-**click**   Holding down ALT and clicking is used in Xara to select underneath objects. If you have, for example, a small object beneath a large one on a layer, and you know it's there but it's hidden, ALT-clicking selects beneath the current object on top (the cursor turns upside down as a visual indicator of the action). If more than one object is hidden, you can repeat the ALT-click to toggle to the next hidden object, or use TAB to do the toggling.

- **Toggle full-screen mode**   Full-screen mode is marginally larger than normal view—full screen hides the Windows interface "padding" and the menu. You might never need to assign this mouse gesture to the right button, because the pop-up right-click menu provides you with the Full Screen command (the keyboard shortcut is 8 on the number pad).

- **Push Tool**   Other ways to quickly toggle to the Push Tool (which pans the document window) include dragging with the mouse wheel and holding the Spacebar. Therefore, changing the right button's action is truly a matter of personal work preference.

Set Snap Options

On this page, you can set the amount of "magnetism" your cursor reacts to during a snap-to operation. Snapping to is the onscreen result of getting your cursor close to but not exactly touching an object or guideline—the Snap-To feature (which you can enable and disable by using the horseshoe magnet button on the Standard bar) guides you from "close" to exactly the onscreen position you desire for object alignment. The Magnetic Snap Radii options can be set for snapping distance for both points and lines you draw in Xara. It's probably best to leave the default settings as they are for this option: higher amounts will make your drawing tools snap to other objects and points that can be clear out of view.

View Options

The View tab in Options provides a lot of preferences for setting how bitmap images in Xara appear and are written. Also, you can set visibility options for interactive screen feedback—creating and editing with immediate feedback is one of the unique powers of Xara, and there's really no need to disable this power with today's processors.

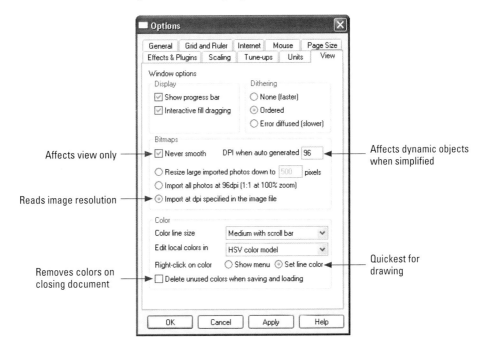

Affects view only

Reads image resolution

Removes colors on closing document

Affects dynamic objects when simplified

Quickest for drawing

Display and Dithering

At top, the Window options are to show or not show a progress bar. The progress bar in Xara appears at the bottom left of the interface, but with the exception of exporting artwork to a 40MB TIFF image, you probably won't notice the progress bar. Xara Xtreme is a very fast application, even on older machines. Leave Interactive Fill Dragging enabled. When you drag on a selected object with the Fill Tool to create and edit gradient fills, updates onscreen are immediate, and this feedback is usually a good thing. If you're used to a drawing program that does not update fills until you release the mouse button, you can uncheck this box.

Live Drag View Option

When you drag, resize, or otherwise transform a shape, it would be nice to preview exactly what you're about to do before releasing the mouse button. Live Drag is related to items on the View tab, but you won't find the feature there. You enable or disable Live Drag by double-clicking the tiny arrow-in-a-circle icon at the bottom right of the interface, to the right of the status line. Enabled, Live Drag shows you an outline of the object plus a dashed red outline of the proposed transformation before you release the mouse button. It's handy; you should use it.

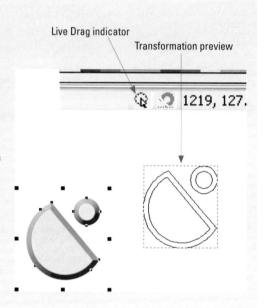

Live Drag indicator

Transformation preview

Dithering can be left at its default value. On inexpensive notebook computers, you might see banding in gradients you apply to shapes, and dithering breaks up the banding onscreen. However, in general, when you're using even a modestly priced video card in your PC, you won't see banding or Xara's dithering compensation feature.

Bitmaps are smoothed by default when you import an image or drag it into a drawing window from a file folder. This can make small bitmaps easier to work with, but smoothing bitmaps can also lead to inaccuracy if you're manually tracing over them. The DPI When Auto-Generated option is important if you're going to convert an object that has a drop shadow or other effect dynamically attached to it. By default, effects that you need to convert to bitmap format for any reason are created at 96 pixels/inch resolution (*dpi* and *ppi* are usually synonymous). The result, were you to export your design at a printing resolution of 300ppi, would be that the shape exports just fine to 300ppi, but the drop shadow part is going to look coarse because it is of insufficient resolution. The remedies for this are:

- Don't ever convert a shape that has a dynamic effect applied to it.

- Don't use dynamic effects.

■ (*Correct answer*) Remember where this setting is, and type an appropriate value in the box whenever you need to work with both vectors and bitmaps for print.

If you're only doing work for the screen and the Web, 96dpi is fine and you won't have to change this preference.

Bitmaps

The next three options on the list are relevant to building Web graphics (covered in Chapter 10). If you choose Resize Large Imported Photos Down To ___Pixels, you'll never bring in an image any larger than that—Xara auto-scales a copy of the image. This is fine for Web work, but not accurate or desired for print and other high-quality design work. By choosing Import All Photos At 96dpi, you're assured that all images you bring in match screen and Web resolution, and you won't have to manually adjust the size or resolution of the imported piece. However, this is not such a good idea if you're designing pieces for print: although Xara doesn't change the resolution of a copy of the bitmap, resolution is inversely proportional to the size (usually measured in inches) of a bitmap. For example, if you have an image that's 8 ½ by 11 inches at 300ppi, Xara will import the photo to 96ppi, thus increasing its height and width by more than 300%. The result is that the photo doesn't fit on a standard drawing page—an inconvenience, but an inconvenience you don't have to live with. If you choose Import At DPI Specified In The Image File, image file formats that contain resolution information (TIFF, PSD, PDF, JPEG, and occasionally PNG) will import exactly as the image was created or photographed, in scale and resolution. Common and older file formats such as BMP, GIF, and others will import at 96ppi regardless of your View settings because these file formats don't have the structure to handle resolution information.

The Color Section

You can choose from sizes at which the color line is displayed. Medium With Scroll Bar is fine for 1024×768 displays and slightly higher; you might want to choose Large if you're running Xara on a notebook. Choose Edit Local Colors In HSV color model so that every time you need to create or adjust a color by using the Color Editor, you'll go to work in HSV and not RGB or CMYK.

Right-click On Color allows you to specify a right-click action to choose a selected object's outline color, or to show a context menu. The menu might not include enough options

you seek to justify setting the color line behavior this way:
many of the Xara Grand Masters use a right-click to set outline
color—it's fast and one less shortcut to remember. It's up to
you, the way you want to work and possibly a drawing program
convention you're already familiar with.

The Delete Unused Colors When Saving And Loading
option is *important* to consider. With this box checked, the next
time you reopen a drawing, only colors used in your artwork
will appear as swatches on the color line. This means any really
neat color you might have created but didn't use in your design
is gone. With this bo*x un*checked, all new colors, whether
they're in your design or not, appear on the color line. The
downside to using this preference is that your color line will
soon become quite crowded.

Page Size Options

On the Page Size tab, you'll find everything as you'd expect
in a desktop publishing or other design program. You have the
Paper Size drop-down list that provides you with a good working
supply of standard U.S. and international paper sizes as well as
sizes for Web pages. If you need a specific size, particularly if
you're going to use this size often, type the Width and Height
values in the appropriate fields. If the unit of measurement from
Units makes calculating your ideal page size difficult, type the
abbreviation for the unit after the value in the boxes (don't use
spaces). For example, an 11in width results in an 11-inch wide
page even though the Width field initially offers 1024pix. In
the future, you will not access your custom page size from the
Page option; instead, save this (blank) document via File | Save
Template and then use the File | New menu to open a copy of the
page. Additionally, you have options for creating outer margins
commonly used for margin (or pasteboard) around the page.
Bleed Margin shows the margin the color would bleed off the
page edge. You might use it for magazine artwork (when the art
bleeds edge to edge, but the presses need a margin for gripping
the physical sheet and trimming it to bleed). You can also specify
a double-page spread so you can easily visualize how art might
span a spread in a physical publication.

Other Options

Some options not previously covered have to do with building
animations and previewing them, as well as previewing Web
pages and controlling how Xara taps into your system resources.

On the Tune-Ups tab, you have the Redraw options of letting Xara take as much as needed from system resources or setting a limit. Unless you're working entirely with camera RAW photos, or your drawing is astronomically complex with thousands of shapes, redrawing (refreshing after editing elements) is seldom a problem. Today's computers usually ship with 1GB and usually 2GB of RAM and a 500GB hard disk; in short, you probably will never be pressed with sluggish redraws, but the feature is here if you find your system is slowing down. Gallery Cache relates primarily to thumbnails of graphical items found in the Bitmap and Clipart galleries; caching has no impact on, say, the Color gallery. If you have indexed a lot of Xara artwork in one folder and want the folder available for opening and importing artwork, you might want to speed up the process by allowing more items (the default is 25) to be auto-cached (updated). The Undo allotment for system resources controls how many Undo steps you can perform on a file. When you're first starting out with Xara, you might want to set this figure high so you can backtrace a lot of steps. Because Xara artwork can be entirely made up of vectors, and vectors are comparatively small as digital artwork goes, a figure of 100MB will serve you well. In the Cache Control area, you can specify how much system memory is used to update layers, effects, and other dynamically changing visual data. If you want to set a high value, such as 50% of the current available RAM, you'll work quickly, but be advised that you might not want to have your e-mail browser open or burn a music CD while you're working. These are memory-intensive processes that will compete with Xara for available RAM.

It's usually not worth your while going through 37 Undo steps to revive your original work. Xara does not use a Revert command. To revert a document, you answer Discard to the "Do you want to save your changes?" question in the Closing Document box, or choose File | Open, and then pick the name of the document you're currently working on; you'll get the attention box that offers a Revert option, but Xara has no Revert To Last-Saved command.

The Internet tab is where you can set the amount of system resources you want to dedicate to previewing GIF and Flash animations you create in Xara, for previewing Web pages as a dry run of a Web page design, and for existing pages on the Web. As with caching, you're best off not running other applications while previewing Web media. Set your desired connection speed to simulate download times for Web previewing, set a reasonable amount of RAM for cache (750MB when you have 1GB of RAM on your motherboard is not reasonable, for example), and make sure you revisit this page and flush the cache by clicking Empty Cache after you're through with your Internet work to free up RAM.

The Effects & Plugins page provides you with an easy way to access and use Adobe standard plug-ins directly within Xara. Live Effects work on both vector artwork and imported bitmaps; they can be dynamically changed, and scores of effects are available online. Note that if you own Photoshop and have bought and installed third-party plug-ins, most but not all will work correctly within Xara. Some filters require Photoshop-specific features, and filters that belong to Photoshop will not be listed after you click the Setup button and direct Xara to the location of plug-ins on your hard disk. This page also offers a resolution-setting option for effects; you probably should stick with 96dpi for the screen unless you plan to convert an object that has an effect to an editable shape for exporting it to bitmap. If this is the case, know what resolution you need and select it from the drop-down list before converting the object in your design. The only real reason for choosing to lock an effect at a specific high resolution would be if you intend to work very close to this object at a high magnification onscreen. Finally, on the Photo Editing tab, you have your choice of where you want to edit bitmaps that you import to a Xara document. By default, the Xara Picture Editor (XPE) is called whenever you choose Utilities | Bitmap Editor (when an imported bitmap is selected), and it's called within the document window. However, if you prefer to edit images by using a different bitmap editor installed on your hard disk, you can choose one instead.

Bear in mind that launching an outside application takes system resources. XPE takes only a moment to load and you're editing from within Xara.

Make Your Own Guides

A Guides layer is automatically created and accessed through the Object gallery the first time you drag a guide from a ruler. However, a guide doesn't have to be a line; it doesn't even have to be a vertical or horizontal line. Guides in Xara can be any object you like: one you create directly on the Guides layer by using any drawing tool, or a vector object you import. You can make and save a document as a template with guides in place, and you can create diagonal and curved guides to help you create unusual and freeform shapes.

The Snap To Objects button (the horseshoe magnet) on the Standard bar has nothing to do with shapes you move snapping to guides. By default, Windows | Snap to Guides is enabled. Uncheck this option, or press 2 on the keypad to toggle guide snapping on and off.

Here's something of interest if you're a designer who works in a manufacturing enterprise: a product that has not been manufactured yet might have a CAD drawing available. Many CAD and modeling applications can export files to EPS vector-type formats, which Xara can indeed import. Here's how to make quick work out of illustrating something that cannot be photographed for advertising yet:

1. In a new document, click the Minimize/Restore button at upper right of the UI so you have an unobstructed view of both the Xara Xtreme document and your Desktop.

2. Drag the mug.eps file into the document window. By default, the CAD drawing is given its own layer; open the Object gallery now.

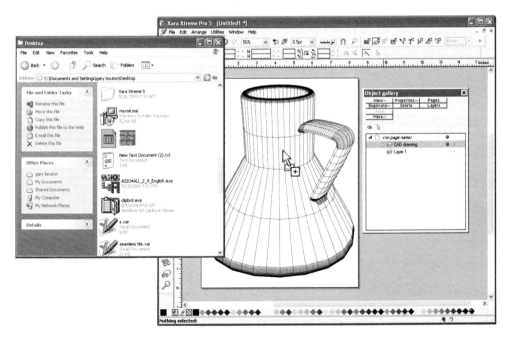

3. Rulers have to be visible to create guides: press CTRL-L if you have no rulers in the document. Drag a guide from a ruler to create a Guides layer in the workspace. This is

only to prime the pump and create a Guides layer in the document—you won't use this guide (and can drag it back into the ruler to delete it).

4. Open the CAD drawing layer's contents by clicking the title's triangle on the Object gallery.

5. Drag the Group title up to the Guides layer title; the Guides layer now has the CAD drawing.

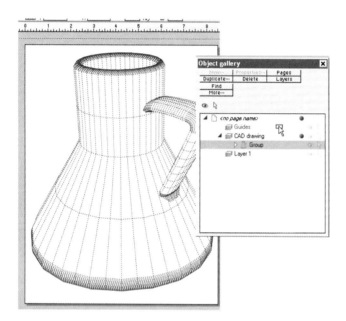

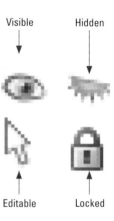

6. Lock the Guides layer from editing—click the Editable icon (arrow) on the Guides layer to toggle or change it to a closed lock.

7. Click the default Layer 1 title on the Object gallery, making it the active drawing layer. You're now all set to illustrate over the wireframe guide; everywhere you direct a drawing and editing tool cursor, there will be magnetic attraction to the mug guide as long as Window | Snap to Guides is enabled.

Realistically, this is only Chapter 2, and you're not expected to draw a finished travel mug right now. But when you've finished this book, it will certainly be within your skills. Figure 2-4 shows one approach to illustrating the mug. Open Futuristic travel mug .xar and take a look at how it was illustrated. Although a lot of

FIGURE 2-4 Guides are of tremendous help when you need to accurately illustrate a product that is only in its prototype phase.

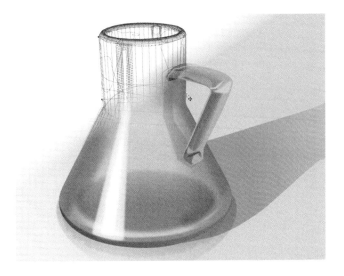

blends and objects were used in drawing this piece, significant time was shaved off because the guides were used for proportions and an accurate silhouette of the product.

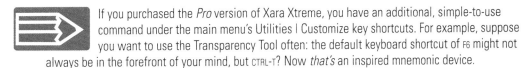

If you purchased the *Pro* version of Xara Xtreme, you have an additional, simple-to-use command under the main menu's Utilities I Customize key shortcuts. For example, suppose you want to use the Transparency Tool often: the default keyboard shortcut of F6 might not always be in the forefront of your mind, but CTRL-T? Now *that's* an inspired mnemonic device.

3

Working with Paths

Vector paths are the underlying structure for everything the drawing tools in Xara can produce. Unlike bitmap painting programs—where a click of a tool produces a colored dot on a canvas—producing great artwork in Xara is a two-step process.

1. You design the underlying geometry of your composition with *paths*.

2. You apply *properties* to the paths so your design is visible. A vector is a type of geometric equation that has a direction and a distance, but not a skin. This is where Xara line properties come in.

Often, you'll find these two steps indistinguishable from one another; you can build a path and apply a property to it at the same time, but you shouldn't confuse vector artwork with a pixel painting.

This chapter first discusses how to draw the underlying structure of a vector shape (with some property application here and there for fun) and then adds things you can *apply* to a path: outline width, color, making the path dashed lines, adding arrowheads, even applying shapes to the path shape to make your lines look like chalk and watercolor.

 Download and extract the contents of Chapter03.zip, which contains everything you need to work through this chapter's tutorial steps.

The Components of a Path

Xara gives you three tools for drawing paths:

■ **The Shape Editor Tool**   Offers the smoothest curves and performs double-duty as a path-editing tool. As you'll see shortly, you can adopt a work technique where you alternate drawing with editing as you build a path.

- **The Pen Tool**   Has the act and feel of drawing tools you might have used in other applications. With this tool, creating absolutely perfect curves is more difficult than with the Shape Editor Tool. However, drawing shapes that have both straight lines and curves along various segments of the path is easier.

- **The Freehand and Brush Tool**   The closest thing you'll find in a vector drawing program that is used as you'd use a paintbrush tool in a paint program. You can start painting immediately with the Freehand and Brush Tool—the brush styles are shown on the Infobar. However, you can also create a path, as well as brush stroke styles simultaneously with the other drawing tools by accessing the Line gallery.

- Additionally, you can create paths by creating a QuickShape, a rectangle and an ellipse (with the appropriate Toolbar tools), converting the shapes to editable shapes, and then breaking the closed paths at any point you need. This approach is covered later in this chapter.

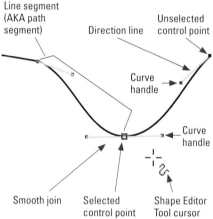

Regardless of which tool or method you use, a path always has a beginning and an end point, and often intermediate control points where the path takes a different direction. Control point handles are associated with curved path segments and do not exist on paths that are made up of only straight-line segments.

- **The Cursor's appearance**   A cursor's appearance in Xara is *a visual indicator of a proposed action*. The Shape Editor Tool is a multi-function tool, as are many of Xara tools. The cursor looks like cross hairs with a squiggly line below when over a blank area of the document and nothing has been drawn or selected. When a path has been started and a point clicked to end a path segment, a plus sign is featured on the Shape Editor Tool cursor, telling you the next point you click or drag is an *extension* of the current selected path. You might or might not want to close a path; an open path can serve a design purpose, such as arrows pointing out map directions. When the cursor is close to or directly over the beginning of a path, the cursor changes to a large plus sign below its cross hairs. If you don't want a path closed, put the cursor over the last point you clicked and then hold SHIFT while you click on this point. The path remains selected. Alternatively, you can end a path by pressing ESC, which also deselects the path. You can also move the points between path segments by placing the cursor over a point and then dragging—in this case, you know your cursor is in position by the move symbol below the cross hairs. Finally, you can change a path segment by clicking and dragging on it directly; your cursor changes to a hollow arrowhead when this action is possible. This is a fast way to change a straight-line segment into a curve and to reshape existing curved path segments.

■ **Path segment**   This is what we call the part of a path that is joined on both ends by control points. A segment can be a line or curved and you can reshape it by moving its control points, dragging on the control point curve handles, and by dragging directly on the segment (with less predictable results than using the curve handles) when your cursor is an arrowhead.

■ **Control point**   A path is made up of at least one segment; multiple segments are connected with control points, which, depending on the point's properties, can signify a sudden or smooth change in the direction of the path. The position of any control point on the page controls the direction of the path segment that follows the point. With the Shape Editor Tool, you can marquee-select (or press SHIFT-click) points and then move more than one path segment bound by the selected points. When a control point is selected, it changes to a hollow red square. Unselected points are represented by solid black squares.

■ **Curve handle (control point handle)**   Depending on the property (curve or straight line) of a path segment as it passes through a control point, there can be none, one, or two control point handles bound to the control point, You can use them to steer the path segment, creating a shallow or a steep curve for the segment. You can also manipulate control point handles while you draw with the Shape Editor and Selector Tools if the points are visible; make sure the Show Object Edit Handles icon is selected.

■ **Direction lines**   These connect the curve points to control points; they're an indicator of whether the control point is a smooth or cusp connection between path segments and are not manipulated directly in any way.

Trace Out a Path

Beginners and experts alike use guides and bitmaps on layers beneath the current layer to *trace out a path*, as it's called in architectural design. Having something to trace is particularly helpful for developing the skill to work with paths in Xara; in the following steps you'll do exactly that.

Open the document, shapes to trace.xar. Open the Object gallery, and notice the file contains a bitmap image on the bottom layer (which is locked) and you have a new Trace layer on top for a little practice with tracing shapes. Click on the Trace layer to select it, if it's not already the active layer. The goal is not to perfectly trace any of the four drawings but instead to develop the skill so that in the future you won't *need* to trace to draw.

How Many Points Make the Best Path?

You can click (or click and drag) as many points as you like to create shapes; however, too many control points can result in difficulty making your shape smooth in appearance. Conversely, too *few* control points that make up, for example, an oval, makes *editing* the oval a challenge.

Curve handles behave as levers for what can be described as the fulcrum—the pivot point—a control point along a curve. If you've ever tried to move an object by putting a plank under it and using something round as the fulcrum, you know that the farther the handle is from the fulcrum, the less control you have over precisely where the object will be moved.

What's true with curve handles is true with control points. Usually, you want to create control points at no more than 90° apart on the arc that describes the curve. When you design a curve segment along a path, envision where the center of rotation would be for the curve if it were part of a complete circle or oval. Then imagine the angle created by two lines extending from the center to each control point that makes up the arc. When you're just starting to use Xara, you might get away with 60° between points surrounding a curve, but if you create control points at every 45° or less, your path almost always will look uneven, a little lumpy, and hard to smooth.

Here's how to get a handle on the handles, points, and curves you produce with the Shape Editor Tool, by tracing over the French curve in the document:

1. Zoom into the French curve image, with the left side in clear view; you can begin a path anywhere you please, working clockwise or counterclockwise.

2. With the Shape Editor Tool chosen (press F4), first go to the Infobar and click the Make Curve button and the Smooth Join button.

You can determine whether a path segment is a line or a curve in advance before clicking to set a control point, and you can change connection and segment properties while you draw. You might find it more convenient to memorize the keyboard shortcuts for these buttons. Press c to set a curved path segment, L to set a line segment, z to set a control point to cusp, and s to set the control point to smooth.

3. Click a point at the center left edge of the French curve.

Make Curve   Smooth Join   Click
button   button

4. Click a second point where you pre-visualize that a 90° angle (or less) should exist between your first clicked point and this one. With the Shape Editor, your initial path segment won't be curved. Instead, the curve handles lay flush against the line, but this will change after you click a third control point.

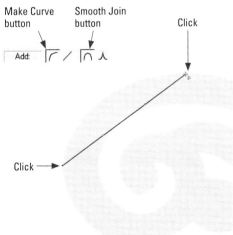

Click →

5. It's showtime now: you create a third control point by clicking and dragging, accomplishing an edit to shape the previous path segment as you place a control point. Watch the previous segment as you drag—a blue preview curve appears, showing you where and how the segment will adjust after you release the mouse button. This is Trick 1 of the two tricks to tracing of the French curve shape. Don't worry if the shape isn't perfect at this stage of the game; the goal is to get a general outline that you will refine and perfect later.

Click and drag to
create control point
Blue preview   and reshape previous
line   path segment

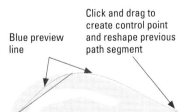

6. When you arrive at a sharp deviation in the French curve's profile (at its top right —peek ahead to the illustration in step 7), set a control point by clicking. Move on to the next control point location you want to set and click again. Then double-back to the smooth join

that should be cusp—there's a sharp change of direction. Double-click the control point; doing this changes its property from smooth to cusp. The Shape Editor draws shapes but is also an *editor*—Trick 2 of 2.

7. Drag first one and then the other curve handle visible when the control point is selected to reshape the two associated path segments. Then return to the last point you set, click it to select it, and proceed to click or click and drag to position the remaining points as needed to complete the profile. You always know if the next action will extend a path if a plus symbol is showing by the cursor's lower right.

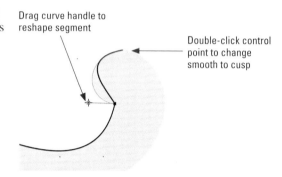

Drag curve handle to reshape segment

Double-click control point to change smooth to cusp

8. To close the path, single-click the first control point you created, when the cursor's plus symbol is visible. Now that you have created the coarse path, you can push and tug at the curves and curve handles with the Shape Editor Tool to perfect the shape. End of experiment; you now know how to draw and edit by using the Shape Editor Tool.

Work with the Pen Tool

The Pen Tool is a logical choice when you have a design that has a mix of smooth curves and sharp corners. Unlike the Shape Editor Tool, you cannot use the Pen Tool for editing curve handles as you draw. However, you *can* backtrack and *move* a control point, and change a straight line segment to a curve (by dragging directly on the line). Additionally, you have a pop-up menu entry while using the Pen Tool—right-click over a control point or a path segment and choose Shape Editor Tool.

The operation guide for the Pen Tool is short:

■ You click and drag in the direction in which you want a curve path segment to follow. Doing this creates a control point with control handles and a smooth join property.

■ You single-click to create a control point whose join is a corner that is neither cusp nor smooth because the control point has no control handles.

■ You single-click instead of clicking and dragging to create straight-line segments.

Precision Control Point Placement

If you're designing a machine part or just need a perfect pattern edge for a card, Xara offers hands-off controls on the Infobar when the Shape Editor is chosen and you've selected some control points along a path. For example, say you need a sawtooth pattern from left to right whose control points are perfectly spaced at 1-inch increments. You create a line (any drawing tool will work), using a guideline, and then click several times with the Shape Editor Tool to approximate where you need the points of the sawtooth design. If you are still using the Shape Editor Tool, click the Make Line button to ensure straight-line points with no handles. Click the second control point, and then, in the top middle field (the X field) on the Infobar, type **2in** and press ENTER. The control point moves to an absolute distance of 2 inches by the page's measure. Do the same for the other points (type measurements of 3in, 4in, etc); the process is shown in Figure 3-1. Then hold SHIFT, click every other point, and use the Nudge feature, pressing the DOWN ARROW key until your perfect sawtooth design displays the appropriate amount of toothiness. You also have fields for setting line length and angle if your design has straight-line path segments, and you can even precisely position curve handles when path segments are curved.

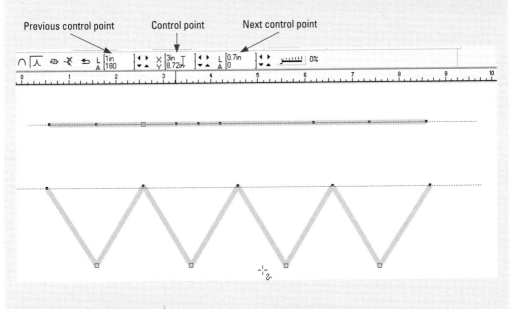

FIGURE 3-1 Use the Infobar fields to accurately position and space control points, line lengths, and curve handles.

In the shapes to trace.xar file, move down and to the left to the cartoon drawing of the crown. Here's how to get a little practice in with the Pen Tool, tracing a portion of the top of the crown:

1. Click and drag just a little, directly to the right, beginning at the point of the crown.

2. Click and drag a second point to the right and down (point at about 4 o'clock) to create a second control point and the path segment between the two points. Watch as you drag—the distance you drag from the control point sets the degree of curvature of the trailing path segment.

3. Repeat step 2, clicking at the tangent, the *apogee*—the farthest distance the curve will travel away from its bounding two control points. The blue preview of the proposed new path segment is an excellent visual guide.

4. Click and drag at the junction of the knob and the top of the crown. This sets a smooth curve control point that you will want to convert to a cusp property.

5. Click and drag at the midway point of the curve making up the top of the crown. Although you can usually continue a path segment to the next change of course in a path—which in this case would be the junction of the crown's top with the band of the crown—doing this would set a smooth control point, which you don't want. So you create an intermediate smooth-join control point at about 45° off the tangent of the curve segment and then single-click at the next junction to set a corner point.

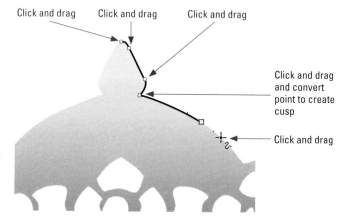

Click and drag   Click and drag   Click and drag

Click and drag and convert point to create cusp

Click and drag

Using the Freehand and Brush Tool

There are absolutely no constraints when you use the Freehand and Brush Tool—the approach is to simply drag with the tool to produce a fairly unstructured series of path segments and control points. The importance of this tool to your design work is that you can achieve a very natural look with paths that can later take custom outlines from the Line Gallery collection.

You have the option at any time to refit a Freehand and Brush Tool stroke, both as you draw (okay, as you *brush*) and afterward. Try this:

1. Choose the Freehand and Brush Tool, and then in a new document window, jitter the tool as you drag from left to right; pretend you're swatting a fly with the cursor. Release the mouse button, but don't deselect the path.

2. Drag the Freehand smoothing slider all the way to the right. Notice that some control points you created disappear. Xara evaluates redundant and superfluous control points and adjusts the path to follow curve handle properties it feels are the most significant, that create the greatest change in the path's segments.

3. Drag the slider all the way to the left. If the slider was at its default of 50 when you began, you'll see more control points created; the new path will tightly conform to just about every nuance of your mouse's movement across the page.

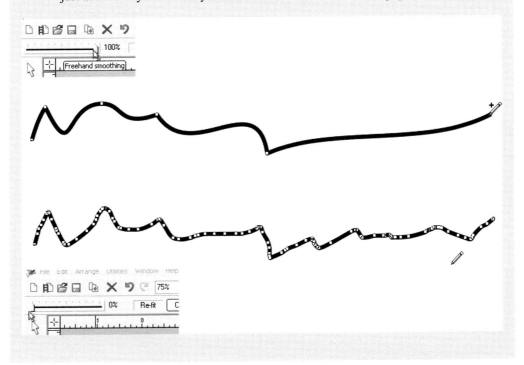

4. Choose the Shape Editor Tool. Marquee-select some but not all of the control points.

5. There is a Smoothing slider in a different location on the Infobar, but it serves the same purpose as the Freehand smoothing slider—you can use it to re-fit any path created by using any drawing tool in Xara. Drag the slider to the left or to the right and see that it affects only the path segments bound by their respective control points.

Use drawing tools in combination to create the art you need in record time. For example, if you want to draw a torn sheet of paper, first draw the jaggy edge with the Freehand and Brush Tool. Then switch to the Pen Tool, click the end point of the selected Freehand path to extend it, click a bottom point and a left point, and then click to close the path at top left.

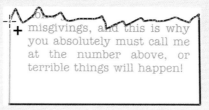

Editing a Path's Components

You have several options for modifying path segments within the overall path. They're available on the Infobar when you use the Shape Editor Tool to select one or more control points along a path. Figure 3-2 shows the area in Xara; detailed explanations are provided in this section.

■ **Current Mode** This area reports what you can do when a control point is selected. For example, when you've clicked on a control point along a path with the Shape Editor Tool, the box says Change; click the beginning or the end point on a path, you'll see Add. When you click a point to start a path, the box says New.

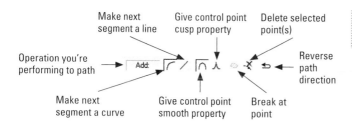

FIGURE 3-2 The Infobar when the Shape Editor Tool is active.

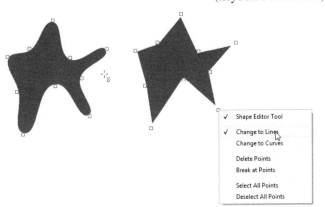

- **Make Curve** (keyboard shortcut c) and **Make Line** (keyboard shortcut L)   When drawing with the Shape Editor Tool, you use these buttons *before* you drag a path segment. Click the Make Line button, for example, if you want the segment you intend to create a straight line. However, the Shape Editor is also an editing tool—you can click or marquee-select several control points and then convert their properties. These two commands are also available by right-clicking after you select all of the points you want to affect.

- **Cusp and Smooth Join**   When you've create curve path segments, they can pass through a control point in a smooth fashion (one side of the curve handle direction line is linked to the other side and they move in tandem like a seesaw), or you can create an abrupt change in the overall path direction—a cusp join, in which the direction line between the curve handles is broken at the control point and both sides operate independently. To see the visual difference between smooth and cusp joins, create a path with the Shape Editor Tool, clicking up and down as you travel from left to right on the page to create sort of a sine wave. Hold SHIFT when you click the final control point to end the path. Marquee-select some of the control points and then click the Cusp Join button on the Infobar. Now when you click a control point to select it and reveal the curve handles, each handle can be move independent of the other and you can create a sharp-crested wave design.

- **Break At Points**   Breaking a path into separate segments can be done at a control point, or you can click directly anywhere on a path to create a new control point and then break the path there. This is an invaluable feature, especially when you've created a QuickShape and want to use the segments as individual paths. Let's run through a short tutorial here on how to create a flower design by breaking a star QuickShape and then applying a Stroke Shape (covered in detail later in this chapter):

1. Choose the QuickShape Tool. Then on the Infobar, click the Radius creation button to draw from the center outward, click the Create Polygons button and the Starred Shapes button, and then set the number of sides to 5. Drag a star shape that is about 450 pixels from top to bottom; release the mouse button when the Size field on the Infobar displays this value.

2. Open the Line gallery (on the Standard bar). Set the line width of the outline to 48 pixels.

3. SHIFT-click a warm color such as brown on the color line to set the outline color, and then left-click the Set 'no color' box to the left of the color line (for a No Fill effect).

4. Press CTRL-SHIFT-S (Arrange | Convert To Editable Shapes). The star loses its dynamic editing properties and is now simply a closed path.

5. In the Line gallery, open the Stroke Shapes/Pressure Profiles folder and double-click the Blip preset. This is *not* an impressive design now, because the Blip stroke shape starts and ends at the complete path of the star.

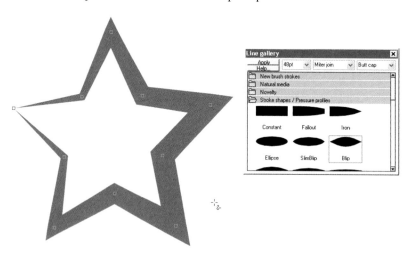

6. With the Shape Editor Tool, marquee-select all the control points and then click the Break At Points button on the Infobar. This command is also available from the pop-up menu (you right-click). The design

is much more interesting now that the Blip preset starts and ends at each individual path segment.

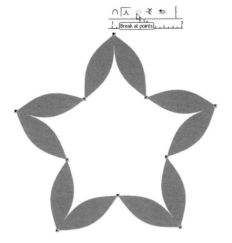

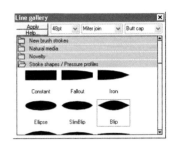

- **Delete Points**   You can remove one or more control points from a path by selecting the points and then clicking this button on the Infobar; you can also press BACKSPACE or use the right-click pop-up menu command to delete a selected point. When control points are deleted from a path, the neighboring path segments change. If the remaining control points on either side of the deleted control point have the Smooth Join property, they retain this property and the resulting shape, making it simple to refine the new shape while keeping the path segments and joins smooth in overall look.

FIGURE 3-3 Use the Reverse paths feature to make the start control point the end point and vice versa.

- **Reverse Paths**   The usefulness of this feature won't become apparent until you apply an outline to a path; you'll be able to see the most pronounced changes by using Stroke Shapes/Pressure Profiles. All you need to do is select a single control point with the Shape Editor Tool and then click the Reverse Paths button. Figure 3-3 shows what happens to a spiral path with the Saw Tooth profile applied at left and then reversed at right. You can achieve different looks for paths with a single click.

Joining Paths

It would be unfair to show you how to break paths without *also* showing you how to put path segments together. You can combine individual paths in Xara regardless of whether the start and end control points meet: you select two paths and then press CTRL-J (Arrange | Join Shapes). This means you can have one path, noncontinuous, with a single outline property; you can, for example, create several map arrows, join them, and then move and edit them—apply a different outline—all in one fell swoop. Perhaps of more use is to create two closed intersecting paths and join them. The intersection areas become negative space and you can apply a fill and an outline to create unusual compositions.

 Xara doesn't care which end of a path you extend it from; you can start at either end, and if the path is reversed from your intended use, use the Reverse Path button on the Infobar.

Here's still bigger news about joining paths: when you have two or more open paths you want connected into one, you can select them all, and then—with the Selector Tool or the Shape Editor Tool—you drag a path's end control point to another selected end point. The plus symbol on your cursor indicates that you're in position to connect the paths.

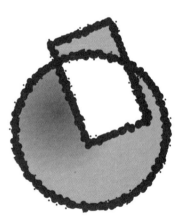

Let's put this wisdom to practical use.

Open the extend and join paths.xar file. Then open the Object gallery. There is a hidden layer on the bottom with design embellishments; leave it hidden for the moment. On top is another decoration: your task is to trace the right side of it, without closing the path. Then you'll see how to flip your trace and join the original with the mirrored copy to complete the decoration in lightning time.

1. Choose the Shape Editor Tool. Click on the Shape layer in the Object gallery to make this the active layer. Click a start point at the intersection of the guide and the top right side of the decoration.

2. Click points, traveling clockwise around the faint green decoration.

3. If your path goes off course, click a control point to reveal its curve points and then drag one of them to fit the curve to the underlying decoration. Alternatively, drag on the line segments to shape them into place when you see the hollow arrow cursor.

4. SHIFT-click when you've reached the end.

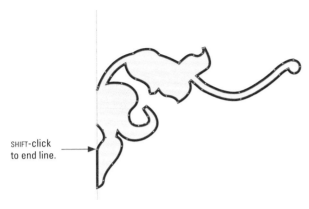

SHIFT-click
to end line.

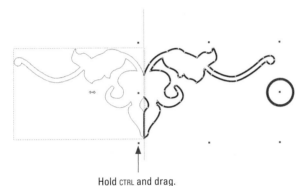

Hold CTRL and drag.

5. Choose the Selector Tool. You're going to perform a combination drop-copy and horizontally flip the copy at the same time. Click the right center bounding box handle of the path; while holding CTRL (constrains proportions of the selection), drag to the left until you see a preview of where the duplicate path will land. Then right-click before releasing both mouse buttons.

6. Hold SHIFT and add the original path by clicking it.

7. With both paths selected, drag one of the path end points to meet the other; you can do this with the Selector Tool or the Shape Editor Tool. You know you're in position and can release the mouse button when your cursor has a large plus symbol at its corner.

8. Now that the two paths are a single one, you can close the path at the top by dragging one end point to the other (the same as you did in step 7).

You now know, not only how to join paths, but also how to close them so they can be filled. However, it would be a shame not to *complete* the design. To visually integrate this elegant shape into the composition:

1. Fill the shape with any color you like, just for a temporary fill.

2. Choose the Bevel Tool and just drag on the face of the shape. You change the bevel by pasting the attributes from the existing dark green shape on the Design layer, but before you can paste an attribute such as a bevel, a shape already has to have a bevel, of any type.

3. Open the Object gallery on the Standard bar. Unhide the Design layer by clicking the Closed Eye icon. Click on the Locked icon to unlock the layer and restore it to the Arrow Cursor icon.

4. Click on the dark green shape's *bevel* and then press CTRL-C to copy it.

5. Marquee-select the shape you completed by using the Selector Tool—drag diagonally over both the shape and its child bevel—and then press CTRL-SHIFT-A to paste the attributes of the dark green shape's bevel (along with the color) to the one you created (see Figure 3-4).

FIGURE 3-4 Cut your work in half when designing symmetrical shapes. Flip a copy and then use the Join Shapes command.

Scale Line Widths

As you get into applying properties in the sections to follow, be aware of a much overlooked feature on the Selector Tool Infobar: Scale Line Widths. You might think that you'd *always* want the width of a path's outline to scale, but no, not always. What if you created a dozen shapes with an outline width thick enough to print well, and then decided you need a bitmap version of the design for the Web? If you scale the drawing down for the Web to a fairly small size, the outlines might scale to less than one pixel in width, and they'd vanish completely from your exported bitmap.

- When the Scale Line Widths button is depressed on the Infobar, outlines scale thicker and thinner as you increase or decrease the size of selected shapes.

- When the button is not depressed, outline width is always maintained as you shrink and grow selected objects.

Adding Properties to Paths

The following sections are as much the icing on the cake as the substance on the skeleton: vector paths aren't very attractive and it's the outline *properties* you assign to them that make your artwork tangible, exciting, and beautiful. You have an incredibly wide selection of properties in the Line gallery, and you can even build your *own* outline, as shown in this section. Imagine that: a path outlined with a path.

Cap and Join Properties

Whenever you apply an outline width to a path, you get to decide on how (in the case of an open path) the ends are built and the manner in which path segments meet at a control point.

Your Set Line Cap options for beginning and ending an open path are:

- **Butt cap**   If you imagine a tangent to the path—a line drawn perpendicular to the path—you create a butt cap ending this way. It is perfectly flat and it ends exactly at the location of the control point.

- **Square cap**   This path ending also ends perpendicular to the path, but it overshoots the control point by half the distance of the outline width. For example, if you give a path an 8-point outline with square caps, it will have 4 points of outline color on one side, 4 points on the opposite side, and 4 points of overshoot distance extended from the start and end control points.

- **Round cap**   This option creates a half-circle at the terminating control point on a path. Like the square cap, the round cap overshoots the control point by half the distance of the outline width.

Control points that aren't at the end of a path—especially along closed paths—often need a special join. Your Set Join Type options are as follows:

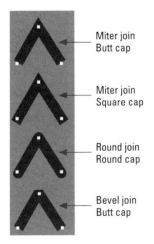

Miter join
Butt cap

Miter join
Square cap

Round join
Round cap

Bevel join
Butt cap

FIGURE 3-5 Use the join and cap properties that best suit a design need.

- **Miter join**   Connects two path segments by continuing the outline width until it self-intersects and ends. The greater the outline width, the more the join overshoots past the direction of the two joined path segments. At high outline values, as you'll see in the next section, a miter join can become a design problem, easily solved by choosing a different join property.

- **Bevel join**   This type of path segment connection truncates the outline as a flat termination perpendicular to the angle at which the path segments meet.

- **Round join**   A good path segment connection type for most of your illustration work. It's similar to the bevel join, but being rounded, it's less visually evident within a design.

Figure 3-5 illustrates the caps and joins.

Caps for path outlines cannot be mixed and matched; if your path begins with a square cap, for example, it will also end with a square cap.

Fancy Outlines for Your Paths

Color and width are only the beginning to outline properties.
You can use both shape and outline properties in harmony to
design outstanding compositions, as the next sections take you
through.

The Lines Gallery Folders: Applying Styles

The Line gallery contains six folders. The New Brush Strokes
folder only contains the default (an even line) unless you've
created a user stroke (you'll learn how to build one later in
this chapter), and new brush strokes are saved locally on a
document-to-document basis.

Figure 3-6 shows the categories of strokes and some of the
previews.

■ **Natural media**   You can apply these strokes while
using the Freehand and Brush Tool; you can also apply
them after creating a path with the Shape Editor Tool or
the Pen Tool and apply them to QuickShapes. Natural
media, Novelty, and Stroke shapes/Pressure profiles

FIGURE 3-6 The Line gallery is
your resource for all the strokes
(outlines for paths) available on
Xara.

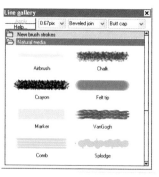
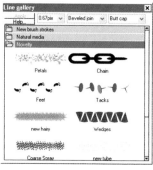
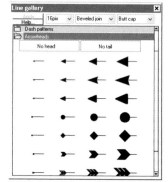
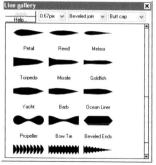
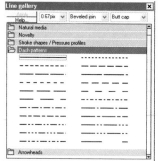

strokes are available as a drop-down list on the Infobar when the you use the Freehand and Brush Tool. Natural media strokes consist of an elaborately designed group of shapes, as do Novelty strokes—you're actually stroking a path with other (closed) paths. Natural media strokes have a default color that you can change by clicking the color line after making a stroke. You can also modify a Natural media stroked path by using Stroke Shapes/Pressure Profiles. For example, you can draw a Chalk stroked path and then apply an additional Bow Tie or Concave profile to the stroke.

You want to pay attention to the outline width when using any of the Line gallery presets. If, for example, you apply the Wedges Novelty stroke to a path but don't see anything, the outline width is probably too narrow. In general, you'll work with the Novelty and Natural media strokes most effectively at 36-point outline width and larger.

- **Novelty**   This collection consists of elaborately designed graphics; they're simply more whimsical in content than the Natural media. For all intents, Novelty strokes behave the same way as Natural media.

- **Stroke Shapes/Pressure Profiles**   This category can only modify Natural media and Novelty strokes, but you can also apply them "straight," with no other preset applied. As a Stroke Shapes/Pressure Profiles preset travels along a path, the contour width of the path changes. You can achieve the look of a felt tip pen and even some media yet to be invented with these presets.

- **Dash patterns**   These are ideal for creating road maps, coupons, and technical diagrams.

- **Arrowheads**   You have both heads and tails at your disposal from this folder. If you find your arrow is pointing in the wrong direction, remember to use the Reverse Paths button on the Infobar when the Shape Editor Tool is chosen—the same is true when using Stroke Shapes/Pressure Profiles.

Creating Your Own Brush Stroke

After this tutorial, you'll be inspired to build several brushes on your own. Consider the real world objects that are randomly peppered around: rocks, coins, even the texture of objects lumped in a pile.

Open Trees.xar. As mentioned earlier, a saved stroke is saved to a document and not as a program entry; therefore, there is a nearly completed stroke above the bare trees in this file, thus making an entry "leaves" in your New Brush Strokes folder. However, it's better to learn how the stroke is created then just to use it, and this is a two-parter. You first define a stroke from a group of objects, and then you edit the saved stroke to make the stroke less predictable in appearance, more natural.

1. Design three or four leaves. The leaves themselves can be made up of more than one shape—group two halves of a leaf to make a whole one with two different colors; this is similar to flipping and duplicating the ornament pattern you worked with earlier in this chapter.

2. Rotate and scale the leaves so the distance between them is random and their locations on the drawing page look random and natural. Make sure their orientation more or less is facing right, as this is the way strokes are built. Press CTRL-A and then CTRL-G to make a group from the leaves; keep the group selected.

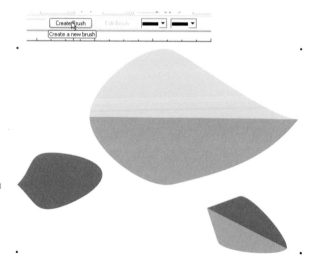

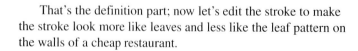

3. Choose the Freehand and Brush Tool, and then click the Create A New Brush button on the Infobar.

4. Name the brush in the following dialog box and click OK.

5. Make a stroke with the Freehand and Brush Tool, and then set the line width to at least 72 points on the Standard bar.

That's the definition part; now let's edit the stroke to make the stroke look more like leaves and less like the leaf pattern on the walls of a cheap restaurant.

1. Click the Edit Brush button on the Infobar: the box has several tabbed areas—let's work through them, beginning with Spacing.

2. Drag the Spacing slider to about 60% and then click Save—*always* click Save when you adjust a parameter or you'll lose it. Alternately, if you type 60% (rather than using the slider), press ENTER before clicking Save. Drag the Random slider so the result is between 60–164%; click Save. If you are not getting the visual feedback on the drawing page that pleases you, your leaf drawings might be of a different size than the ones in Trees.xar. Make changes to the settings, using your artistic judgment; watch the path you drew to preview the changes, and then click Save.

3. Click the Offset tab; here is where you determine how far away from the path your leaf objects can stray. Choose Direction From Line: On Line from the drop-down list, and then drag the Random slider to 0–54%. Click Save.

Click the Randomize button on any tabbed menu if you like to generate changes you might not have considered. If the change looks useful and visually interesting, click Save.

4. Click the Rotation tab. Check the Rotate Along Path check box and set the Rotation changes by: Adding to –16 degrees. You can use this stroke to paint leaves on bare branches, and negative rotation make the leaves splay outward instead of clumping together. Set the Random slider to 0–130%. Click Save.

5. Click the Scaling tab. Set the Random value to 59–168%. This will create leaves randomly whose size vary from one another by a factor of about 300%—some smaller, some larger. Your drawing will take on a depth of field when both small and large leaves are featured. Click Save.

6. Click the Fill Properties tab. Set the Saturation randomness to 0–16% and then set the Hue randomness to 0–52 degrees. If you're familiar with a traditional color wheel, what you're doing is allowing the green in the group of objects to move toward warmer colors, oranges and yellows, but no farther. Blue leaves would look strange. Click Save.

The Tile Fills check box is for when you use bitmaps for stroke fodder. It doesn't do anything checked or unchecked when you're working with vector shapes.

7. Finally, you can add just a little transparency; click the Transparency tab and drag the Transparency slider to about 9%. By doing this, you build up visual complexity in a composition, because some of the leaves allow just a little of the strokes under the current stroke to almost show through. Click Save, and that's it: close the dialog box. Figure 3-7 shows the boxes you just worked through, and a before and after of the leaves stroke.

The payoff to this exercise, naturally, is to paint some leaves on the trees. Go for it; if you want to make one of the trees enjoying a different season than the other, stroke over the branches. Then, while the path is still selected, use the Color Editor to change the hue of the selected path, as shown in Figure 3-8.

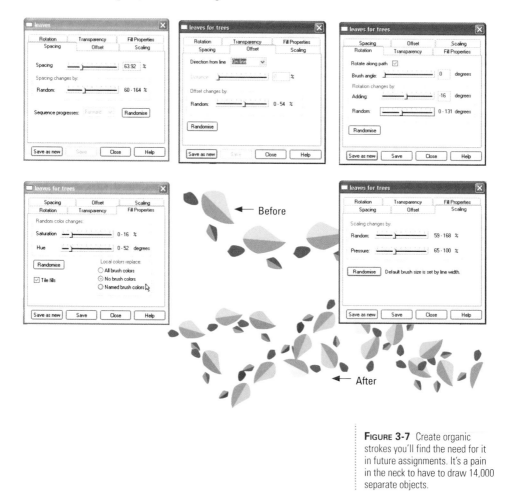

FIGURE 3-7 Create organic strokes you'll find the need for it in future assignments. It's a pain in the neck to have to draw 14,000 separate objects.

FIGURE 3-8 Create a brush stroke in advance of a design you have in mind to quickly populate the design with an elegant collection of shapes.

You'll find working with the Freehand and Brush Tool more rewarding if you press CTRL-SHIFT-O and then in Options check the Give Objects Most Recent Attributes box.

As a treat, play around with Snowflakes.xar; a brush you can build or just use with snowflake designs.

You'll frequently want to make a path that has a Novelty or a Pressure Profile property into a shape. As a shape, the object can then take a gradient fill or a bitmap and can be distorted with the Mould Tool. To change a path into a shape, choose Arrange | Convert Line To Shape.

4

Transforming Shapes

Shapes you draw—or create by using the QuickShape Tool—can be *further* modified through the extensive array of object translation (moving a shape), transformation (changing the shape), and effects features in Xara Xtreme. Once you've created a shape, your inclination is to then *do something creative* with it. This chapter takes you through the tools you use to precisely scale, move, rotate, duplicate in rows and along paths, and other easy routines that provide fantastic results.

Download and extract the contents of Chapter04.zip, which contains everything you need to work through this chapter's tutorial steps.

Moving and Stretching Shapes

One of the wonderful things about designing in vector art programs is that you can rework the art indefinitely. There are no pixels you're obliged to erase after goofing up, and if you've drawn a complex composition in the wrong place on a page, you can pick it up and move it. When you've spent a lot of time drawing something and you discover that it's a little too wide, or that it's crooked, you can scale and rotate shapes without losing any visual detail. The following sections take you through both the precision and manual methods of putting objects where you want them, at the size that suits your need.

Working with the Infobar

Below the Standard bar is the Infobar; it's contextual and offers options specific to the tool you're using currently. Although the Shape Editor performs some shape-editing tasks, it is the Selector Tool you use to move, rotate, scale, and generally alter a shape. When you choose the

Selector Tool, the Infobar offers transformation options you can use to directly change a shape, or enter numerical data for precise transformation.

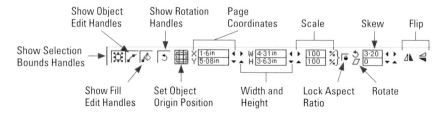

- **Selection Bounds Handles**   This button toggles the handles on and off that you use to scale and rotate objects. There is a Show Rotation Handles toggle button on the Infobar, but as long as the selection's outermost extent is visible—its bounds—if you put your cursor just a little inside the corner handles, you get a double-headed cursor that you can use to drag a rotation angle for the selected shape. Unless your zoom level is very distant from a selected object and you can't clearly drag a different selection handle (such as an object's fill), it's a good idea to always leave handles visible.

- **Show Object Edit Handles**   When toggled on, this option shows the control points along the path of a shape, and the center point of QuickShapes. When edit handles are hidden, you need to use the Shape Editor Tool to move a shape's control points; when toggled on, you can directly edit a path's control points with the Selector Tool.

- **Show Fill Edit Handles**   If an object has a solid fill, there is no advantage to making the fill edit handles visible. However, you can scale, move, and rotate gradients, fractal fills, and bitmap fills with the Selector Tool with this button toggled on. When off, you need to use the Fill Tool to modify the shape's fill.

- **Show Rotation Handles**   For the beginner, this is a good button to toggle on when you need rotation and skew handles to be clearly visible. Curved double-headed arrows at each corner can be dragged to rotate the selected shape. To skew (slant) the shape, you use the 3, 6, 9, and 12 o'clock middle handles. An alternative method for showing rotation and skew handles is to click a selected shape once and click an unselected object twice to display these handles. While this button is toggled on, however, you cannot scale an object.

- **Set Object Origin Position**   This button is actually nine small buttons, and the action you perform on any of the buttons is a single-click and then an action. When you scale, rotate, or perform similar operations on a shape or group of shapes, you have the option of changing the shape relative to its center *or* to its bounds. For example, if you want to rotate a shape relative to its bottom center, you first click the tiny button at 6 o'clock and then drag a rotation handle or enter a value in the Angle Of Selection field (then press ENTER). After performing the transformation, click another object origin position if desired or the center position to reset its default—these nine tiny buttons do not toggle on and off.

- **Page Coordinates (X/Y coordinate of selection)**   This feature is most meaningful if you have the page rulers turned on (press CTRL-L). The vertical ruler marks Y coordinates and the horizontal ruler marks X coordinates. Therefore, if you want an object to be located so its lower-left side touches the lower-left edge of a page, you type **0** in both of these fields and then press ENTER. You can change the origin of zero for both coordinates by dragging the "origin 0,0 point" to anywhere in the document window—not just the page but onto the pasteboard as well.

- **Width and Height of selection**   These fields are used for scaling in absolute increments, as the scale width/height fields are used for scaling relative to the current dimensions of a selected shape. They are also useful references as you work to see how large something is, or should be. By default, the Lock Aspect Ratio button is toggled on; if you type a new value in either field (and then press ENTER), the other dimension of the shape will change proportionately so you're not stretching a shape unintentionally.

Units for the Width and Height scales are set in Utilities | Options | Units, Page units. However, if, for example, your current units are pixels and you want a shape to be 3 inches, you type **3in** in the value field and then press ENTER. You denote pixels by typing **pix**, millimeters by **mm**, and so on, with no space between your value and the unit.

- **Scale width/height**   You use these fields to relatively scale a shape by entering a percentage in either field. The percentage automatically applies to both fields when the aspect ratio is locked, or you can enter percentages in the fields individually when the aspect ratio is unlocked. Relative scaling means that after changing the size of an object, the entry fields reset to 100%, so you have no sense of how much you previously scaled a shape. This is why the Width and Height fields provide instant reference to the absolute size of shapes.

- **Lock aspect ratio**   This button toggles on and off to constrain proportions when you use the Scale and Width and Height controls.

- **Angle of selection (or Rotate)**   Type a value in this field and then press ENTER to create an absolute rotation of an object. As the icon indicates, positive values are counterclockwise, but you can perform clockwise rotations by typing a – **(minus)** before a value before you press ENTER. Absolute rotation values reset after making them; there is no way to reset an object's degree of rotation unless you remember the rotation value. You can apply fractional amounts of rotation by typing a decimal after a whole number value.

- **Skew-angle of selection**   As the icon indicates, positive values entered slant an object to the right, while negative values make a shape skew left. You can enter almost any value in this field, but skew amounts over 90 degrees simply make a shape look weird and put its width clear off your drawing page.

 The increase/decrease buttons next to fields can be used to change rotation, scale, and other properties by a single digit value.

- **Flip horizontally/Flip vertically**   These buttons are used for turning a shape into a mirror image of its former self.

Hands-On with Shape Transformation

Some occasions call for precise transformations, but *manually* adjusting an object is the more organic, artistic approach. To change a shape with the Selection Tool, you need to be sure the

Show Selection Bounds Handles are visible and toggle on the Show Object Edit Handles to restore any QuickShape you might be editing.

 Although you can create rectangles and circles by using the QuickShape Tool, shapes you produce with the Rectangle and Ellipse Tools are also QuickShapes, in that they have special editing properties.

With the Ellipse Tool, hold CTRL and marquee-drag (drag diagonally while holding the mouse button) a circle for a little experimenting now; CTRL constrains ellipse creation to proportionate circles. Fill the circle with a solid color or a gradient so you can better view the transformations you'll perform.

- To scale the circle proportionately—without stretching or squashing it—select the circle with the Selector Tool, and drag any of the corner bounds handles away from the object's center to enlarge it or toward the center to shrink it. It's useful to turn on the Live Drag Indicator at the bottom right of the status line by double-clicking it so the circle is hollow and not blue. If you do this, Xara Xtreme shows you a preview on the page of the proposed transformation before you release the mouse button.

- To scale a shape from its center inward or outward, hold SHIFT as you drag a corner bounds handle.

- To stretch or squash a shape, drag the middle bounds handles away or toward the object's center.

- To *disproportionately* scale *both* sides of a shape simultaneously, hold SHIFT as you drag a central bounds handle.

- To scale an object larger or smaller by a whole number percentage (200%, 3×, and so on), hold CTRL while you drag a corner handle. If you hold CTRL and drag a middle bounds handle, you disproportionately scale the sides equidistantly by a percentage.

Scale proportionately   Scale disproportionately   Hold SHIFT to scale from center

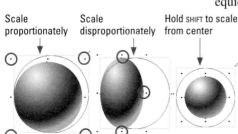

Skewing a shape is performed after you click on a shape that is already selected. Drag any of the middle bounds handles, which look like double-headed arrows. CTRL constrains a skew operation to the value you've specified in File | Page Options | General | Document Editing | Angle Constraint (which also applies to rotation).

Holding SHIFT causes the skew to happen centrally on a shape: the top side slants right while the bottom slants to the left.

CTRL and SHIFT are good keyboard modifiers to commit to memory: you'll find with experience that manually transforming shapes is faster than relying on the Infobar value entry fields.

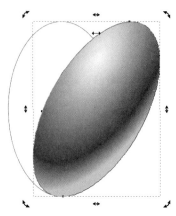

Duplicating and Changing Object Centers

The center around which a shape is scaled and rotated doesn't have to be located at the center of a shape; you'll often find it useful to move a shape's center so it pivots off-center to create complex designs. The following tutorial takes you through the composition of several duplicate shapes that make a pattern. The keys to accomplishing this are to move the center point of an oval and then get familiar with the drop-copy technique in Xtreme.

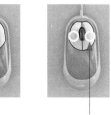

To create a copy of an object in a different area of the page:

1. With the Selector Tool, drag the shape to the duplicate's intended position on the page.

2. While the left mouse button is depressed, tap the right mouse button.

3. Release both buttons.

Drag | Tap right mouse button | Release both buttons

Here's how to put the drop-copy technique to constructive use with the rotate object manual technique:

1. Drag a horizontal and a vertical guide from the rulers (press CTRL-L if they aren't in the workspace) until they intersect at the middle of the page.

2. Choose the Ellipse Tool. Then hold SHIFT, click a few inches above the intersection of the guides, and drag until you have an oval about twice as tall as it is wide.

3. With the Selector Tool, click the selected oval so you can see the rotate/skew handles and also the transformation center.

4. Drag the transformation center to the guides intersection. The snapped indicator on the status line turns to a red horseshoe when the center is precisely snapped to the guides.

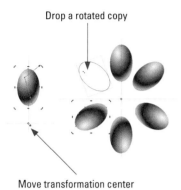

Drop a rotated copy

Move transformation center

5. The oval is still in rotate/skew transform mode: drag the top-right rotate handle down until the preview shows that the intended position is clear of the original position. Tap the right mouse button and then release both buttons to drop the copy of the oval.

6. Repeat step 5 a few times, each time with the new duplicate selected, working clockwise. In no time, you've created a fairly symmetrical pattern. If you want a perfectly symmetrical pattern, hold CTRL as you drop copies to constrain the angle of rotation.

Transforming QuickShapes

You can do some exceptionally neat things to modify QuickShapes—rectangles, ellipses, and polygons—because these shapes have internal behaviors you can change in a dynamic way that's totally reversible. You'll see the advantages of changing a shape that can be *un*changed in the following sections.

Undoing a QuickShape Transformation

When you create a QuickShape with the Rectangle, Ellipse, and QuickShape Tools, notice that the shape has control points that look exactly the same as control points along a path you'd draw with the Shape Editor and other tools. However, you don't use these special control points to steer paths but instead to create modifications to the entire shape.

Double-click a control point to restore proportions

Try this: With the Ellipse Tool, drag an oval, making it very short and wide. Now with the Ellipse Tool, Selector Tool, or QuickShape Tool, double-click on any of the control points. The oval becomes a perfect circle because that is the native state of this type of QuickShape. You can perform this on any ellipse you've distorted with the Selector Tool too; skewed ellipses also return to perfect circles with a double-click on a control point.

Create Round-Corner Rectangles

A rectangular QuickShape has a different editing property than an ellipse because it has corners. You can round the corners of a rectangle by double-clicking a corner point. A second double-click on the corner returns it to a 90° intersection of adjoining lines.

Be sure you don't attempt disproportionate scaling of a round-corner rectangle by dragging its middle object bounds handles: doing this disproportionately scales the rounded corners and the resulting shape looks awkward.

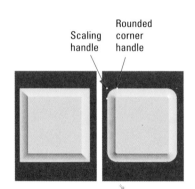

- To scale a rounded corner rectangle, drag the control point between the rounded corner control points.
- To adjust the amount of corner roundness, drag the rounded corner control points.

QuickShapes and Modifying Polygons

The QuickShapes Tool provides an Infobar that lets you create circles, rectangles, and symmetrical polygons—both the sort you see in a chemistry class and *star-shaped* polygons. Figure 4-1 shows the Infobar when the QuickShapes Tool is chosen and some examples of the interesting polygons you can create after clicking the Polygon button.

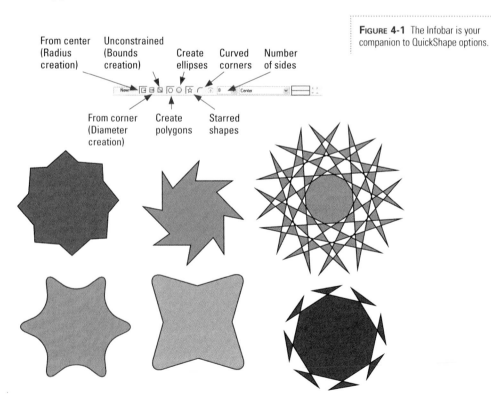

FIGURE 4-1 The Infobar is your companion to QuickShape options.

The first three buttons are fairly self-explanatory: they control from which direction a QuickShape is created when you drag.

- **Create Polygons**   Click this button before you begin dragging to create a shape that has anywhere from 3 to 99 sides. You set the number of sides by using the Number Of Sides drop-down list, which is also an entry field in case you want a polygon with more than 10 sides.

- **Create Ellipses**   Clicking this button basically produces a circle, which you can also create by using the Ellipse Tool. However, when you use the QuickShape Tool, an ellipse you create can become a polygon at any time. This is not true when you use the Ellipse Tool.

- **Starred Shapes**   As with the Create Polygons button, clicking the Starred Shapes button lets you produce a pointy polygon; you use the Number Of Sides list to specify the number of points, not the number of sides. After creating a starred shape, you can alter the degree of stellation from extremely star-like to practically a circle by dragging the control points away or toward the center with the Selector or QuickShape Tool. You cannot access the Starred Shapes button without first clicking the Create Polygons button.

You will see that a four-sided polygon, in starred shapes mode, does not look like a rectangle. Four-sided polygons in starred shapes mode actually have eight sides.

Because the Polygon QuickShape obeys the same editing properties as a rectangle, you can blunt the points of a polygon and a starred polygon by double-clicking a point. You can also drag an inner control point on a starred polygon (not the pointy part but the point *between* the outer points) inward and past other points until the interior of the polygon self-intersects. Several examples of the fascinating op-art geometry this creates are shown in Figure 4-1.

Converting a QuickShape

You might reach a point in editing a QuickShape when you want to remove its symmetrical properties and actually edit the control points along its path. The command to allow this is CTRL-SHIFT-S (Arrange | Convert to Editable Shapes). Make sure you have your rounded corners and everything a QuickShape can transform into before using this command; after simplifying the object, you've let the magic out.

Open the file, QuickShape editing.xar. In the Object gallery, the bottom layer is active and the cartoon "Thwack!" is locked on the upper layer. The following simple tutorial shows how to make an irregularly shaped burst behind the cartoon sound effect, which is also useful to put behind "Sale" and "Now New 20% More Free."

1. With the QuickShape Tool, click the Create Polygons and Starred Shapes buttons on the Infobar. Then type **15** in the Number Of Sides field and press ENTER. Fill it with red by clicking the color swatch on the color line. Then press SHIFT and click on the Set 'no color' icon to the left of the color line to remove the outline of the shape. Click the Bounds Creation button.

2. Drag on top of the word "Thwak!" until the starry polygon is a little larger than the phrase, so you can see the points.

3. Choose the Selector Tool. Then while holding SHIFT, drag the left or right middle handle outward until the starry shape is much wider than it is tall.

4. Press CTRL-SHIFT-S to convert the shape to a regular closed path.

5. Click the selected shape to put it into rotate/skew mode and then rotate it a little counterclockwise so it matches the angle of "Thwak!".

6. One point at a time, select a few control points along the starry object's path, and then move them until the path takes on a natural, irregular appearance.

Aligning and Distributing Shapes

Between dropping copy and creating different versions of a shape by scaling and other operations, you'll soon have a lot of objects on a page. It would be nice to be able to *arrange* these shapes, and the Object Alignment palette helps you do that. With more than one object selected on a page, press CTRL-SHIFT-L (Arrange | Alignment on the main menu).

At the top of the Object Alignment palette is an interactive proxy box that you can use in lieu of the drop-down lists.

Clicking in any of nine "hot spots" in the box aligns selected objects to the center, left center, top right, and so on. If you hold CTRL while you click in the box, you specify only vertical alignment. Hold SHIFT and click to set up only horizontal alignment. Before doing this, however, it's best to specify the *extent* to which objects are placed on the page by clicking a choice in the Within area.

How Far Can Xara Align Objects?

You use the Within area to specify the extent on the page to which objects are automatically moved, aligned, and distributed.

- **Selection Bounds**   The default setting. Regardless of how you align objects, they always stay within the outermost area of your selection.

- **Bounds Of Back Object**   The back selected object is not affected, but instead determines the boundary limits for the alignment of the *other* selected objects.

- **Page(s)**   Aligns and/or distributes objects to the boundary of your current page—or pages if you have a multi-page document set up. This is a good way to pepper an entire page with shapes.

Spray, a small application designed by Dmitry Malutin, can instantly create hundreds of random ellipses. You can download it at http://xaraxtv.at.tut.by/spray.htm and then align all the objects to a page for instant background designs.

- **Spread**   This option performs the same alignment operation as Page(s) but does so when you have a spread set up for magazine or other publication layout. To create a spread, press CTRL-SHIFT-O, click the Page Size tab, choose a Page Size from the drop-down list, and then click the Double Page Spread check box.

Alignment vs. Distribution

The Aligning drop-down lists give you styles for both alignment and distribution of objects selected, and you can mix and match alignment with distribution. **Alignment** is the *arrangement* of objects in a row or column, while **distribution** specifies the *spacing* between objects. Alignment is visually intuitive, but distribution deserves a little ink here.

- **Distribute Top Edges**   The tops of the objects are evenly spaced with this option. It's useful in design work when used in combination with Within Bounds Of Back Object to vertically distribute the top edges of a selection, while choosing Align Left to make quick charts and graphs.

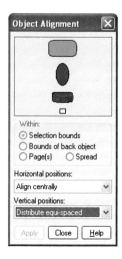

- **Distribute Bottom Edges**   The bottom of the objects are evenly spaced.

- **Distribute Left and Right Edges**   Respectively, the left and right edges are used as the basis for the distribution.

- **Distribute Centers**   The centers of the objects are evenly spaced. You will achieve a different effect than by simply aligning objects to center.

- **Distribute Equi-spaced**   The objects are evenly spaced from each other.

 If you see that you've made a mistake in alignment options after clicking Apply, click in the document window to change the focus from the palette to the page, and then press CTRL-Z to Undo.

Here is a remarkable example of alignment and distribution; open the file, align ruler.xar. It's a drawing of a traditional ruler, with the tick marks scattered all over the place. If you've drawn several open lines or objects in the proper left-to-right order but have messed up on their spacing and relative alignment, the Object Alignment palette can sort it out in one or two clicks. There are only two prerequisites for aligning objects in order:

1. The objects need to be in the right *sequence* from one side to the other.

2. The objects at either end need to be in their final selection position. In this ruler file, the 1-inch tick is aligned to the *1* on the ruler, as is the tick above the *5*.

Here's how to prove to the design community that Xara rules:

1. With the Selector Tool, marquee-select all the lines above the ruler while being careful not to select any of the ruler parts.

2. Press CTRL-SHIFT-L to display the Object Alignment palette.

3. CTRL-click the bottom of the proxy box to align all the selected shapes to the bottom horizontally. Choose the Within: Selection bounds option if it's not already selected.

4. Choose Distribute Equi-spaced from the Horizontal Positions drop-down list. Click Apply. You can close the Object Alignment palette now.

5. Hold SHIFT and then press the DOWN ARROW (↓) key about six times. By default, the Nudge distance is 1 pixel in Xara; holding SHIFT increases the distance by 10 times.

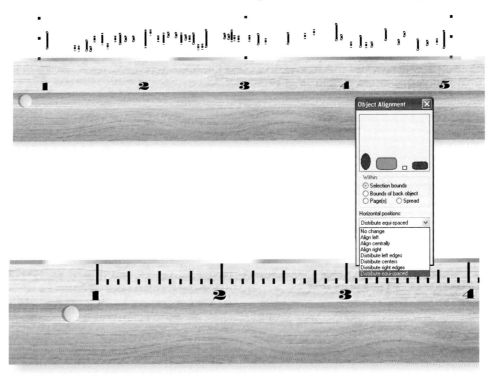

Combining Shapes

Adding and subtracting from a shape by using a different shape is called a *Boolean operation*, after mathematician George Boole, who devised algebra statements that use logical, plain English declarations to describe conditions, such as "Show me B but without any of A showing" and "Show me A and B united." In addition to the Join Shapes command in Xara (CTRL-J), you have four such Boolean operations called Combine Shapes on the Arrange menu. All Xara operations for combining shapes can also be displayed on a control bar, which you should display now to witness some of the speed and power of putting shapes together. Choose Window | Control Bars, scroll down the list, and then check Arrange if it's not already checked. The Arrange control bar appears above the Standard bar; if you prefer to work with a floating bar, drag by the edge of the bar into the drawing page.

You need to know three things before combining shapes:

1. The object that affects the outcome of a combination is always the top object. For example, if a square is on top of a circle and you choose Subtract Shapes, the result is a donut with a square hole.

2. The object that affects the result shape is deleted. When, for example you subtract a square from a circle, the square goes away.

3. The result object inherits its properties from the top object when you're adding shapes and from the back object when you're subtracting shapes. When you subtract an orange square from a blue circle, your donut with the square hole is blue.

When you use Join Shapes or Subtract Shapes, if the top object is completely surrounded by the underlying shape, you can retrieve the top, deleted shape. Press CTRL-K to clone the result shape, move it away from the result shape, and then choose Arrange | Break Shapes. You now have both original shapes. This trick doesn't work when you use Subtract Shapes if the top object only partially intersects the bottom shape.

Figure 4-2 visually demonstrates four object combinations that, with the artistic creation of special shapes, can quickly produce exactly the result shape you need for a composition.

A Shape Combination Exercise

The following steps show a very practical working example of Boolean shape combination. You're going to use all the skills you've learned so far in this chapter and design an international Walk sign—a stylized human figure with rounded corners—as a single object.

Open the document, walking.xar. The Object gallery shows a bottom locked layer that contains an image of a mannequin approximating the classic pose symbolizing "It's okay to walk now; you're not going to get run over." Also, there is a hidden layer; in case you get into a jam, all the individual pieces for this tutorial are provided for you.

FIGURE 4-2 Combine shapes to arrive at the shape you need.

Two shapes   Add   Subtract

Intersect   Slice

Here's how to build the symbol by creating pieces, modifying them, and then combining them:

1. You'll be most comfortable creating shapes with an outline but no fill so you can see the mannequin for geometric positioning of shapes. With the Walking.xar document open, set the line width to 2 or 4 pixels on the Standard bar. If Xara alerts you that nothing has been selected and asks if you would like to use this property as the default, click Set, which means "Yes. Please." All future shapes will have a green outline, but only in this document.

2. Similarly, SHIFT-click on a bright green swatch on the color line and click Set in the attention box. Then click the No Fill icon to the left of the color line and click Set in the Attention box. You're good to go now.

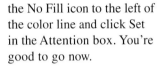

3. Choose the QuickShape Tool, and then click the Radius Creation (from center) and Create Ellipses buttons on the Infobar.

4. Drag from the center of the head outward until you've produced a circle a little larger than the head of the mannequin.

5. Switch to the Rectangle Tool, and then drag a rectangle about the proportions of the torso of the mannequin.

6. With the Selector Tool, move the rectangle until its top-right edge is over the top right of the mannequin torso. Click on the rectangle to put it in rotate/skew mode.

7. Move the transformation center to the top-right corner, and then rotate the rectangle until it fits over the mannequin torso.

8. Double-click any corner to make this QuickShape a rounded rectangle and then adjust the roundness of the corner by dragging on any rounded corner control point. You can fill the head and torso with a solid color for easier viewing now.

9. The arms can each be represented by two rectangles; create and move them into position as you just did with the torso. Move their transformation centers, rotate them, and then round the corners to a severe extent so they look like capsules.

10. You should have four rectangles for the two arms now. It's okay to move them a little away from the mannequin to make a slightly stylized anatomy. The mannequin is a reference for the pose and not an absolute guide. These international symbols never look exactly like humans.

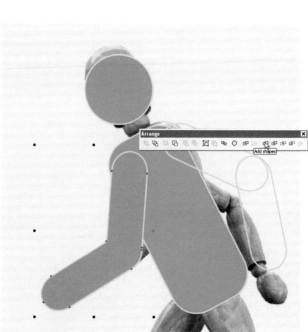

11. Select both left-arm rectangles and then click the Add Shapes button on the Arrange control bar. You can fill the result shape with a solid color now. Do the same with the right-arm rectangles.

12. Select both arms and the torso. Click the Add Shapes button. Because the torso inherits the properties of the top shape, the entire torso and arm shapes are now filled.

13. Create the legs exactly as you did with the arms. With the legs selected, press CTRL-B to put them to the back of the layer, and then use the Add Shapes button to make the legs and torso one object. The resulting shape inherits the fill.

14. Select the head and the body and then press CTRL-J (or click the Join Shapes button on the Arrange bar) to join them. Alternatively, because these two shapes don't overlap, you could click the Add Shapes button and get the same result: one object.

Alternatively, you can make your design a sign and not just a symbol.

1. With the Rectangle Tool, hold CTRL-SHIFT and then drag, beginning at the center of the figure you've drawn. You've created a centered square that is rotated 45 degrees because you used both the Draw From Center key modifier and the CTRL (constrain proportions) modifier.

2. Using the Selector Tool, scale the figure to fit within the rotated rectangle. Double-click a corner of the rectangle with the Selector or QuickShape Tool to round the corners, press CTRL-B to put it behind the figure, select both shapes, and then click the Subtract Shapes button.

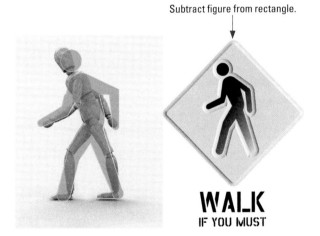

Subtract figure from rectangle.

WALK
IF YOU MUST

Run, don't walk, to Chapter 5, to learn how to *fill* your design.

5

Working with Fills

Xara Xtreme goes way beyond the definition of traditional vector drawing program "fills." A shape can be filled with solid colors, color-matching formulas for pigments from PANTONE specifications, gradient fills, images, fractal patterns—and you can even fill an object with a different object. This chapter shows you the artistic uses for fills in Xara, and along the way you'll learn how to add color to a composition in a way that mimics everything from traditional art to photorealism.

 Download and extract the contents of Chapter05.zip, which contains everything you need to work through this chapter's tutorial steps.

Applying Solid Color Fills

You can apply solid fills to shapes by using any of three different resources in Xara Xtreme:

- **The Color Line** The strip at the bottom of the interface can display a collection from any of those in the Color Gallery; right-click over a Color Gallery library and then choose Show In Color Line from the pop-up menu. You can apply colors on the Color Line to a selected shape by single-clicking a swatch. Alternatively, you can recolor a filled shape by dragging a swatch on top of the shape. You don't have to select shapes to fill them when using this technique.

- **The Color Gallery** You can double-click a folder icon to extend a color swatch library, and then double-click a swatch to apply it to a selected shape. Alternatively, with any solid filled shape, you can drag a swatch from a library on top of a shape to change the color.

- **The Color Editor** You can specify any local color you like by using the color component fields and then apply this color by dragging the bottom or top swatches (at the right side of the box) on top of a shape, whether it's currently selected or not.

When a shape is selected and you mix a color by using the Color Editor, the selected shape immediately changes to that color; you can click the reference swatch above the current color swatch to undo any color change—you drag this swatch on top of the shape. You can also color unselected filled shapes by dragging a swatch from the Color Editor to any solid-filled object.

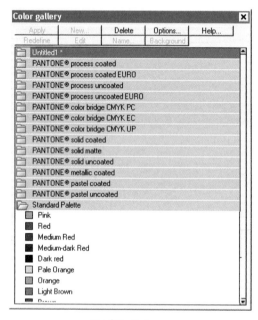

The Color Gallery

The Color Editor

Displays the Color Editor

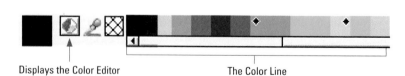

The Color Line

Shapes filled with gradients, fractals, and bitmaps will not take a solid color unless you select the shape and then click a color on the Color Line; drag-dropping swatches doesn't work. The reason for this is that you need to change the *type* of fill before applying a solid color.

Identifying Items on the Color Line

The Color Line does more than show off a nice collection of swatches; it's also your guide to what type of colors you have on tap and what the current fill color is and a resource for copying and mixing up colors.

 To color an outline around a shape, you can SHIFT-CLICK a swatch on the Color Line.

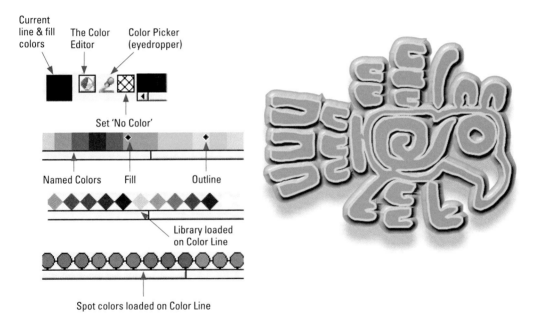

Current line & fill colors

The Color Editor

Color Picker (eyedropper)

Set 'No Color'

Named Colors   Fill   Outline

Library loaded on Color Line

Spot colors loaded on Color Line

■ **Color Editor**   You can toggle the Color Editor display on and off by clicking the button whose face is a tiny color wheel.

■ **Color Picker**   The Color Picker is always available for sampling a screen color and immediately applying the color you've chosen to a selected object. Note that with gradient fills, the eyedropper is contextual; you must select a control point along the gradient line to set that point in the gradient with a color you sample by using the Color Picker.

- **Current line & fill colors**   This box at the lower left of the interface (not precisely a part of the Color Line) indicates from moment to moment the color of the outline and the fill. It shows the currently selected color attributes; it shows the default values if no object is selected and an object's color attributes if a shape is selected. If several shapes are selected and they have different fill and/or line properties, this box shows nothing. Similarly, if a selected shape has no fill, this box is blank. Line color is displayed by an edge around the box, and the current fill color is displayed inside this color edge. With gradients (discussed later in this chapter), this box is split horizontally: the start color is shown at bottom and the end color is shown in the top half.

- **Set 'No Color'**   You click this box to the left of the color swatches to remove the fill of a selected shape. You can also drag the Set 'No Color' swatch on top of an unselected shape to remove its fill. SHIFT-CLICK the Set 'No Color' box to remove the line color.

- **Special shapes for different swatches**   By default, the Standard Palette colors are listed on the Color Line; they're indicated by a diamond swatch shape as are most library colors you load on the Color Line from the Color Gallery. To load a color library, you right-click the folder icon on the Color Gallery and then choose Show In Color Line from the pop-up menu. Named colors are colors local to a document and a template; they are represented by a square color swatch on the Color Line and are not loaded to the Color Line from the Color Gallery unless you choose Show In Color Line from the right-click options. Naming colors is demonstrated later in this chapter. Spot colors are additional colors to the standard CMY and K color plates used in commercial printing; for example, many commercial goods such as snacks use packaging printed with CMYK inks and then a special ink for the logo. The logo might be a PANTONE color-matching metallic ink and this spot color is shown on the Color Line in a circle (a *spot*).

Examining the Color Editor

The Color Editor is your resource for mixing up custom colors and adding them to the Color Line as named colors. However, the Color Editor performs several *other* convenient functions, so this is a good time to discuss solid colors and the editor. Open the Color Editor by clicking the color-wheel button to the left of the Color Line.

■ **Show/Hide Advanced Options panel**   Use this button to toggle between a simple and advanced view of the Color Editor's features.

■ **Color Model drop-down**   Use this list to choose from a color model within which to define colors. In this book, HSV is used extensively as a color model because of its ease of use. However, there will be occasions when you need to use the subtractive color model CMYK for specifying printing ink values, the RGB color model (when you need to match a client or co-worker's specifications), and Grayscale, ideal for working accurately for black and white output. Color models in Xara Xtreme are synchronous—there is no out-of-gamut concern when you switch between colors defined in CMYK and those defined by using HSV—Xtreme provides a general "domain" for user colors that work with one another.

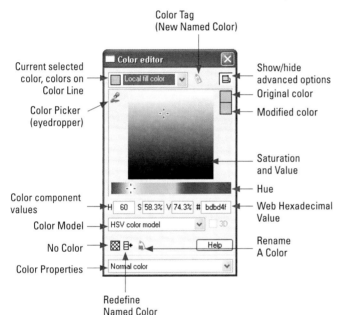

Color Tag (New Named Color)

Current selected color, colors on Color Line

Color Picker (eyedropper)

Color component values

Color Model

No Color

Color Properties

Redefine Named Color

Show/hide advanced options

Original color

Modified color

Saturation and Value

Hue

Web Hexadecimal Value

Rename A Color

■ **Saturation and Value field** (HSV color model)   *Shades* of a specific color are usually based on a combination of Saturation and Value (brightness, luminosity). Use the large field in the center of the Color Editor when you use the HSV color model to create shades of a defined hue much the same way you mix black or white with paint or other pigment to create a shade of a color. Drag the cross hairs in this color field to specify the color components you need to modify the Hue component.

■ **Hue slider**   Drag the cross hairs along this area to set a hue, and then work your way around Saturation and Value to define a color you need.

- **Color Component values**   These value boxes not only give you numerical data about colors you choose, but you can also type in these boxes to precisely redefine color. For example, if you like the hue and value you've defined for a color and only want to change its saturation: you type in the S field to do so.

In Options I Units, you can choose from Percent or 0–255, and this has a bearing on the display of color components in the Color Editor. Because monitors usually can display only 24-bit color (8 bits per channel), you might have an easier time using the 0–255 color units. Setting this option to 0–255 breaks RGB and HSV color models into increments (256 units is 2 to the 8th power) that match 24-bit color depth. Three channels of 8-bit-per-channel color equals 24 bits.

- **Web Hexadecimal Value**   When defining colors for Websites, this field is invaluable for discovering and also defining the colors declared in the HTML document that makes up the Web page. For example, if you want to match a color the Website designer specified as a21c1c (a brick red), you type this into the Hexadecimal Value box and the Color Editor presents you with the values in HSV, CMYK, or RGB amounts.

- **The Color Picker**   This is the eyedropper icon available both next to the Color Line and on the Color Editor. To sample a *screen* color—but not the *actual* color of an object with transparency in a blending mode—drag the eyedropper from the Color Editor to the area on the page from which you want to sample color. The sampled color is immediately available as a modified color swatch on the Color Editor.

When using the Color Picker, you'll perform two operations at once (one possibly unintended) if you have an object selected while using this tool. Sampling a color when an object is selected also *applies* the sampled color to the selected object or group of objects. So if you only want to sample a color for naming and adding to the Color Line, don't have an object selected during this action (or press ESC to deselect all objects before using the Color Picker).

- **Original and Modified Color Swatches**   The color of a selected object or the default color is displayed as a swatch at top right on the Color Editor. This is an active screen element and you can drag and drop this swatch to any object on the page to recolor it. Conveniently, when you mix a color, this is considered a modification of the current color and is shown as a swatch below the current color swatch. This swatch, too, can be drag-and-dropped onto objects in your composition. You have Undo capabilities at your disposal here and also a good reference between where you were and where you are color-wise.

- **Current selected color and colors on Color Line**   The drop-down list at the top of the Color Editor shows the current local color (as shown in the Color Editor). If you drop the list down, you can select any color from the Color Line, plus a color to apply to an object's outline, and Contone colors (covered later in this chapter).

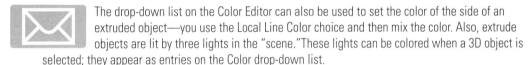

The drop-down list on the Color Editor can also be used to set the color of the side of an extruded object—you use the Local Line Color choice and then mix the color. Also, extrude objects are lit by three lights in the "scene." These lights can be colored when a 3D object is selected; they appear as entries on the Color drop-down list.

- **Color Properties**   There are Named Colors, Local Colors (unsaved colors, not named), Tints, Shades, and Links To Other Colors. You use this drop-down list to create dynamic links to named colors, which is a very quick way of recoloring a complex composition of scores of colored objects.

- **Color Tag (New Named Color)**   You click this icon at the top of the palette to name the color you have currently defined in the Color Editor, covered later in this chapter.

- **Redefine Named Color**   To use this button, you first name a color. With the named color loaded, click this button and a copy of the named color is created. You can then redefine the color by dragging in the color field and using the Hue slider, except it's a different color. This will make sense when you get into naming colors—it's a terrific way to create a lot of variations on named colors without accidentally overwriting one you've saved.

- **Rename A Color**   Because the Redefine Named Color feature auto-names variations on named colors, you click this button *after* redefining a color to make the name easy to locate in your future work.

Using the Fill Tool

Although Flat Fill is a Fill Tool option for returning a gradient or other fill type to a default, the Fill Tool in Xara Xtreme (unlike paint programs) is not just for filling shapes with a solid fill. Rather, it opens a gateway to filling objects with everything except the kitchen sink (the kitchen sink is coming in Xara Xtreme 6). You can design gradients you can then edit to add intermediate colors, use fractal patterns you can edit to create anything from puffy clouds to gritty concrete, and any bitmap you've imported can serve as a shape fill. The following sections take you through working between the Fill Tool, its options, and a little use of the Color Editor and the Color Line.

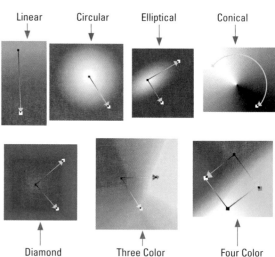

Options when Fill Tool is chosen

Working with Gradients

A *gradient* is a continuous transition from one color to a different one across the dimensions of a shape. Unlike object blends, a gradient does not display banding or clear demarcations between one shade of color and the next, and Xara Xtreme has seven different types of gradients you can use, depending on your design requirement.

Linear   Circular   Elliptical   Conical

Diamond   Three Color   Four Color

To apply a gradient fill to one of more selected objects:

1. With the objects selected, choose the Fill Tool on the Toolbar.

2. Choose the gradient Fill type from the drop-down list on the Infobar. A default gradient appears, centered relative to the single object *or* to *the outermost boundary* of *all* the objects.

3. To set the location of the gradient's start color, click and drag the control handle that doesn't have the arrowhead. The start point for the gradient can be moved outside of the object(s), frequently a useful strategy for creating very subtle variations in colors.

4. To set the location of the gradient's end color, click the control point attached to the direction arrowhead and then drag it, similar to moving the starting color.

5. To set a different color for either the start or end of the gradient, click the control handle to select it, and then click a color on the Color Line, double-click a color swatch in any Color Gallery library, or dynamically change the color by using the Color Editor. You can also drag and drop a swatch onto a color gradient

control handle, although your target is quite small and consequently not the most foolproof method. Note that with the Three Color and Four Color gradient types, you have more than two control handles to which you can assign colors.

6. To make the color transition broader or steeper, a basic method is to position the start and end control handles more closely together or farther apart. The other method is to use the Profile box, covered later in this chapter.

7. To constrain the direction of a gradient to the angle specified in the File | Page Options | General tab in the Document Editing | Angle Constraint option, hold CTRL and drag a control handle.

Suppose you have several objects and you want them all to have the same gradient fill in the same position. Selecting the objects and applying a gradient only fills the objects as a group, each with a fill relative to the group. However, try this: Fill an object with a gradient the way you like it, press CTRL-C to copy it, select all the objects (CTRL-A), and then press CTRL-SHIFT-A to paste attributes.

Making Rainbow Gradients

When the Fill Tool is active and a gradient-filled object is selected, you have a number of additional customization features at your disposal on the Infobar. One such feature is how the start color makes the transition to the end color. The Fill Effect drop-down offers Rainbow and Alt Rainbow in addition to the default of Fade (from the start to the end color). One or two conditions need to be met to successfully play Weather Wizard or Witch with the Rainbow Effect:

▨ The default gradient colors of white to black aren't going to produce any sort of rainbow. You need to set colors (ideally, brilliant and saturated colors) for the start and end gradient points.

▨ Rainbows are created in nature by cycling through the visible spectrum of light; the old acronym Roy G. Biv describes the primary hues in a rainbow. In Xara, the Rainbow Effect cycles counterclockwise; therefore, if you set the start color to red and the end color to blue, a gradient will cycle from start to finish showing red, violet, and then blue. This is where the Alt Rainbow setting comes in handy: Alt Rainbow cycles the spectrum *clockwise*.

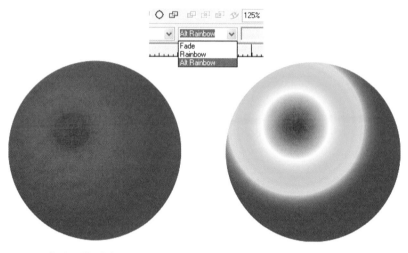

Red-to-blue Rainbow   Red-to-blue Alt Rainbow

 The standard Fade effect for gradients can occasionally produce muddy transition colors, because the start and end colors are not neighboring colors on a color wheel. This is where you can use the Rainbow effect to clean up a muddy transition. Alternatively, you can put intermediate colors along the gradient direction line, described later in this chapter.

Repeating a Gradient's Colors

By default, the gradient's Fill Tiling option is set to Simple—a transition across an object from start to end color, and that's it. However, when the Fill Tool is selected and a gradient-filled object is selected, on the Infobar you have the Fill Tiling option, which you can set to Repeating. When you do this, the start point of the gradient is used to position the beginning location for the gradient, but the end control point controls not only direction for the fill but also the number of times the gradient repeats within the object. Here's how to use Repeating:

1. Create a circle.

2. Apply the Circular type gradient to it by using the Fill Tool and the Styles Fill Type drop-down list on the Infobar.

3. Set the start point as a medium yellow and the end control point for the gradient as a rich red.

4. Click the Fill Tiling drop-down and choose Repeating.

5. Drag the end control point toward the start control point. Be careful not to accidentally hypnotize yourself while doing so.

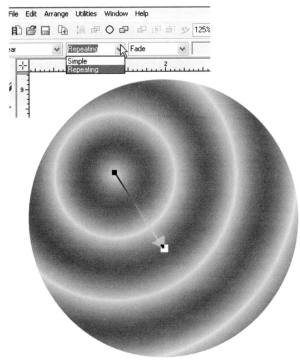

Creating Intermediate Gradient Color Points

Xara Xtreme has no gradient editor *per se*; like most effects in the program, *you're* at the controls and you build custom multi-stage gradients manually, using the tools you see onscreen. Let's say you need (or even faintly desire) to make a dimensional-looking shaded sphere, one that not only has light falloff from the source of the lighting in the scene, but also with the suggestion of a *cache light*—sometimes called a "kick light" that's pointed in the opposite direction as the main light to help reveal deeply shaded areas and give a sense of roundness to a surface. Here's how:

1. With the Ellipse Tool, hold CTRL (to constrain proportions) and then drag down and right.

2. Choose the Fill Tool, and then choose the Circular Fill Type style from the Infobar drop-down list for the gradient.

3. Drag the start control point for the gradient to about 11 o'clock, and then drag the end control point toward 5 o'clock.

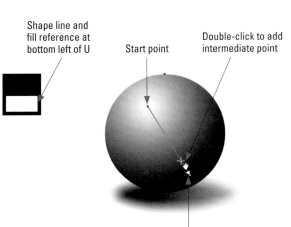

Shape line and fill reference at bottom left of U

Start point

Double-click to add intermediate point

End point

4. Double-click a point on the gradient direction line that joins the start and end control points. Your visual cue that you're in the correct position to add the point is that the cursor features a hand below the cross hairs. Doing this adds an intermediate color point to the gradient; its color is the same as the end point.

5. Click the end point, open the Color Editor, and then mix up an interesting light color.

6. Click the intermediate control point, and then choose a deep, contrasting color. To complete the scene, you can make a shadow by adding a black oval behind the circle and then applying the Feather feature on the Standard bar—you drag the slider all the way to the right to create an extremely soft edge to the ellipse.

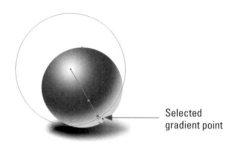

Selected gradient point

To remove an intermediate color point, select it by using the Fill Tool and then right-click. Alternately, press the DELETE key on the keyboard, but *not* the BACKSPACE key.

A Primer on the Transparency Tool

When it comes time to add shading to a composition, the Transparency Tool is the Fill Tool's alter ego: you not only have the same styles (called from the Transparency Shape drop-down list on the Infobar), but you also have the capability to build multi-stage transparencies. You do this the same way you add intermediate color points with gradient fills: Create a transparency gradient for an object, double-click a point on the direction line by using the Transparency Tool, and finally, set the amount of transparency for this new (selected) point by using the Transparency slider on the Infobar.

Consider the creative possibilities of building an object with a gradient fill and then applying a different multi-stage transparency. Figure 5-1 shows a sphere very similar to the one you designed using a gradient in the previous tutorial, but the effect uses a solid circle, with a duplicate circle in a contrasting color placed over it. The shading in this example is shown on the left in front of a gray rectangle. Using different transparency values for a circular gradient transparency type, the sphere is a little more attractive and visually interesting than the previous example. Also consider the visual complexity you can achieve with a gradient-filled shape, with a duplicate placed over it, with a multi-stage transparency to add different colors in different areas.

Understanding Profiles

Profiles might be a feature better *experienced* than explained. However, to make your adventures using Profiles for gradients more predictable, here's a little quasi-technical explanation

Circular	⌄	Mix	⌄	Simple	⌄		⌄	◆	Ramp transp			76.5%

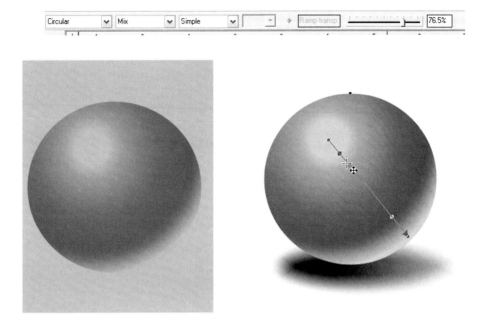

FIGURE 5-1 Use transparency in combination with fills to create a vector composition that *looks* like you used a paint program.

of them. A curve can usually be described as a beginning point and an end point, with some sort of influence over the shape (or it would travel in a straight line). The two most common influences that shape a curve are called *bias* and *tension*:

- **Bias** The preference of one side over the other, similar to what we see in politics. With curves, Bias determines whether the curve slopes toward the beginning point or the end point.

- **Tension** Think of a rope being held by two children (or adults). When there is tension, there is a close adherence to a straight-line vector between one end and the other. Without tension, the curve deviates away from the straight-line vector; the rope sags toward the ground.

Bias and tension are shown to you every time you create a curve in Xara Xtreme. The control handles for the curve determine bias when you drag, for example, the end-point control handle toward the curve segment. Tension is created and released as you move the control handle away from the curve itself. Similarly, a gradient by default travels linearly, and here's where Profiles change this, and all you need do right now is apply a linear gradient to a rectangle to see how you can use Profiles to your design advantage:

1. With the rectangle selected and the Fill Tool chosen (so the Infobar displays tool-specific options) click the Profile button; the Profile panel contains presets you might want to try out on the drop-down list, and an upper and lower slider. The top is Bias and the bottom controls Tension, which when applied to colors might also be called *contrast*.

2. Drag the top slider to the left and then to the right. Notice the graphic representation of bias and how first the start color and then the end color is more prominent in the graduated fill as you drag the slider.

3. Drag the bottom slider a little to the right. Notice how the transition between the start and end colors is more relaxed; the transition colors spread out from the center. This is sort of "relaxing" the contrast of the gradient.

4. Drag the bottom slider to the left. Notice how the transition between colors becomes sharp toward the center; contrast (tension) is increased.

Figure 5-2 shows a linear profile applied to a gradient and then, from top to bottom, bias to the left, bias to the right, increased tension, and finally relaxed tension. A really useful trick when using a circular gradient is to set the bias to prefer the start point's colors. You can use this setting when illustrating sharp specular highlights on glass and other lens-type effects.

FIGURE 5-2 Use the Profile panel to distort a gradient and to change its acceleration.

Defining Fractal Fills

The term fractal was coined in 1975 by Benoît Mandelbrot from the Latin meaning "broken" or "fractured" to describe geometry not easily performed with Euclidean math, which involves straight-line functions. Fractal patterns characteristically reveal two common elements: they show *self-similarity*—one branch of a fractal pattern looks a lot like another branch, and they *recursively subdivide*—in English, as they move across a distance, they branch into smaller, very similar structures as the root of the geometry.

Xara Xtreme offers two fractal types for filling shapes: Fractal Clouds and Fractal Plasma. One creative use for fractal fills is using fractal geometry to simulate natural textures: trees, lightning, clouds, and wood bark all display the visual phenomenon of branching self-similarity in their organization.

Your options when you choose Fractal Clouds or Fractal Plasma from the Fill Type drop-down list can be seen by working through the options as steps:

1. Create a shape, choose the Fill Tool, and then choose Fractal Clouds from the Fill Type drop-down list on the Infobar.

2. Click the control point on one of the direction arrows: this is the local end color for the fractal pattern. Click a color swatch on the Color Line to define a different color—try a deep blue because the Fractal Clouds fill type resembles clouds, so the sky "behind" the clouds should be an appropriate color.

3. Click the start color control point, the point that doesn't have an arrowhead. Click a pale blue on the Color Line or define a very pale blue by using the Color Editor.

4. Drag an end-color control handle left or right to rotate the pattern; then drag either end-color control handle away and then toward the center (start-color) control handle—this is a quick way to scale the pattern.

5. Click the Fill Tiling drop-down list and then choose Repeating Tile. You'll see a difference in how the fractal pattern appears in the shape. The default option, Repeat Inverted, mirrors the fractal pattern both horizontally and vertically. You'll see a creative use for Repeat Inverted shortly in this chapter, beyond its use to create a different overall fill pattern in an object.

The Single Tile option will not fill most large shapes entirely and you're left with a small rectangle of fractal fill surrounded by transparency. However, you can scale the Single Tile fill to fit the object: drag a direction handle away from the shape.

6. Click the Fill Effect drop-down and then choose Alt Rainbow. The straight Rainbow effect won't produce a noticeable difference because the start and end colors for the color mapping of the fractal are of similar hue, but Alt Rainbow produces a fill that looks a little like a mineral such as agate stone. It's most useful to define colors other than blue for the fractal start and end colors: use shades of brown and you'll have a nice cobblestone pattern in no time.

7. Here's a Big-Time Trick: Click the cursor just a little away from the start control point, between the end point control handles, the crux of the branch, so to speak. On the Infobar you'll see two new fields light up. The first is the resolution of the fractal; if you type a large value in this field (and then press ENTER), the pattern grows smaller. Small values enlarge the pattern. The other field controls fractal graininess of the pattern: Type **1** to get a very smooth fractal cloud fill and then try typing **7** (then press ENTER) to make a very coarse pattern.

8. Try steps 1–7 using the Fractal Plasma type fill. Fractal Plasma is good for adding grain to an illustration, while Fractal Clouds are put to good use for marble, clouds, and other materials that have a gaseous or wafting structure.

Figure 5-3 shows a few examples of the two types of fractal fills, with the values listed that appear to produce markedly different results.

Mix and Match Fill Textures with Transparency

If you peeked ahead, you know that both Fractal Clouds and Plasma are available as transparency types; to create super-detailed illustrations, you can mix different object fill types with transparency fill types. This is only one of the results you can achieve, shown in Figure 5-4.

Take a look at how the effect was accomplished in pill.xar, by moving the pieces around. At left, the drawing of the pill is okay: Transparency and gradients are used in combination with overlapping shapes to get a dimensional look. However, at right, the shadow has been filled with Fractal Plasma at

Fractal clouds
Repeating Tile
105 dpi
Graininess 1

Fractal Clouds
Repeating Tile
100 dpi
Graininess 5

Fractal Plasma
Repeating Tile
350 dpi
Graininess 7

Fractal Plasma
Repeating Tile
223 dpi
Graininess 2

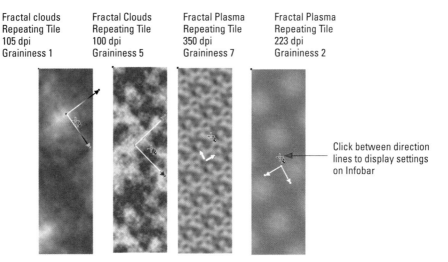

Click between direction
lines to display settings
on Infobar

FIGURE 5-3 Fractal fills can simulate natural textures because fractal patterns are found in nature.

FIGURE 5-4 You can draw small objects with a few more photorealistic qualities if you add noise via a fractal fill.

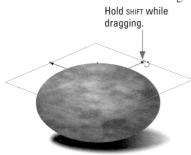

Hold SHIFT while dragging.

high graininess, and a linear transparency is used to create the shadow fall-off toward the object's right. Similarly, the Fractal Plasma is used for a piece that lies on top of the illustration of the pills to add a diffuse quality to the work. In real life, nothing is perfectly reflective and shiny, so you can use fractals to add noise to a drawing to achieve the desired simulated object complexity.

Distorting a Fractal Fill

On the Xara install CD are several examples of natural and industrial textures created by overlaying fractal-filled shapes using different degrees of opacity and transparency types. Many of the fine pieces of illustration were accomplished by using a trick; you can disproportionately scale and skew fractal fills by holding the SHIFT key while you drag a fill handle. Doing this can lead to fill effects that look like polished aluminum, fine-grain wood, and other useful textures.

To disproportionately scale (stretch or squash) a fractal fill, hold SHIFT-CTRL (CTRL helps constrain any unintended rotation) and then drag one of the fractal control points.

To proportionally skew a fractal fill, hold CTRL and then drag on a control handle away from the control point's direction line.

After you've distorted a fractal fill's scale, the disproportion remains this way the next time you simply want to scale the pattern by dragging a control handle. However, unless you use SHIFT while altering a skewed fractal fill, it will snap back to its proper orientation when you try to scale it.

Open sunset painting.xar and move the objects around, and then click on them with the Fill Tool and the Transparency Tool to see on the Infobar what the Fill Type is. As you can see in Figure 5-5, this drawing looks more like it was created with a paint program, but only a few shapes with a creative use of Xara's fills produced the picture.

FIGURE 5-5 Draw your way to a painting with fractal fills.

Using and Customizing Bitmap Fills

The easiest way to make a texture look as though it's on the surface of a shape in Xara Xtreme is to use a bitmap photo of that texture. The following sections lead you through how to import, use as a fill, and modify any bitmap so it seamlessly tiles in shapes.

Adding Bitmaps to a Document

You'll find scores of bitmap fills in the Fill Gallery, and here are two ways to fill an object with a bitmap:

1. If you have a folder in the Fill Gallery (you should if you installed Xara with all the options), open the folder. If no folders are showing, you might not have installed them from the CD. If you bought the download version of Xtreme, click the Get Fills button at the top of the gallery box to download categories of fills, provided you have an active Internet connection.

2. Create a shape.

3. Drag the thumbnail of an image from the folder in the Fill Gallery on top of the shape. If the shape you created doesn't have a fill, right-click on the texture in the Fill Gallery and then choose Apply As Fill from the pop-up menu.

That's it: you can now rotate, scale proportionately, or smoosh the fill, using the steps covered in Fractal Fills earlier, and skew the fill. When the Fill Tool is chosen, make certain that the Fill Tiling choice on the Infobar is set to Repeating Tile.

Here is a way to fill a shape with a bitmap, without using the Fill Gallery:

1. Press CTRL-ALT-I (Import) and then navigate to a place on your hard disk that has the photo or other bitmap you want to use as a fill. Click the filename and then click Open.

2. The bitmap is in your document now, which means when you save this file, a copy of the bitmap is actually in the file. Move the bitmap, scale it down, and move it out of the way for the moment.

3. Create a shape you want to fill. With the shape selected, click the Fill Tool.

4. On the Infobar, choose Bitmap from the Fill Type drop-down list, and you're going to get the default fill, a nice Xara logo, which is probably not what you anticipate. The Xara logo is a very small bitmap used as a placeholder for whenever Bitmap is chosen for a fill type.

5. Click the Bitmap Name drop-down list, and then click on the bitmap previously loaded in the document to fill your shape. You can delete the copy of the image on the page now, because when you save the document, the copy of the bitmap is referenced within your filled shape, so the bitmap is automatically saved within the *.xar document.

Bitmap fills are subject to modification with the Photo Tool. So, if your bitmap is too light or too colorful, select the shape, and then choose the Photo Tool—use the controls on the Infobar to make a good fill look even better.

Avoiding Bitmap Edges in Shapes

You'll find that images tend to tile, spoiling the appearance of a filled shape. Many of the stock images in the Fill Gallery have been carefully edited so the image content wraps and repeats around its four sides to eliminate this problem. So what do you do with your own favorite photo of a texture that displays visible tiling? You follow these very simple steps:

You'll use Non-Tiling Inferno.jpg, a small nice image that suggests fire, and Alarm.xar, a document set up to take a bitmap fill in the following tutorial. Work through these steps to see how useful the Repeat inverted Tiling choice is:

1. In a new document, press CTRL-ALT-I to import Non-Tiling Inferno.jpg. The weird and wonderful thing about Xara is that although this image was imported as an image, it is also evaluated as a rectangle with a bitmaps fill.

2. Choose the Fill Tool and, with the image selected, look up at the Infobar. It's a Bitmap as a Fill Type and a Single Tile as a Fill Tiling, and the Bitmap Name drop-down has a tiny thumbnail of the image. Click the center control point and try dragging the fill around. You'll see that as a single tile, the image disappears within its boundaries. This is only cool for a limited few design situations.

3. Choose Repeating Tile from the Fill Tiling drop-down list. Now drag by the center control point a little. Well, oops: Xara is doing its job, but the image itself wasn't designed as a seamless tiling image.

4. Choose Repeat Inverted from the Fill Tiling drop-down. *This* is what you came here for. The four sides of the inferno image mirror themselves when they tile, producing a seamless image. The pattern might be detectable if it repeats more than twice, but this trick can save you a lot of time using a paint program as an alternative.

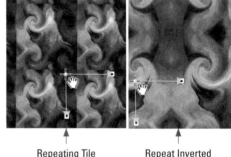

Repeating Tile   Repeat Inverted

Here is how to put a seamless tile to a practical purpose.

Xara Xtreme 5 offers to match named colors when you import an Xara file to an existing Xara document. This is a convenience that's especially useful when you're adding Xara clipart to new documents and you've used specific design colors. However, you can dismiss the attention box when you import XAR files. The result is that any named color used in the imported graphic is added to the new document's Color Line.

1. Press CTRL-ALT-I to import the Alarm.xar document. After clicking Open, click the Merge button in the following query box to put the Xara artwork directly on top of the bitmap (hiding it) without putting the file on a new page. If you receive a dialog box that asks if you want to match colors, this has no impact on the tutorial (see previous note), and you can safely click the Match button.

2. With the Selector Tool, click the word "Alarm" to select it. Then choose the Fill Tool.

3. On the Infobar, choose Bitmap from the Fill Type drop-down, and then click on the Bitmap Name drop-down. Click the inferno thumbnail to apply it as the text's fill.

4. Choose Repeat Inverted as the Fill Tiling style. Now you can scale and rotate the fill to suit a design need.

5. Repeat steps 2–5 with the mirrored text. It will fade even when filled, because apart from its fill property, it also has a gradient transparency property.

Working with a Contone Image

"Contone" is an abbreviation for *Con*tinuous *Tone* image. Most bitmap file formats save continuous tone data; the only time you'll see something *other* than neighboring pixels expressing the full range of colors is in a newspaper that has to use *halftones*. Halftones

trick the human eye into visually integrating one color ink on one color of paper into a representation of a continuous tone.

A Contone in Xara Xtreme is a process by which you can remap a 24-bit full-color digital color image into an 8-bit photo, using only the brightness component of the photo and any light and dark Contone colors you please.

Open Contone example.xar, a serviceable mock-up of a CD jewel case insert. Suppose after all your layout work (the work is finished on a locked layer in this file, with only the image selectable), your client tells you that they only have money for a one-color print job.

The good news is you get to choose the one color. Follow these steps to make quick adjustments to the composition so you can quit work early today:

1. Select the image by using the Selector Tool.

2. Open the Color Editor.

3. Click the upper-left drop-down list of colors on the palette.

4. You'll see that Light Contone is selected, but the color has yet to be defined. Drag the cross hair in the color field to white. You'll see that the image has become grayscale; white—and shades of white down to the dark Contone color (which is currently at its default of black)—are mapped to color brightnesses in the image. And because pure white has no color saturation component, there is no color to the image.

5. Make life easy on yourself: the CD cover already has text in shades of green. Drag the Hue slider's cross hair and the cross hair in the Saturation/Value field over to create a light green.

6. Click the drop-down arrow next to the Light Contone entry and then choose Dark Contone. If the color model choice shifts to CMYK, click the drop-down Color Model menu to revert back to HSV. Then drag the cross hair to a deep forest green color.

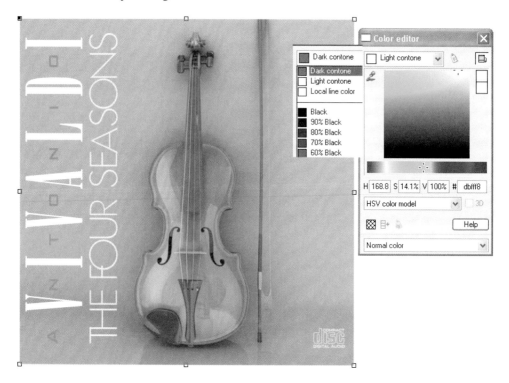

 If you want the Color Editor to always use the same color model, choose Window | Options and then, on the View tab, choose your favorite color model from the Edit Local Colors In drop-down list.

Naming Colors

Giving a name to a color you mix by using the Color Editor does more than simply make it easy to find on the Color Line: a *named color*—tagging a color value—lets you *redefine* the color wherever you use it in an illustration. Yes, this process takes marginally more time than whipping up a color value and applying it to shapes. But if you consider all the time you invest in designing, for example, a terrific MP3 player and then want to see it in several color schemes—you can *change* named colors in your original drawing at whim in literally no time at all.

Let's walk through the process of naming a color, and then hunker down to a practical example of how robust and useful this feature is. To name a color:

1. Create a shape on the page to more easily see the process.

2. Open the Color Editor. Mix a color; any color is fine for these steps but you might want to mix a color you think will be useful.

3. Click the Tag icon on the top of the Color Editor.

4. In the New Named Color dialog box, type a name for the color, and then click Create.

Open icosahedron.xar. The file contains a drawing of an icosahedron (a Platonic geometric that many people simply call a "soccer ball having a Bad Hair Day") and a rendered image of the model for reference with respect to the shading this object might have when a light is shown on it.

If you don't have a named color all set up yet, this is okay. The following steps show you how to name a color, apply it to one of the faces of the icosahedron, and then use linked shades of this color to complete the illustration. Then it's on to fun *changing* the named color.

1. Open icosahedron.xar and then open the Color Editor. The triangle shapes have all been filled with a solid light shade of gray (10% black) to make them easy to select.

2. With the Selector Tool, select a triangle in the drawing that's medium in tone when compared to the photo image in this file. If you are more comfortable mixing colors in HSV or another color model, choose your model from the drop-down menu.

3. Mix a new color for the selected triangle; a powder blue is shown in Figure 5-6 but use any hue you like.

4. Click the tag icon and then name the color you've mixed.

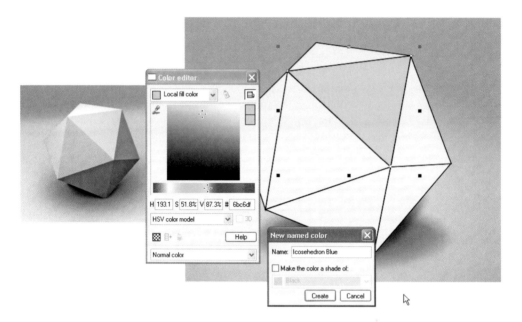

FIGURE 5-6 Name the current color.

5. The new color swatch appears in the Color Gallery. You can right-click on the Color Gallery folder (with the same name as the file), choose Show In Color Line, and then drag the new color swatch on the Color Line to the start of the swatches. Doing this makes the color easier to choose both on the Color Line and in the Color Editor's drop-down list of colors.

It's often easier to drag a swatch on the Color Gallery to the top to put a color at the far left of the Color Line instead of trying to perform this action directly on the Color Line, particularly if you have a large number of local colors on the Color Line.

6. Click on a different triangle, and then click the named color on the Color Line to apply the same color as the first triangle.

7. Clearly by referencing the image, this second triangle is a different shade than the first. With the triangle selected, on the Color Editor, click the bottom drop-down arrow next to the Normal Color entry, and then choose Shade Of Another Color. The Color Editor chooses the first color on the Color Line. Click the drop-down in the bottom Parent: area of the Color Editor and choose your named color.

8. Now you're free to drag in the Saturation/Value field to choose a darker or lighter shade of your named color, as shown. Note that when you're defining a shade, changing hue in the HSV color model is not possible, nor is selecting colors by using the Color Picker in the Color Editor.

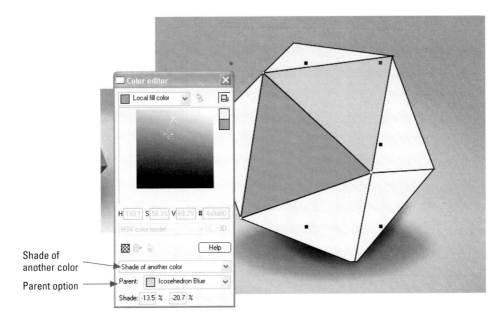

Shade of another color

Parent option

9. It would be nice to add a linear gradient to the lower-right triangle; there is some lighting fall-off in the reference image in this area, and you can indeed use a gradient made up of shades of named colors. With the Fill Tool, drag on the face of this triangle to set the direction (it runs from about 7 to 2 o'clock).

10. One at a time, click the start and then the end control points for the gradient, and then set them to the named color by clicking the swatch on the Color Line.

11. One at a time, click the gradient control points and define them as a shade of the parent named color. Then adjust the Saturation and Value by dragging in the color field on the Color Editor. Both shades of the parent color can be changed in the future. Repeat steps 9–11 for the lower-left triangle.

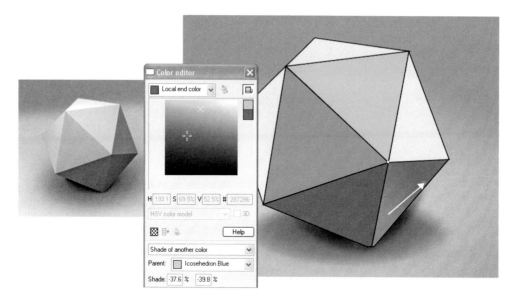

12. A tint is a color mixed with white when using physical pigments; the result is always a lighter color we sometimes call a *pastel*. You can also link a tint to a parent named color. Select the top triangle with the Selector Tool and then choose Tint Of A Different Color from the Parent: drop-down list and choose the named color.

13. Adjust the color, using the slider presented in the Color Editor.

14. Save the file when you have colored all the facets of the icosahedron.

Ready to perform a feat of minor magic? With no object selected (press ESC to deselect all shapes), on the Color Editor, choose your named color from the drop-down list at top left. Then drag the Hue slider, adjusting the Saturation and Value to your taste. Figure 5-7 has been edited to show you a night-and-day difference in your coloring work—the icosahedron at left would change color as well as the one on the right if its shapes were named colors.

Download Train.xar, a finished illustration that uses two named colors. Take the first two colors out for a spin and change the composition's colors. Figure 5-8 is just an example of the multiple use of named colors and the unparalleled flexibility your drawings can have when you tag colors you define.

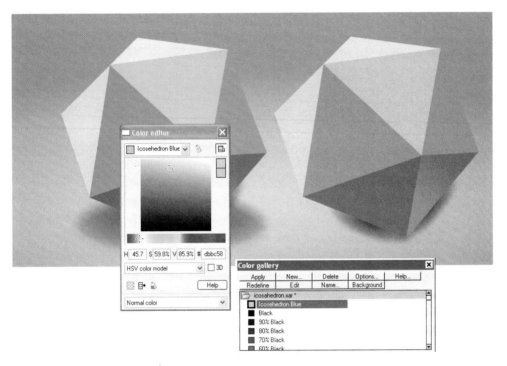

FIGURE 5-7 Create dramatic changes to illustrations when you've tagged colors.

Options for Named Colors

A few more items need to be explained with named colors. You can do the following with features not covered in the preceding steps:

- **Linked To Another Color**   This is not quite the same as a Named Color. You can fill a shape with a named color (let's call it the *child color*) in the top drop-down list in the Color Editor. Then choose to make this shape's color linked to another color from the Parent: drop-down list to choose the parent color to link to. You then will see an Inherit field at the bottom of the Color Editor, based on your color model. You can choose—by unchecking— to select Hue, Saturation, Value, or any combination of color model components. Then (without any items selected) if you edit the named parent color (by choosing it in the top drop-down list of the Color Editor), you'll see *really* dramatic changes to the linked (child) colors as well. The changes might be unexpected if linked colors are not harmonious, but with a little practice you'll achieve the ultimate in color-editing flexibility.

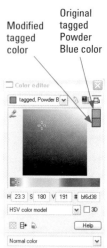

Modified tagged color

Original tagged Powder Blue color

FIGURE 5-8 Blue is orange and red is green, and never the train shall meet.

■ **Redefine A Named Color** This button on the Color Editor creates a local copy of a named color chosen in the top drop-down list. This new color copy name will be preceded by the layer a filled object is on. You can then change a local color on a layer without changing the colors of named objects on a different layer. Just make certain that a named color fill is within an object on the layer you *intend* it to be on.

■ **Rename A Color** The button to the right of Redefine A Named Color on the Color Editor is useful for removing the ambiguity of several redefined colors all with similar names. You can also rename a named color by clicking the Name button on the Color Gallery.

 If you recolor a child color in a shape, you break the dynamic link between the fill and its parent named color.

6

Basic Magic: Blends, Contours, and Moulds

The first (and probably second) time you visited a funhouse hall of mirrors, you thought there was some magic going on. You might have been amazed at the way you and the objects around you multiplied and distorted, and yet the magic lay in the *organization* of the shards of objects all around. It's time to learn how to produce a little magic of your own in Xara Xtreme compositions, using the Blend, Contour, and Mould Tools. You'll get a handle on creative uses for these features, and artistically match the mathematical perfection produced by these tools with the visually interesting results.

 Download and extract the contents of Chapter06.zip, which contains everything you need to work through this chapter's tutorial steps.

Multiply Your Art by Using Blends

You use the Blend Tool to create duplicates between two objects. It has many uses: as a shading tool to achieve airbrush-like fills in irregularly shaped composition areas and to create fancy borders using a single design element you've drawn.

To use the Blend Tool, you must first have two objects selected. These objects can be made up of *groups* of objects, and bitmaps can be included within groups containing vector shapes.

To create a basic blend   Choose the Blend Tool, and then drag from one selected object (or object group) to the other. The default number of intermediate objects created is 5. Depending on how close the objects are from one another, you might get intermediate blend objects that overlap. If they do, they will overlap in order from the direction in which you dragged the tool. In other words, the object you dragged to might have a blend shape beneath it.

- **To redirect a blend**   If you made the blend in the opposite direction you wanted, click the Remove Blend button on the Toolbar and then do the blend again in the intended direction.

- **To increase or decrease the number of intermediate blend shapes**   Type a value in the *n* Steps field on the Infobar after creating the blend and then press ENTER.

- **To change the distance and position of the parent blend objects after creating a blend**   Hold down CTRL- and click on a parent object with the Selector Tool, and then move it. You can also rotate and scale a parent blend object after CTRL-clicking on it while the status line says "1 *something or other* (inside) on Layer *x*."

- **To control intermediate colors**   If the two blend parent objects are different colors, the blend objects will display a transition between the colors—by default, the Fade Color blend effect. However, you can choose Rainbow or Alt Rainbow from the drop-down list on the Infobar when the Blend Tool is chosen and a blend has been created. The Fade option makes a linear transition between the parent shape's colors, mixing the first color with a percentage of the second color. Depending on your object colors, occasionally you will get muddy intermediate colors. The Rainbow option fills the intermediate objects with the shortest route along the outside of a traditional color wheel, while Alt Rainbow takes the longest route to cycle through a color wheel's hues.

Fade

Rainbow

Alt Rainbow

You have additional control over both the distribution of the intermediate shapes and how much of the blend is influenced by the color of either control object. Click the Position Profile button on the Infobar for these options:

(Position profile)

- **To move the blend objects to the last parent object**   Drag the top slider to the right.

- **To move the blend objects to the first parent object**   Drag the top slider to the left.

- **To gang the blend objects toward the middle of the blend**   Drag the bottom slider to the right.

- **To position the blend objects toward each parent object and away from the center**   Drag the bottom slider to the left.

- **For some interesting distributions of the blend objects**   Check out the Presets drop-down list.

Figure 6-1 shows a QuickShape rectangle blended to a duplicate whose corners are so rounded that the shape looks like a circle. You can see that the original blend makes an even transition, and at bottom the blend has been modified for its intermediate positions. You can also access an Attribute Profile panel by clicking its button, to the right of the Position Profile button on the Infobar. Use this panel exactly as you do the Position panel; it "prefers" parent shapes and colors the way the Position Profile panel is used to "prefer" distribution of the blend shapes between its parent shapes.

FIGURE 6-1 Use the Profile boxes to create custom blends.

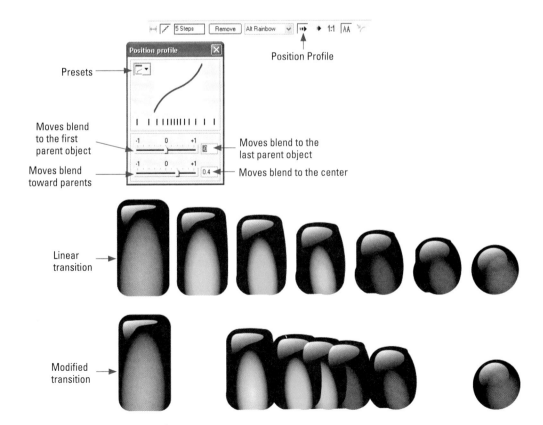

Blending Between Dissimilar Control Points

A good demonstration of the power of blends in art is to map a control point on the beginning shape to a point on a duplicate shape that *doesn't* correspond to the other. Although you can usually drag between two shapes and not worry about the control points that make up the shapes' paths, when you have Show Object edit handles enabled on the Infobar, you can see the control points, and you can drag from one control point to a different one to create an effect.

When you drag between two shapes, you might notice a tiny check mark on the cursor, an indication that the blend operation is valid. You will see this regardless of which two control points you blend between. You won't see the check mark if the two shapes are very close together, the default number of steps will create overlapping intermediate shapes, and you've dragged from a top object to an object below it in the hierarchy of shapes you have on a layer.

Creating a complex geometric pattern for a background is as hard as drawing two straight lines and then "improperly" mapping the paths' control points, as follows:

1. In a new document, choose the Pen Tool. Set the outline width on the Standard Bar to about 4 points.

2. Click a point on the page, and then click another point without dragging so the path is a line and not a curve. Hold down SHIFT and click on the end point now to finish it.

3. Repeat step 2 to create a second line, but make it travel at an odd angle to the first line.

4. Press CTRL-A to select all, and then choose the Blend Tool.

5. Drag from the first control point on the first line to the first control point on the second line, and then type **60** in the Steps field on the Infobar (then press ENTER). You now have an interesting blend; perhaps it looks like a fan, but here's the cool part…

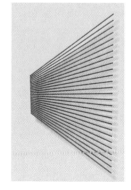

6. Drag with the Blend Tool from the start point on the first line to the *last* point on the second line. Clearly, the second Blend technique provides a more visually interesting pattern.

Let There Be Neon!

Neon lettering is a valuable element in commercial design, and it requires a little skill and the Blend Tool to accomplish with a degree of photorealism. What does neon actually look like? For research, go to the Blarney Stone Pub on 9th Avenue… onnnnly *kidding* here. Neon tubing is quite brilliant at its core, but the illumination tapers off at the edges of the tubing so you can clearly see the edges of the glass. The effect itself is often perceived as a glow *behind* the tubing, and the following steps show you how to illustrate neon.

Open Neon motel sign.xar. The illustration of the scene is locked on a layer and there are two groups of paths you can select. You use the Blend Tool in the following steps to make neon tubing to light up the classy motel sign. In your own assignments, consider how to create the paths for any type of neon effect, and be sure to read Chapter 3.

- Manually, trace the center of a typed message or drawing to serve as the core of the neon effect. Make regular breaks in the path; in real life, neon messages are often composed of two or more individual piece of tubing. You group (CTRL-G) the paths as a final step.

- You duplicate the path and give it a much wider outline than the center, original group of paths. Then you ever-so-slightly offset their positions so the final blend is not exactly from the center but instead shows the hottest part of the neon just a little to one side, suggesting perspective to the audience.

You create a copy of the original before blending the first two. Assign the duplicate a very wide outline width (1 inch is usually good), and then choose Arrange | Convert Line To Shape. The result is a shape that has no outline and it's used as a final enhancement to the neon blend effect. Here's how to light up a scene:

Thin path   Wide path

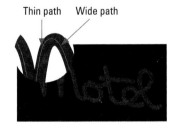

1. Zoom way in until you can clearly see a section of both groups of paths. Using the Blend Tool is easiest when you have a clear view of both target shapes. In the motel illustration, a 600% zoom will do the trick.

2. Choose the Blend Tool, and then drag from the thick to the thin path. On the Infobar, type at least **16** in the Steps box for a smooth-looking effect and press ENTER.

3. Select the large red shape behind the neon letters and in the Change Size Of Feather Region box (to the right of the gallery buttons), drag the Feather slider to about 25 pixels in this example.

4. The final touch gives a little dimension to the neon. It probably isn't photorealistic but rather a very nice illustrative touch. With the Shadow Tool, drag down and to the right on the neon blend objects. As you can see in Figure 6-2, the shadow lifts the tubing up and accentuates the contrast between the tubing and the glow it produces.

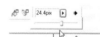

FIGURE 6-2 Create neon, argon, and other gaseous sources of illumination by using the Blend Tool trick.

Blending a Blend

Just as you can have groups of groups in an Xtreme composition, you can nest blend groups too. This capability offers you the design option to create (among many things) a blend group of shapes that blend around a circle or other shape. The following tutorial is a real-world design example: You're going to create ticks for a watch face and then pattern them so they travel across the face of an image of a wristwatch.

Open Wristwatch.xar; the image layer is locked and there is a new layer on top for you to design the watch ticks.

1. Create a small shape you think would be good for the hour tick marks on a very expensive watch. The figures in this section show a QuickShape 3-sided polygon (a triangle) because you can do something interesting with a blend and an odd-sided polygon. Make the shape about ¼ inch high and/or wide; once you've built a shape, select it and then type **.25in** in the W or H field on the Infobar, and then press ENTER.

2. Duplicate the shape by holding CTRL and then dragging the shape to the right by about 5 inches. Before you release the mouse button, tap the right mouse button, and then release both buttons to drop a copy, a duplicate.

3. Select both objects and then, with the Blend Tool, drag from one shape to the other. Big-Trick Time: Because you will blend the blend group around a circle, and a watch typically has 12 hour tick marks, you need to set the number of blend steps on the Infobar to *11*. Type **11** in the steps box and then press ENTER. Blending intermediate shapes around a circle puts the parent objects in exactly the same location—although the result is 13 shapes, you'll only see 12 unhidden.

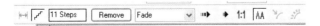

4. With the Ellipse Tool, hold CTRL-SHIFT and then drag a circle until it more or less fits over the watch face.

The wonderful thing about vector graphics is that you can scale them ad infinitum without loss of detail or focus. Remove the fill by clicking on the No Fill box to the left of the color line now.

5. Select the blend group and the circle, and then choose the Blend Tool.

6. You have your choice of designs now if you chose to use a triangle tick mark. On the Infobar, click the Blend Along A Curve button. Doing this puts the ticks exactly where needed for a watch face design. However, all the triangles are in their original orientation; it might be novel to make them all point toward the center of the watch. Easy enough: While the Blend Along A Curve button is toggled on, click its neighbor, Rotate Along Curve.

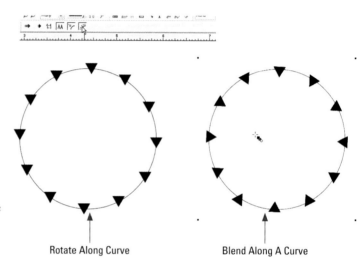

Rotate Along Curve

Blend Along A Curve

7. First, with the blended blend selected, click a good color on the color line for the ticks. Doing this also fills the circle, so with the Selector Tool, hold down CTRL- and click on the circle, and then click the Set 'No Color' swatch.

8. Choose None from the Outline Width drop-down list on the Standard Bar to hide the circle's outline.

9. Because the watch image is angled, the ticks don't align. Yet. The Mould Tool Perspective function is covered later in this chapter, but there's no reason not to test-drive it right now to complete the assignment. With your design selected, choose the Mould Tool, and then click the Default Perspective button on the Infobar.

10. You can use the Mould Tool, Selector Tool, or Shape Editor Tool to align the bounds of the tick marks to the watch face, as shown in Figure 6-3. Take your time and look at this figure carefully to see where you should locate the corners to make the drawing appear to be on the face of the watch.

Figure 6-3 Blending shapes around objects is the solution when your shapes aren't text so you can't use Fit Text To Curve.

Using the Contour Tool

The Contour Tool creates multiple copies of a *single* object, radiating equidistantly from the object's edge in either an outward or inward direction. Contouring is great for creating thick outlines to headline text, for creating a feathering effect to soften a shape's appearance, and for creating fake topological survey maps. In the next steps, you'll work with the Contour Tool and a file provided for you to build a suggestion of ocean depths surrounding the Bahamas Islands.

1. Open Bahamas.xar in Xara. The artwork is on a locked layer beneath the shape of the islands on the top layer. There is also a hidden layer on the top of the composition you'll use at the end to complete the illustration. Select the Island object by using the Contour Tool.

2. Note that there are control handles surrounding the islands object, and that the handles are two-headed arrows, indicating that you can drag them inward or away from the object. Drag them outward until you see on the Infobar that you've reached about 24 pixels of

Contour Width in an outward direction, and then release the mouse button.

Drag away from shape

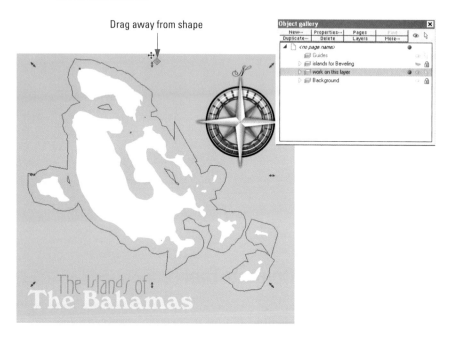

3. Type **4** in the Number Of Steps In The Contour box on the Infobar and then press ENTER.

4. Clearly, this default contour isn't doing the artistic thing intended, because by default, the outermost contour is white, but it should blend into the ocean color to indicate the ocean is getting deeper away from the islands. With either the Selector Tool or the Contour Tool, click on the outermost ring of the contour. The message "1 contour on *layer name:*" will appear on the status line.

5. Click open the Color Editor, the rainbow circle icon at the bottom left of the UI.

6. Click the Color Picker (Eyedropper) on the editor and drag it over any of the ocean area. The outermost object of the contour effect is now that color and the topography of the near waters in the Bahamas looks terrific. To give the outer contour a slightly darker color than the ocean, drag the Color Picker cursor slightly down until the color is a more appealing, darker tone.

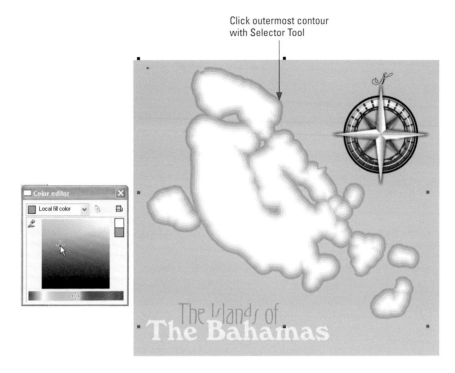

Click outermost contour
with Selector Tool

The Islands of
The Bahamas

7. Unfortunately, you cannot recolor the islands object a nice warm sandy color because it's the control object for the contour effect—it would look just plain wrong for the contour to traverse from brown to ocean blue. Fortunately, there's a spare set of islands on a hidden, locked layer on the top of the composition. Click the Object Gallery button now to reveal the palette.

8. Click both the Visibility and Lock icons for the islands for Beveling named layer. You can select the object; the composition looks nice now, but could look better. Keep the document open for the exercise in the section to follow.

Creating Bevel Shapes

The Bevel Tool is a "Jiffy Button Maker" for Web pages, but also has other creative uses, one of which you'll play with in the following steps. Like the Contour effect, you can create an inner or outer bevel for an object, and the Bevel Tool offers a number of edge styles as well as controls for setting the lighting direction. The concept here is to make the Bahamas illustration look more dimensional, like those plastic relief maps the teacher would hang on the wall in 3rd grade (China was always a pale cream color with a lot of Himalayan bumps).

1. With the Bahamas selected on the top layer, choose the Bevel Tool on the Toolbar.

2. Drag any control handle a little toward the center of the object. By default, the Flat Bevel Type style has been applied, a little too harsh for the soft beaches of Nassau.

3. Click the Bevel Type drop-down list on the Infobar and choose Rounded.

4. Click and drag the red dot at the end of the direction handle for the bevel effect until it points at about 11 o'clock.

5. With the Bevel Tool, click directly on the bevel edge, not the object itself, to select the bevel.

6. Click the Round Join button on the Infobar, shown in Figure 6-4. By default, control points on paths are represented in the bevel with a bevel join connection to prevent spikes along the edge of the bevel shape. However, a round join works best in this example, further smoothing the coastline in a pleasing 3D sort of effect.

FIGURE 6-4 Use tools in combination with each other to produce exactly what you have in mind.

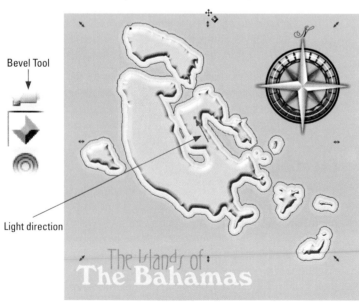

Using the Mould Tool

The Mould Tool extends the transformation capabilities you enjoy in Xara; as you can scale and rotate shapes with the Selector Tool, the Mould Tool enables you to do unthinkable things to shapes. Imagine if you could heat up a Xara drawing to its melting point (yes, imagination is good here) and then reach into the page and mush shapes like you did with that child's toy that came in an egg. That's the essence of the Mould Tool, in an eggshell.

The Mould Tool operates in two different, mutually exclusive modes:

- **Envelope**   Text and objects conform to the shape you create.

- **Perspective**   Creates the appearance of reading a sign or a logo around the corner of a building.

The Envelope, Please

You must meet certain conditions to use the Envelope mode of the Mould Tool:

- **Four points define an envelope**   As you can see with the presets on the Infobar, only four points (4-sided shape) can be used to define an envelope.

- **Special effects objects must be simplified**   Groups of objects can be enveloped, but effects such as blends, contours, bevels, and so on, cannot be enveloped. However, if you convert these shapes into *editable* shapes (CTRL-SHIFT-S), they lose their special editing properties but then qualify for enveloping.

- **Candidate must be vector, and not a bitmap**   You can apply an envelope to a bitmap, but the effect only crops the bitmap—it doesn't produce a liquid distortion. To alter a bitmap in an envelope style, you'd use the Live Effect Tool.

There are two ways to distort an object (or group of objects) when using the Envelope mode of the Mould Tool:

1. After selecting the object with the Mould Tool, click a preset button on the Infobar. The shape immediately

conforms to the Circular, Elliptical, Concave, or Banner preset. The left button on the Infobar in the Envelope presets—Default Envelope—creates no change; instead, you can make your own distortion by dragging on the envelope control points. When using the Mould Tool to build a custom envelope from the Default preset, you are limited to moving the envelope control points. This exposes control point handles at each of the four corners, which you then drag to shape the envelope. However, you can use the Selector Tool and the Shape Editor Tool at any time to reshape the envelope after you apply it. The Shape Editor Tool is particularly useful because you can reshape the bounding lines and curves of the envelope by dragging directly on them. Also, with the Shape Editor Tool, you can lasso more than one envelope point and perform complex edits by dragging the envelope points.

2. You can create your own envelope shape and then copy it to the Clipboard. You then select a shape with the Mould Tool and click the Paste Envelope button on the Infobar. From this point, you can modify the envelope exactly as though you created it from one of the presets.

Envelope handle   Envelope point

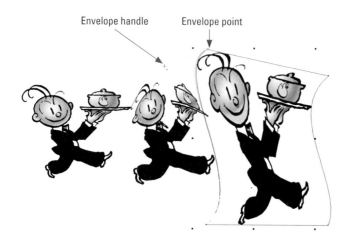

If you've applied the Concave or Banner envelope, you'll notice that two envelopes sides are curves and two sides are lines. This can be *changed* with the Shape Editor Tool. Although you cannot change a curve into a line, you can drag with the Shape Editor Tool on a side that is a line and thus convert it to a curve.

Adding Perspective

The Perspective mode of the Mould Tool is similar to the Envelope except all four bounding lines are straight, and this cannot be changed. Additionally, when you apply a Perspective mould, you will see vanishing point marks outside the mould. You can drag on these marks to create the impression that a shape vanishes at an imaginary horizon on the page; usually when you can see a vanishing point on the page, the degree of perspective applied to the shape is so severe that the composition looks unrealistic. It's often best to use the Default perspective and adjust the perspective bounding box points manually.

Mould Options and Guides for Making Your Own Mould

Whether you have applied a Perspective or an Envelope style mould to a shape, you have options that affect the mould itself:

- **To remove a mould at any time**   With the Mould Tool chosen, click the Remove Mould button.

- **To copy a mould and then apply it to a different shape**   With the Mould Tool and the object selected, click the Copy Mould Shape button to the right of the Remove button (the pages icon). Then select a new object, click the Mould Tool on the Toolbar, and click the Paste Perspective or Paste Envelope button (the clipboard icons on the Infobar).

- **To rotate the target shape**   It's not uncommon for a pasted mould to rotate the target shape. Click the Rotate Contents button; each click rotates the shape 90 degrees clockwise within the mould.

- **To pick up a little editing speed**   Halt instant redraws of moulds by clicking the Detach Mould button to toggle the mould to a frozen state. You then edit the mould, click the button again to toggle it off, and the mould updates and continues to update as you edit.

- **To use Perspective mould guides**   You can toggle on a guide within the shape to get a better idea of the perspective as you edit. The Toggle Mesh button turns the mesh on and off within the shape; it's for preview and is not editable in any way.

You can edit a Perspective mould at any time by using the Shape Editor or the Selector Tool.

Creating your own moulds is fun and can be very productive. The rules for the natures of envelopes and perspectives apply: an envelope shape can only have four sides and four control points, but the line segments can be curves or straight lines. The Pen Tool is probably the best tool for creating moulds, because you can achieve straight lines by single-clicking and make curves by clicking and dragging. Perspectives can only have straight line sides.

The other important rule is in the creation of a Mould shape: Your first point must be located on the relative page closest to the 0,0 origin, usually the bottom left of the page. This means that if you click at the lower-left point first, which is representative of the 0,0 bottom left origin on a page, and then work clockwise, life is good and you can then copy and paste the shape to deform an object you have selected with the Mould Tool. If you create a shape starting at top right or left, or work counterclockwise, the contents of the moulded object will be reversed or rotated. You can correct this by using the Rotate Content button, but why not get it right on the first go?

Open envelopes.xar. This document contains a few template shapes you can copy and paste to deform objects. Make sure the target shape is approximately the same shape and size as the template shape and the result will be predictable. Alternatively, you can scale, rotate, and stretch the template shape in this document to suit your design need.

7

Creating Photorealistic Effects

Using Xara Xtreme, it's not difficult to visually suggest a design that doesn't look like a "vector drawing." You can achieve practically any photorealistic effect you desire, lifting your subjects and objects off the drawing page through the use of perspective, shadows, highlights, and textures. This chapter takes you through the steps to building reflections and transparent objects such as water droplets. Overall, you'll gain a better understanding of *lighting*—natural lighting we observe in the real world—to make your graphic ideas come alive.

 Download and extract the contents of Chapter07.zip, which contains everything you need to work through this chapter's tutorial steps. Optionally, download environments.zip, is a bonus collection of images you can use when creating shiny 3D objects.

Working with Shadows

Shadows in an illustration are a visual clue to the viewer about how objects are ordered, from near to distant, by hiding and revealing areas. Shadows suggest a light source cast into a scene, and the accurate placement and shape of a shadow orients the audience. Xara Xtreme offers two modes of auto-shadow creation—Floor and Wall Shadows—that you can adjust to simulate shadows cast on smooth or rough surfaces.

Using the Shadow Tool

 The Shadow Tool has three modes, plus sliders to customize the shadow you create. By default, when you choose the tool and then drag directly on an object, you apply a Wall Shadow (a drop shadow) with default values for color, opacity, and the amount of blurriness the shadow has.

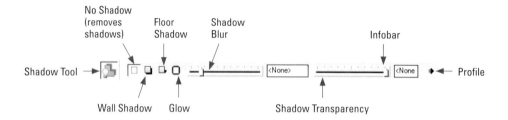

No Shadow (removes shadows) · Floor Shadow · Shadow Blur · Infobar · Shadow Tool · Wall Shadow · Glow · Shadow Transparency · Profile

The Profile box is used with many effects, including contours and gradients. See Chapter 6 for details on how you can use Profiles to change the distribution of the components of effects.

When we view a shadow produced by a plane, parallel to a surface behind it, the default Wall Shadow type produces the most photorealistic effect, as you'll perform with a picture frame drawing in the steps to follow. However, it would look strange to apply the same Wall Shadow effect to a nail holding a picture frame to a wall, and stranger still for the frame to produce a shadow … but not the nail. This is where the Floor Shadow type effect comes in useful, as you work through the following steps:

1. Load frame that needs a shadow.xar in Xara. The frame is grouped and is separate from the grouped objects that make up the nail.

2. Choose the Shadow Tool, and then decide on a direction for the shadow. Because this simple drawing shows no strong indication of a light source, you're free to drag in any direction; however, down and left or down and right will produce a Wall Shadow most audiences are comfortable with (a shadow casting upward suggests a gothic horror scene). Also, subtlety helps in this instance—the farther away the drop shadow, the larger the implied distance between the object and the surface. In this case the frame is close to the wall surface; therefore, the shadow should come close to hugging the frame.

3. If you feel the shadow isn't dense enough, drag the Shadow Transparency slider from its default value of 75% (transparent) to the left, increasing opacity.

4. The sharpness of the shadow has an artistic effect; we see crisp edges on shadows in broad daylight, but shadows have soft edges when subdued lighting

illuminates a scene. Additionally, the surface upon which the shadow falls can be smooth, producing a sharp shadow, or soft, such as fabric, which produces soft shadows. Drag the Shadow Blur slider to the right to increase softness if you'd like to suggest rough wallpaper. Conversely, if you want the look of smooth wallpaper, drag the slider on the Infobar to the left.

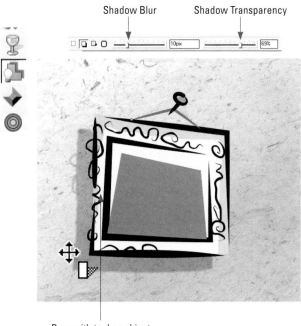

Shadow Blur   Shadow Transparency

Drag with tool on object

5. Drag on the nail now. By default, you're creating a Wall Shadow, but the nail is *projecting* from the wall; it's traveling *toward* the viewer and not simply lying against the wall. Therefore, you use the Floor Shadow, also called in photography a *cast shadow*, a shadow casting *into* a scene—it has perspective.

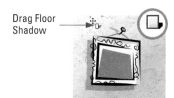

Drag Floor Shadow

6. With the nail selected, click the Floor Shadow button on the Infobar. Now drag on the shadow—when the Shadow Tool is selected, you cannot move the parent object to the shadow. Point the shadow to the same direction as the Wall Shadow that belongs to the picture frame.

Shadows are not always black; in reality, shadows often take on a tint from ambient lighting in a scene. Shadows outdoors on a sunny day are often a deep, desaturated blue, acquiring a hue from the sky. To make a shadow any color you like, with the shadow selected, use either the Selector or the Shadow Tool to click a color on the Color Line, or use the Color Editor to change the color of a shadow.

Applying Shadows to Multiple Objects

A group of objects can produce a single shadow. However, when you select several *ungrouped* objects and apply shadows with the Shadow Tool, you create an individual shadow for each object, thus making the collections of shapes take on a very deep 3D perspective. Try this:

1. With the frame selected with the Shadow Tool, click the left button (No Shadow) on the Infobar to remove the shadow.

2. Switch to the Selector Tool.

3. Press CTRL-U to ungroup the group that makes up the picture frame.

4. With all 32 objects still selected, choose the Shadow Tool and then drag on the selected objects. If you drag a great enough distance from the selections, one of the objects has partial opacity. As a result, its shadow has show-through areas and isn't as dense as the shadows of the other shapes. You can now tweak the individual shadows for sharpness and density and, in a composition of your own, make even simple stuff look visually rich and complex.

Putting Things in Perspective

Earlier it was mentioned that the Floor Shadow mode of the Shadow Tool produces a cast, or *perspective* type shadow. Perspective shadows beg for an illustration of a ground or floor below the shadow-casting object. The Perspective Mode of the Mould Tool is ideal for making planes that match Floor Shadows, and the following sections show you how to design an elaborate floor and add perspective to it.

Creating a Grid Plane

A grid design is a very easy, basic, and effective way to suggest depth in an illustration. You'll use a grid twice in this chapter. One is provided for you in the Chapter 07.zip archive, but why not learn how to build one yourself?

1. Press CTRL-N to start a new document.

2. Choose the Rectangle Tool; hold CTRL to constrain the rectangle to a square and drag until you have a square of about half an inch, or 36 pixels if your rulers are set up to pixel units.

3. Set no outline for the square; you can choose None from the Standard Bar. There is no gap between a duplicate and its original when there is no shape outline.

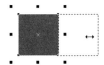

4. With the Selector Tool, select the square, hold CTRL, and then drag the middle left control handle directly to the right. Right-click before releasing the left mouse button to drop a copy of the original square.

5. Select both squares and then repeat step 4.

6. With the four squares selected, hold CTRL and drag any upper-middle control handle down. Right-click to drop a copy before releasing the left mouse button.

7. Repeat step 6 until you have four rows and four columns.

8. With all the squares selected, give the squares a 4-pixel outline on the Standard Bar's Set Line Width drop-down list.

9. Choose Arrange | Convert Line To Shape. Because outlines travel to the outside of a shape's path, all the shapes now overlap; this is key to creating a grid that appears to travel in three dimensions. The fills automatically disappear—the outlines are now shapes and no longer outlines to which you could add a stroke.

10. Press CTRL-1 (Arrange | Combine Shapes | Add Shapes). You have one large grid object now.

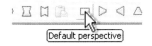

11. Choose the Mould Tool from the Toolbar, and then click the Default Perspective button on the Infobar. The problem with adding perspective to outlines is that they don't accept perspective—the Mould Tool can *distort* shapes, but outlines always remain consistent. They're not filled shapes.

12. Press ' (the apostrophe key) to select Show Grid and then press the period/decimal character *on the number pad* to enable grid snapping.

13. Drag the upper-left mould handle down and to the right until it snaps to a grid point, and then drag the upper-right handle down and left until you have a symmetrical 3D grid. Optionally, with the Selector Tool, you can make the 3D effect more obvious by dragging the top center object bound handle down. Notice that the lines you converted to shapes are now wider at the bottom than at the top, a nice photorealistic effect.

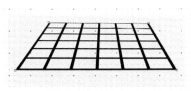

Working with Floor Shadows

Open Floor shadow example.xar; the scene has several individual objects and the perspective grid is already on a locked layer. The steps to follow demonstrate effects you can create by using the Shadow Tool in combination with other Xara Xtreme features.

Ideally, the Floor Shadows you create should match one another. Here's a very quick way to accomplish this goal:

1. With the Shadow Tool, click any of the objects, and then click the Floor Shadow button on the Infobar. A default Floor Shadow is the result, facing right, and this direction is fine for this example.

2. With the Shadow Tool, drag on the shadow itself until your eye tells you it's in proper perspective compared to the grid on the locked layer. A position anywhere from pointing at 1 to 2 o'clock works well, and you'll notice that the shadow is anchored to the bottom bounds of the object.

3. Set the Shadow Blur to about 20 pixels and the Shadow Transparency to 50% for a nice rich effect.

4. With the character to which you applied the shadow selected (use either the Selector or the Shadow Tool), press CTRL-C to copy the object.

5. Select a different object, and then press CTRL-SHIFT-A to paste the *attributes* of the copy on the Clipboard, but not the object itself. However, you cannot avoid pasting the attributes of the fill along with the shadow. In this drawing, artistically, this is good— the characters *need* the pasted gradient attribute to help separate them from the background and from each other. If you don't want the gradient in other characters, click a color solid on the Color Line now.

CTRL-C to copy object

Select and then CTRL-SHIFT-A

You might be looking for a particular front-to-back order for all your 3D perspective objects, and you might run into the problem of a character casting a shadow *on top* of a different character. You can create a ClipView that eliminates the shadow problem in a jiffy, as follows:

1. With the Shape Editor Tool, begin a closed path at the edge of the object receiving the shadow, tracing around the object until your path segment reaches the top and bottom extent of where the shadow should not be.

2. Continue the path, looping to enclose the object casting the shadow, and then close the path.

Exclude area where shadow shouldn't cast.

3. Select the object casting the shadow and then put that object at the top of the order of objects, above the shape you drew; press CTRL-F ("to front" is the mnemonic).

4. While the object is still selected, hold SHIFT and click the path, adding it to the selection.

5. Press Q to apply a ClipView; the bottom object clips the top object.

6. Hold CTRL and use the Selector Tool to click inside the ClipView object. Look at the status line. If the object is selected, press TAB to toggle to the path you drew. If you hit the clipping path on your first try, move on to step 7.

7. Select the path only surrounding the object and give the path no fill and no outline. The illusion is perfect now; the character in front is casting a shadow, but not on the character "behind" him. A flat character would not (photorealistically) receive a perspective shadow.

Dynamic Changes to a Shadow

A Floor Shadow is anchored to the base of an object for a very good reason: regardless of the scale, position, and degree of rotation you apply to the object later, the shadow dynamically reorients itself to reflect any change. Try these maneuvers on one of the subjects in this party scene:

1. Choose an object in the scene that has a Floor Shadow attached. Try an object that has a gradient fill to learn an additional trick here.

2. Click on the selected object to put it into Rotate/Skew Transformation mode.

3. Drag a corner handle. Although the object rotates, the Floor Shadow's orientation remains the same, dynamically changing shape to cast the current shadow on an imaginary floor.

4. Hold the minus keypad key and rotate the object a little more. The gradient fill remains the same while the object rotates and the shadow updates, a useful design technique and a great way to produce an animated GIF or Flash file. You can press CTRL-Z to undo the changes if desired.

Creating Glass and Liquid Drawings

From the airbrush posters of the late 1960s to computer interfaces, we all love a good illustration of chrome and glass. This section walks you through how to draw a glass, and then you'll create not just a handsome water droplet but a custom brush stroke from water droplet drawings. You'll then be able to hose down any illustration that calls for a Wet Look.

Making a Tinted Glass Button

There is a formula for creating the classic glass-button look, a good stepping stone in your education to then move on to illustrating more complex shiny looks. Here is how the formula goes:

1. Using the Rectangle Tool, create a rectangle by dragging until the Width and Height fields on the Infobar tell you it's about 400 pixels wide and 300 pixels high. This is just a background shape you'll delete later, so the size is an approximation. Click a Pale Blue swatch on the Color Line to fill it.

2. Choose the Ellipse Tool and then drag a tall oval. Fill it with white.

3. Choose the Fill Tool, and then choose Elliptical from the Fill Type drop-down list on the Infobar.

4. Click one of the outer control handles for the gradient, and then click a deep color on the Color Line. Maroon is a good choice, just for this example.

5. Drag the center gradient handle down and to the right until the brighter areas of the gradient fall at about 5 o'clock within the oval. This area will become part of the most transparent areas of the glass button and also suggest the mirroring that glass buttons display. The highlight will be at top left and the refraction area at the opposite direction and position.

6. Click the Profile button on the Infobar. ➡

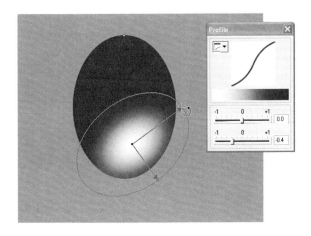

7. You can leave the top slider alone; it's used for tone mapping, preferring one color over the other in the gradient. The bottom slider controls the distribution (the contrast) of the gradient; drag the slider left to about –0.4, and then work with the size of the elliptical gradient. Angle the gradient until it's pointing toward the upper right, and enlarge it a little from its default position by dragging the control handles.

8. Choose the Transparency Tool. Set the type of transparency to Elliptical.

9. Click the center transparency point and drag the Transparency amount on the Infobar to 100%. Then click the outer control point and drag the Transparency slider from 100 to 0%.

10. Click the Profile icon. Drag the top slider (the tone curve, which gives more emphasis to the start or end points in the transparency) to about –0.6. Notice how the lighter areas of the gradient fill contribute to the overall complexity of the drawing: you now have both a center and a lower-right transparency, because the white in the gradient appears to fade out more than the color in the gradient.

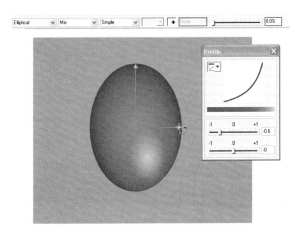

To embellish your good beginning to the drawing, you'll add shading and highlight objects to make the droplet dimensional and truly glossy in appearance:

1. Create an oval by using the Ellipse Tool, click on the selected object with the Selector Tool to put it into Rotate/Skew Transform mode, and then rotate it so its width runs at about 8 o'clock to 2 o'clock.

2. Fill the object with white, no outline width.

3. With the Transparency Tool, drag, beginning just outside the top left and finishing the drag just outside the oval at about 4 o'clock. Assign it the Bleach Transparency type from the drop-down list on the Infobar. Place it over the top of the large droplet shape.

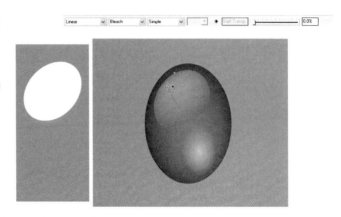

4. Create a drop copy of the original large oval; drag it away from the original, and then right-click before releasing both mouse buttons.

5. Create another copy and place it above the first copy so the area revealed on the first copy is an upward-pointing crescent.

6. With both copies selected, perform the Subtract Shape operation, either by clicking the button on the Infobar (if you put it there) or by pressing CTRL-2.

7. Place the object at the bottom of the glass button composition so its concave part fits the bottom of the button oval. Then press CTRL-SHIFT-B to move the object back two places in the order of objects on the page.

8. Assign the result shape a deep-tone flat fill of the color of the large oval and assign it a flat transparency type in Stained Glass type (about 50% transparency is good). Then feather it—a 2-inch tall button can use about a 20-pixel feather value—just drag the Feather slider until it looks good (see Figure 7-1).

FIGURE 7-1 Create a shadow for the button.

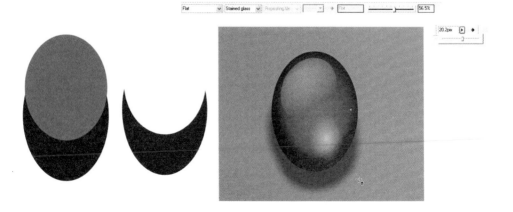

9. Duplicate the feathered shadow (CTRL-K) and then type **50** in either the W or the H field on the Standard Bar (then press ENTER) to scale the duplicate.

10. Assign the duplicate a bright shade of red from the glass button object. With the Transparency Tool chosen, set the Transparency Type to Mix instead of Stained Glass, and then drag the Opacity slider back and forth until this object looks like a bright accumulation of light as it passes through the glass, as lenses are prone to do. If needed, nudge the shadow copy piece to adjust proper positioning. Try grouping the four objects, create new colored backgrounds, and then move the glass button around to see how it interacts with different colors and even bitmaps from the Fill Gallery.

Multiply Your Glass Effect: Making a Brush Stroke

At a small size, the glass button you created in the previous section resembles a droplet of water if you remove all strong hues from the shapes. This leads to a wonderful design opportunity: let's say you need to illustrate the "sweat" (advertising lingo for condensation) on a bottle, can, or other packaged good. You could certainly duplicate your illustration scores of times. However, it's much simpler to build a custom brush stroke from your work and then add condensation to a drawing by dragging the Freehand and Brush Tool around a few times.

First, now that you know the formula for creating droplets, you should play around with the formula. Create some irregular shapes, not exactly ovals—the Freehand and Brush Tool is good for this. Then alter the shape and position of the highlights and even add more than one highlight to suggest multiple reflections from surrounding droplets. Build four different droplets, and then group each one. Here's how to make a water droplet brush:

1. Select a droplet, and then press CTRL-SHIFT-C, the shortcut to Create Bitmap Copy. Feathering and other special effects don't work perfectly as vectors in a custom brush, but bitmap copies work fine. If a warning pops up, click Continue.

2. In the Create Bitmap options box, make sure True Color + Alpha is chosen in the Color Depth field, or the droplet won't feature transparency. If you're doing high-res print work, click the Bitmap Size tab and then choose 300 from the dpi drop-down list. If you primarily do Web work, 96dpi is fine; click Create. Again click Continue if the warning dialog box appears. Certain transparency settings for vector shapes don't translate to *bitmap* transparency as you might expect, but in this example, it's okay.

3. Repeat steps 1 and 2 with the other groups of variations on the vector shapes suggested earlier.

4. Hide, move, or just get the vector originals out of the way for this process. Rotate the droplets now so they are oriented in landscape; arrange the bitmaps in an uneven row to suggest random droplets when you use the brush. A row is recommended because this arrangement follows the order of samples used with the New Brush Strokes Line Gallery in Xara.

5. Select all the bitmaps and then choose the Freehand and Brush Tool from the Toolbar.

6. Click the Create Brush button that now appears on the Infobar.

7. In the Create New Brush dialog box, all you do is name your brush. It will appear later in the drop-down list on the Infobar whenever you have the Freehand Tool selected, and you can also access it through the Line Gallery in the New Brush Strokes folder. Hang on; there are more steps to *complete* the brush.

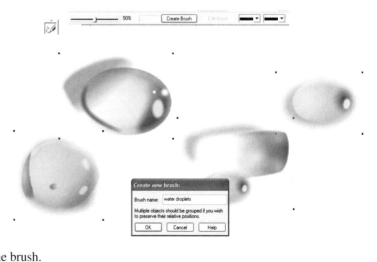

8. There are options for the brush, characteristics you need to define. Click the Edit Brush button now.

9. Make a stroke by using the Freehand and Brush Tool now, from left to right. You do this to see the changes you need to make. Set the outline width to a size such as 72 points on the Standard Bar.

10. Click the Fill Properties tab, and then uncheck the Tile Fills check box. The stroke on the page is going to look much better now. Definitely click Save right now to save and apply this important change, but *do not* close the Brush dialog box yet.

11. Click the Spacing tab. Drag the Random slider to about the 65–152% range, and choose Random from the Sequence Progresses drop-down list. Then click the Randomise button a few times, watching how the selected stroke on the page changes. Stop clicking when you have a nice random arrangement and then click Save, but don't close the box yet.

12. Click the Rotation tab, and make changes similar to those you made with Spacing. Make the rotation a little random as the brush stroke travels. Click Save, and you can now close the Brush box.

FIGURE 7-2 Fewer calories than ordinary illustrations, less filling due to object transparency.

Open up Xara Xtreme Stout.xar if you'd like to apply your water droplet brush to an appropriate target illustration. As you can see in Figure 7-2, the droplets enhance the drawing of the bottle without obscuring the label, due to the transparency built into the brush droplets. Strokes you create are local to a document and, therefore, you need to have both the Xtreme Stout file and the file in which you created your brush stroke to apply your strokes to the bottle file. You choose the Freehand and Brush Tool, choose the brush stroke from the drop-down list on the Infobar, set the outline size on the Standard Bar, and then go to town. The Xara Xtreme Stout document has water droplet strokes within it, with some sample strokes applied to a hidden locked layer in the file. Unlock and unhide the layer to use these strokes and to see how they were built.

Creating Chrome and Building Reflections

The slang for the popular highly mirror-like objects you frequently see on Websites and print ads is "chrome." This section shows you the best possible way to simulate dimensional reflective objects, beginning from the ground up. Because chrome is predominantly mirror-like, a good chrome effect needs to be designed around an environment that reflects *into* the chrome object. Geometry is almost a secondary consideration when drawing a chrome block of text, a lamppost, or other object: it's the *fill* that you need to devote quality-time to constructing.

Two examples are covered here; the first contains the steps to drawing a chrome ball—curved surfaces reflect with more distortion than flat ones. The second example is a dimensional extruded block of text with a mirror finish, perfect for getting a logo or headline noticed when you don't own a 128-point super-heavy typeface.

Designing a High-Tech Chrome Piece

Get the grid design you created earlier in this chapter out now. It will serve as both the ground for an illustration of a chrome pinball and some of the visual content of the pinball itself, the reflection into it from the floor.

1. With your own grid (or you can use a grid.xar), choose the Mould Tool on the Toolbar, and then click the Default Perspective button on the Infobar.

2. Design an interesting, nonsymmetrical perspective by dragging the upper-left and upper-right control handles down and toward the center of the page. Then drag the lower-left or lower-right control handle up or down and away from the center of the page. Usually, a good traditional design rule is: Asymmetrical is more visually interesting than symmetrical. Asymmetry leads the viewer around to different areas of the drawing.

3. Fill the grid with white.

4. With the Rectangle Tool, drag a rectangle to cover the page, and then send it to the back (CTRL-B). Fill it with black.

5. Select the grid and then, with the Transparency Tool, start toward the bottom of the grid and drag upward. The grid apparently vanishes into an undefined horizon, a visual "cheat," but a very effective one.

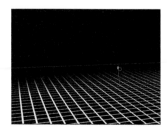

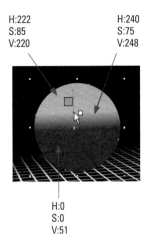

H:222
S:85
V:220

H:240
S:75
V:248

H:0
S:0
V:51

6. Press ESC to deselect all objects. With the Ellipse Tool, hold CTRL (constrains shape to a circle) and then drag a circle on top of the background.

7. With the Fill Tool, drag a gradient vertically.

8. Click the end control point handle for the linear gradient (the bottom one), and then click a near-black color on the Color Line (or use H:0, S:0, V:51 with the Color Editor).

9. Click the start point and then apply a dullish blue. H:222, S:85, V:220 is good.

10. Double-click on the gradient control line near the top of the object to set a new additional gradient color point. Once you have established the point, set the color to H:240, S:75, V:248, slightly lighter than the top color. What you've done is set up the base color scheme for the chrome ball. Traditional artists use a "sky, then horizon, then ground" formula.

Save your work, but don't close the file. There are embellishments to come.

There are two effects to manually create now that a "base coat" fills the soon-to-be chrome pinball.

■   **Let the ball reflect the grid on the ground**   This will visually locate it in space and to set up a good part of the reflection effect.

■   **Shade the edges of the circle to make it look dimensional and contain edge lighting**   Like water and other shiny materials, metal tends to bend highlights. Any edge lighting is often seen as a curved one following the contours and outward distortion of spherical shapes.

1. You don't need a large grid object; perhaps 12 columns and rows will do the job here. Create a copy of the grid and create a rectangle on top of the grid copy. Select both objects and then use the Intersect Shapes command (CTRL-3 is the keyboard shortcut).

2. Give the new object a dull color, a little bluish. In the real world, as the reflections become smaller, they lose illumination. Place the grid directly over the circle.

3. Choose the Mould Tool and then click the Default Envelope button on the Infobar.

4. Choose the Shape Editor Tool; pull the lower-left corner away from the circle, and then pull the lower-right bounding box corner away from the circle.

5. Drag the left bounding box line toward the circle, and then do the same thing in the opposite direction with the right bounding box line.

6. Drag the bottom bounding box until you can see that the grid more or less lines up with the grid on the background. You're not striving for geometric accuracy here, which will likely go unappreciated by your audience. You'll design several other areas of interest, and the grid is so distorted now that only three people on earth will notice the lines don't perfectly line up.

7. Select both the circle and the grid object and then press Q to clip the grid to the interior of the circle.

Add some edge shading now:

1. Press ESC to ensure nothing is selected on the page. Choose the Ellipse Tool and then, on the Infobar, click the Radius Creation mode button, which lets you draw perfect circles from the center outward. Drag, starting at the center of the ball with the grid in it, and drag until you see only a fraction of the underlying ball. Give the circle a white outline with no fill. If necessary, nudge the circle to center it over the ball.

2. Open the Line Gallery. In the Stroke Shapes/Pressure Profiles folder, double-click the Ellipse thumbnail to apply it to the circle. Then set a width for the stroke. In the figures in this section, the ball is 300 pixels wide and a 17-pixel outline for the circle works. Therefore, make the outline width about 15% of the width of the underlying pinball illustration.

3. Set both the join type and the line cap to round.

4. With the circle selected, press CTRL-SHIFT-S (Arrange | Convert to Editable Shapes). The circle loses its dynamic editability and you can now break the circle into path segments (arcs).

5. With the Shape Editor Tool, marquee-select the entire shape and then, on the Infobar, click the Break At Points icon shown in Figure 7-3. You have four tapering arcs, idea for representing edge highlights—with a little editing.

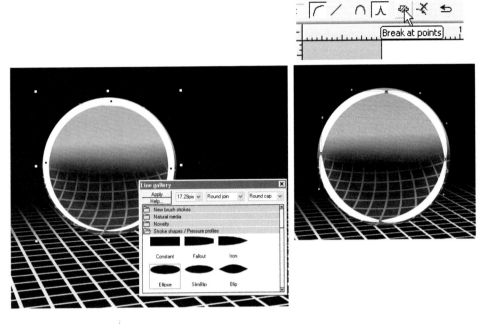

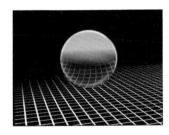

6. Select all four segments, and then choose the Transparency Tool. Give the arcs about 50% transparency in Bleach Transparency type. Then apply a little feathering.

7. Try applying a dull orange-red to one of the bottom arcs—often a contrasting color is used artistically to draw attention to an aspect of a drawing, and red contrasts with the blue in the pinball.

It's time to add a highlight and a little reflection of the ball on the grid now. You'll be surprised at how much more the pinball will pop off the page when reflections and highlights contextualize its dimensions and position in the drawing:

1. With the Ellipse Tool selected, click on the Bounds Creation button. Create an oval, with a bluish color, 16-point outline, no fill and use the default outline stroke (in the New Brush Strokes folder in the Line Gallery). If necessary, set the feather size to None and transparency to 0%.

2. Press CTRL-K to duplicate it. Scale it to about 70% of the original, and position it so it fits inside the first oval, centered, touching the first oval's top.

3. Choose the Blend Tool from the Toolbar, and then drag from the outer larger oval to the inner one. The default number of blend steps (5) is fine.

4. Choose the Transparency Tool and drag vertically, top to bottom, on the blend group of ovals. Then click the start control point for the linear transparency and set the amount to 65%. Leave the end control handle at 100%.

5. Place the blend group under the pinball drawing to create the impression that the edges are reflecting on the grid. Then with the Transparency Tool selected, choose Bleach Blending mode for the group.

6. Create a circle, fill it with black with no outline, and then feather it approximately 24pix (use your judgment to what looks visually correct).

7. Give the circle about 50% opacity by using the Transparency Tool—Flat Transparency shape, and Stained Glass for type. Then put the circle beneath the pinball drawing. You do this to create a slight shadow and to obscure the underlying perspective grid.

8. Create a very small circle, fill it with white, no outline, and then feather it as needed.

9. Put the circle at about 2 o'clock within the pinball to create a highlight.

Here's a nice touch: open Clouds.xar. The drawing was created by using Xara's Bitmap Tracer under the Utilities menu (see Chapter 12). Although the pinball's looking good now, you want it to look *great*. A few clouds above the horizon reflected in the pinball adds visual context to the composition.

1. Copy the grouped objects, and then close the Clouds.xar file.

2. Press CTRL-V in your pinball composition. Then move and, if necessary, scale the group of objects until they neatly fit inside the upper hemisphere of the pinball.

3. Press CTRL-SHIFT-B to put the clouds to the back of the stack of objects until it is just above the ClipView of the circle and the grid inside the circle that represents the body of the pinball. If you go too far and the clouds go behind the circle, press CTRL-SHIFT-F to move the grouped objects up one level in the stack of shapes.

4. Hold SHIFT and select both the ClipView circle and the clouds, and then press Q to nest the clouds group as a clipped object within the ClipView object of the grid and circle. You *can* hierarchically nest ClipViews. And because the feathered arcs are on top of the shapes, they are smooth at their edges and not clipped by this step.

Creating a cross-star highlight at the edge of the pinball is the final touch. This is not a difficult procedure, and adds an element of "wow" to the overall drama of this photorealistic yet surreal scene.

1. Create a circle about 1/20 the size of the pinball. Make it white or very pale yellow with no outline.

2. With the Pen Tool, draw two separate lines that form an X at the center of the circle that extends way outside of the circle. Click a point, click the end point to make the line, and then hold SHIFT and click the finish point to let Xara know you're finished with the line. Then click two points to define the intersection of the X.

3. Select both lines with the Selector Tool, and then in the Line gallery, in the Stroke Shapes/Pressure Profiles folder, double-click the Ellipse profile. Give both lines about a 12-pixel width with round caps. Yes, these are very fat lines now for a cross-star effect, but you'll feather them, and feathering always moves toward the center of a shape.

4. Apply about 25 pixels' worth of feathering to the circle and approximately an 8-pix amount to the two lines, and then make a group of the three objects (temporarily move the Set View Quality slider to the left if it helps you select the objects and return the Set View Quality slider to the right when finished).

5. Place the group over the pinball at about 2 o'clock as shown in Figure 7-4. Done!

Creating Extruded Metal Text

In the next set of steps, you'll create a shiny, metallic piece of extruded text, complete with a mirror plane to add to the visual impact.

Chrome-coated 3D text looks awful when the point of view your drawing suggests is parallel to the audience. The following example uses the Extrude Tool and a slight angle to the text so the audience has a two-sided perspective on the chrome text: the top

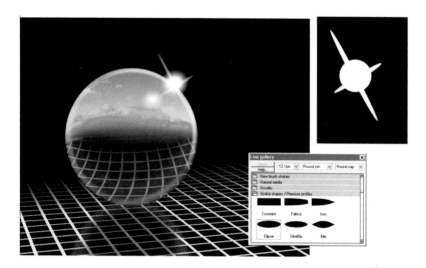

FIGURE 7-4 Have an absolute ball with Xara Xtreme.

and the front. Second, mirror planes don't simply flip the object they are mirroring. The geometry of a reflected shape is mirrored, but the *perspective* is continuous. This is why you can sometimes see a hidden face of an object when you look into a mirror placed near the object. Figure 7-5 shows a viewer, an object, and the proper perspective of the mirror image of the toy train.

Open Art.xar. This file contains the word "Art" in a stylized font that was converted to objects and also a bitmap of a rendered scene. This scene will serve as the reflection, the interior of the extruded word "Art." If you'd like your own phrase, a typeface of your own choosing, you can certainly run the steps to follow to make your own creation. Make sure you use a very bold font. There are also other environment images you can experiment with if you unpack environments.zip. You can definitely go out and take an environment photo and use it in your work; use the Panorama button on the Infobar when the Photo Tool is selected and you've imported and selected several overlapping photographs (see Chapter 14).

FIGURE 7-5 Although mirrored images display opposing geometry, the 3D perspective of the mirrored object is the same as the object itself.

Preliminary Work

Begin by setting up the scene for extruding the text. The text needs to be duplicated and mirrored, and the environment also needs a little editing with the Photo Tool:

1. Move the image out to the pasteboard area of the drawing window. Select the text, and then with the Selector Tool, hold CTRL (constrains proportions) and drag the top center control handle down, clicking the right mouse button to drop a copy before releasing both mouse buttons.

2. Hold CTRL and then drag the mirrored copy down until there is about 1-inch clearance between the two objects.

3. Move the image back onto the page so it covers the top word.

4. Choose the Photo Tool. With the image selected, drag the Sharpness slider on the Infobar almost completely to the left, blurring the daylights out of the image. The reason for doing this is twofold: You diminish the visual importance of what will become the surface of the chrome word so the audience sees the geometry of the word first and you also suggest a slightly rough surface for the word. In the real world, only your next-door neighbor's car—you know, the vintage auto freak—has perfectly reflective chrome. On his car.

5. Optionally, decrease the saturation of the image.

6. With the Selector Tool, hold CTRL and then click and drag the top center bounding box handle down, releasing the mouse button after right-clicking to drop a copy.

7. Move this photo down to cover the mirrored text (holding CTRL to constrain the movement). Then choose the Photo Tool, and decrease the brightness of the duplicated image by about –30.

8. Select both the top image and its underlying text, and then press Q to clip the image to the profile of the word. Then do the same with the mirrored text and its image.

1 ClipView group on Layer 1: Click select; Clic

Extruding Multiple Items

It's time now to dimensionalize these shapes. Follow these steps to extrude the objects in a proper perspective:

1. Select both objects and then choose the Extrude Tool.

2. Hold CTRL-SHIFT (constraining the extrude to centered horizontally and up and down motions only), and then drag on the face of the top object downward to extrude both selected objects in continuous perspective.

3. On the Infobar, with Extrude Depth chosen from the Extrusion Parameters drop-down list, set the Extrude Depth to about 50 by dragging the slider to the right. Then set the Bevel type to 30° Bevel from the drop-down list and make the bevel's size about 60 by dragging its corresponding slider to the right.

4. Click the Extrusion Parameter drop-down box and choose Perspective. Set the Perspective to about 54. Optionally, click the Show Lights button on the Infobar and, one at a time, drag the light arrows to change the lighting until the text looks very shiny. When you select more than one light, and then you drag one, such as the white one, the other text's light changes identically. Take a break for a moment (CTRL-S is a good idea now). Click the Show Lights button to toggle the lights off when you're finished.

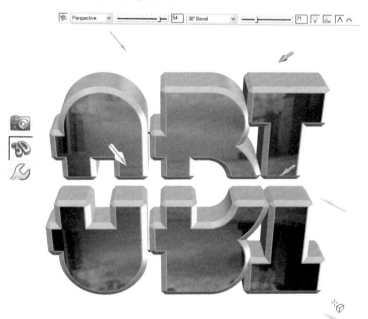

Adding Photorealism to the Text

In the steps to follow, you'll visually integrate the mirrored bottom text into what will become a very rich illustration. You're going to create an object that represents a mirror plane but actually doesn't do anything at all except suggest the plane, because the mirrored text is going to serve that purpose. Let's do some editing now:

1. Select the mirrored bottom object and then press CTRL-SHIFT-C (Create A Bitmap Copy).

2. In the Create Bitmap options box, just make certain that the Color Depth is set to True Color + Alpha and then click Create (or press ENTER).

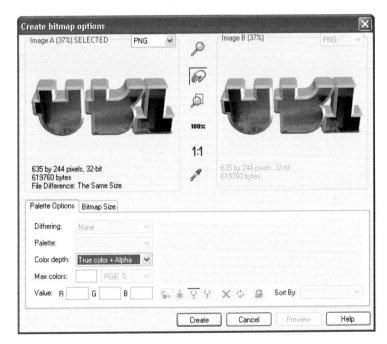

3. You can delete the bottom mirrored ClipView shape now.

4. Position the bitmap so it almost touches the bottom of the extruded text, and then press CTRL-B to put it behind the text.

5. With the bitmap copy selected, choose the Photo Tool. Drag the Sharpness slider all the way to the left.

6. With the Ellipse Tool, drag an oval until it includes the bottom bitmap and about half of the top ClipView object. Fill it with 50% black, no outline, and then press CTRL-B to send it to the back of the two text shapes.

7. Select the bitmap by using the Transparency Tool, and then click and drag perfectly vertically on it (hold CTRL if you need to constrain movement to the first direction in which you move this and most Xara Xtreme tools). Now choose the Stained Glass Transparency Type on the Infobar. If necessary, adjust the start and end transparency control points.

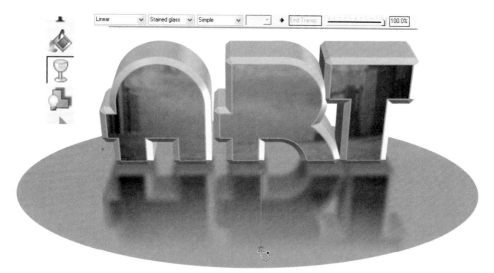

8. To complete the overall design, create a black rectangle to fill the page size behind the shapes and give it an elliptical gradient from near-white at the center to near-black at the edges. Position the center so it eclipses the top extruded text shape. This is simply a design suggestion; there is no reason for this step other than creating a nice artwork mood.

Suggest Bevel Edge Reflections

The front faces of the composition look terrific, but the bevel edges of the extruded text looks more like plastic than metal. The reflections from edges of metallic items are discontinuous from the other faces; they catch and hide light in a manner independent of the other faces. The good news is that the mirrored metal text is so blurry and its edges so nearly hidden that no real editing is needed, so let's address a Xara feature that can quickly create edge reflections.

You can use the Fill Tool's Conical Gradient type to simulate reflections viewed at extreme angles. All you need to do is create the shape to hide a specific area of the extrude's edge, make a multi-stage Conical gradient, and then position the shape's center point so the color variations in the gradient gently fan out.

1. Create a circle; it's the easiest shape to preview a Conical gradient and you can trim it to fit the illustration later.

2. With the Fill Tool, select the circle and then choose Conical from the Fill Type drop-down list. By default, the Conical fill runs from black to white.

3. Double-click on the Conical Fill Gradient arrow to create three points on the arc. Click and drag a shade of black from the Color Line and drop it on one of the control arc points of the Conical fill. Then drag white and drop it onto a different location (almost any location is fine) on the control arc, and perhaps add one more shade of black so the fill looks so visually complex your audience only sees the fill as a collection of reflections in the finished illustration. Press CTRL-C to copy the circle and move the circle out of the way to the pasteboard.

4. Create a shape to fit over a bevel edge on one of the extruded characters.

5. Press CTRL-SHIFT-A to paste the attributes of the Clipboard circle to this new shape.

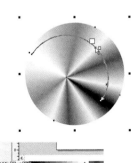

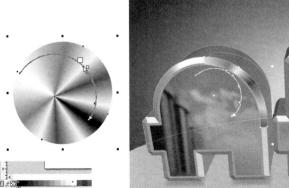

6. With the Fill Tool, drag the center gradient control handle to adjust the fill's center and then make other shapes to suit your taste. Paste the Conical Fill attributes to these new shapes. Optionally, add a Transparency to the conical fill objects for a more subtle appearance.

Add Texture to the Mirror Plane

Suggesting brushed aluminum for the mirror plane oval is quite easy when you use one of Xara's fractal fills. Follow these steps to enrich the look of the composition and to conclude your adventures in chrome:

1. Drop a copy of the oval mirror plane object away from the drawing.

2. Fill it with about 60% black.

3. With the Transparency Tool, select the object and then choose Fractal Clouds from the Transparency Shape drop-down list on the Infobar.

4. Hold SHIFT and drag the top transparency handle downward. Doing this breaks the proportions of the fill. Drag down until the fill looks like thin horizontal lines and then, while holding SHIFT, drag the handle just a little to the right to offset the fractal pattern, adding a little more photorealism in its irregularity.

5. Put the object into Stained Glass transparency mode and then move it until it's aligned with the original mirror plane oval. Play with the Transparency slider to get an appealing visual tone.

6. Press CTRL-SHIFT-B to put the transparency oval shape behind the top text and its conical fill pieces. Figure 7-6 shows the finished piece.

FIGURE 7-6 Yes, it looks nice, but is it Art?

8

Logos and Typography

Typography isn't an art easily separated from the art of illustration; text and graphics have coexisted on the printed page for centuries. When text is used to complement a graphic in a logo, signage, or other piece of art, the combination must be in harmony, and text should be handled with the same finesse as drawing beautiful shapes.

This chapter takes you through the Text Tool in Xara Xtreme and the features you access from the Infobar. Typography rules such as hyphenation, punctuation, justification, and line spacing are covered. You'll see how to communicate with text as aptly as you do with graphics. You'll learn how to design a logo using text you customize. Your choice of fonts is the dressing in which your message appears, and Xara Xtreme is the boutique where you shop for accessories for your dressed-up message.

 Download and extract the contents of Chapter08.zip, which contains everything you need to work through this chapter's tutorial steps. Then install the typefaces in this archive.

Working with the Text Tool Infobar

In design and layout work, there are two categories of text: *headline text* and *paragraph (body copy) text*. Xara Xtreme offers three ways to begin text you type or paste from the Clipboard:

- **Single-click insertion points**   When you click with the Text Tool, you begin a line of text that has no right margin. Therefore, you're not advised to paste a large portion of text after clicking an insertion point, particularly if you want to paste a paragraph or two of text you've copied that don't contain hard returns. If you work in the United States, the text will end somewhere in Australia. Single-clicking is best for inserting a short headline and text you want to use in a logo.

- **Click and drag text insertion (column text)**   By clicking and dragging to the right, you establish a left and right margin for the text you then type or paste. At any point, you can drag the right margin control point (the red dot) to the left or right with the Text Tool to adjust the column width.

- **Marquee-drag paragraph text insertion**   By dragging diagonally (marquee-dragging) with the Text Tool, you establish a paragraph text box whose margins on all four sides you can adjust at any time. Additionally, you can break paragraph text into different blocks while retaining a link. You can easily justify columns, edit in-place text, and design freely with paragraph blocks, graphics, and imported images. Paragraph text is covered thoroughly in Chapter 9.

 You adjust text margins with the Text Tool, and not the Selector Tool. You *distort* text (which is fine by intention) by using the Selector Tool.

Checking Out the Text Tool Infobar

It's hard to imagine any sort of text adjustment you'd need that isn't right at hand on the Infobar when the Text Tool is selected. Text handling in Xara goes way beyond that of a word processing program, and if your desktop publishing needs run from modest to medium-intensive, Xtreme can provide all the DTP features you'd ever need. You have the best of both worlds in Xtreme: the structure you need for creating legible text messages, combined with the flexibility of a drawing program steering most any effect you choose to embellish your message.

Figure 8-1 shows the run-down of the Infobar settings and options after you've typed or pasted some text on a page:

- **Font menu list**   When you have text highlighted with the Text Tool, you can choose and apply typefaces you've previously installed from this list. Alternatively, you can open the Fonts Gallery and then, from the Installed Fonts folder, drag a font preview and drop it on text. You do not have to select the text to change the typeface of what you've typed, but unless you are zoomed into the text or the text is very bold, you can miss the typed text and no change happens. Double-clicking a font preview in the Fonts Gallery applies a typeface to selected text.

 When you install a typeface family, they are *grouped* on the menu. You can click on the small black triangle at the right of a font's entry in the list to display a submenu where you can select the style of that font that you want to use.

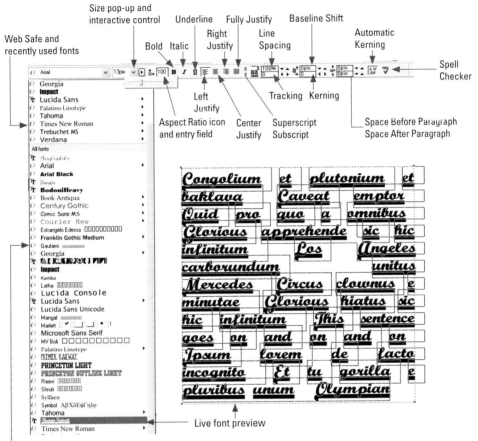

Font menu list

FIGURE 8-1 You have text-handling options similar to those in a desktop publishing program in Xara.

■ **Live font preview**   Deciding on a typeface you want to apply to text you've typed on a page is totally goof-proof in Xara; you're not committed to *applying* a typeface to highlighted text until you click on a font name in the Font menu list. You preview what text *might* look like by hovering over (not clicking) a typeface name on the menu.

■ **Size pop-up and interactive control**   The Size combo box offers typeface size presets from 8 to 72 points (there are approximately 72 points to one inch). Alternatively, you can choose any size you like by directly entering a value in the box on the Infobar and then pressing ENTER. The interactive control offers scaling of highlighted text without the constraint of whole-number values. You click the button to reveal the slider and then drag to set a minimum value of 2 points to a maximum of 32 points.

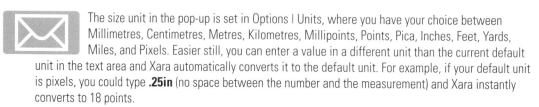

The size unit in the pop-up is set in Options | Units, where you have your choice between Millimetres, Centimetres, Metres, Kilometres, Millipoints, Points, Pica, Inches, Feet, Yards, Miles, and Pixels. Easier still, you can enter a value in a different unit than the current default unit in the text area and Xara automatically converts it to the default unit. For example, if your default unit is pixels, you could type **.25in** (no space between the number and the measurement) and Xara instantly converts to 18 points.

- **Bold and Italic**   Use these buttons on the Infobar to specify a family member of a font used in the text that is highlighted. However, the Bold and Italic buttons will produce nothing except a warning when you've chosen, for example, to call a bold member of a typeface that has no bold member. You can remove italic and bold attributes from text by highlighting the text and then toggling the button to its original state.

- **Underline**   The Underline feature adds an underscore as an effect, which is useful for legal documents— underscores are *not* used in good logos and other design work. Although Underscore is an effect, an underscore becomes a very real shape if you convert text selected with the Selector Tool to Editable Shapes (CTRL-SHIFT-S).

- **Left Justify, Center Justify, Right Justify**   Justification (aligning successive lines of text) works with normal, column, and paragraph text. It is worthy here to mention that in most Western World countries, of these three justifications, left justified text is most quickly read. Try to avoid long lines of centered text to spare your readers from visual whiplash as they scan uneven lines. Right justification can be used effectively in design work, but you need to be a seasoned layout person *in addition to* an accomplished typographer to cast column text in right justification so it can be read without inducing headaches.

- **Fully Justify**   Full justification is flush left and flush right with respect to columns and paragraphs—this option does nothing for plain, regularly entered text. Full justification looks professional and polished but often produces *rivers*—jagged white spaces running vertically through paragraphs. However, if you expand kerning values in problem lines of text, the result can look exactly like magazine and book layouts for text. Full justification *is not* recommended for any text that you will export as part of a web page; browsers don't display fully justified text properly.

■ **Aspect Ratio** This feature changes the width of characters in typed text. You can change the aspect ratio of a character to make it look narrow (condensed) or wide (extended). Generally, you can condense or expand characters by 20% and the font still looks faithful to the original in its design. You can also play with the width of text by dragging one of the control handles on headline, column, and paragraph text with the Selector Tool.

■ **Superscript and Subscript** This feature moves the baseline of the selected text up for superscript and down for subscript, and scales the text to about 75% of the full cap height, although the Text Size box will still indicate the original text size.

■ **Line Spacing** Also called *leading*, this control changes the distance between lines of text in a text column you've highlighted with the Text Tool. Line spacing is often decreased to tighten up the spacing between lines of a stacked headline, or increased to expand the spacing between lines of in a paragraph to increase readability or for aesthetic reasons. Introductory paragraphs are sometimes set with 180% line spacing to draw a reader into a magazine article or a chapter in a book. Line spacing is dependent on how much "headroom" is coded into a typeface. When working with headlines and stacked single works in logos, you can often get away with *less* than 100% line spacing.

■ **Tracking** You can use this feature to increase or decrease the amount of space between all the characters in a highlighted selection. Select some text and then change the interspacing between all characters in a selection by clicking on the arrow buttons to the right of the Tracking Area text box or by entering a value directly in the text box. Tracking is measured in ems/1000, thousandths of an em. An *em* is the width of the lowercase *m* in a specific font. If you want to adjust the spacing between two characters, use kerning instead.

- **Baseline Shift**   The bottoms of characters sit on an imaginary line called the baseline. The Baseline Shift feature moves characters you've highlighted above or below their native baseline. This feature is usually used to fine-tune the alignment of a bullet or symbol—especially if the symbol is a different size than the surrounding text.

- **Kerning**   This feature adjusts the spacing between two characters. Headline text often benefits from the application of kerning rather than tracking. A classic example of a word in need of kerning is HAWAII, where there is too much space on either side of the *W* and not enough between the *I*s.

- **Space Before Paragraph, Space After Paragraph**   This feature is covered in Chapter 9; its real use is with paragraph text and it's not effective with normally entered text. Inter-paragraph spacing is created to the value you choose whenever there is a hard return in your text—where you've pressed ENTER at the end of a literary thought or a list of items. Paragraph spacing is often used instead of indenting the first line in paragraph text. Professional publishing etiquette states that you use paragraph spacing *or* first line indents, but *not* both.

- **Spell Checker**   Covered in Chapter 9. If you select the Check Spelling As You Type option from the Spell Checker button, you'll see the standard word processor-type red-squiggle underline below a questionable word.

- **Web Safe and recently used fonts**   On the font menu list, note the horizontal bar toward the top of the list. Above the bar you'll find typefaces you've recently used in a specific Xara file (but not a single Xara Xtreme session), plus a list of typefaces commonly used in web documents, a handy feature when you're using the web designer features in Xtreme. Typefaces displayed in web browsers are a limited and unique set—you cannot, for example, use Linotype Palatino on a web page without first converting it to a graphic.

An installed font list can get long and hard to scroll through. When the Xara Xtreme font menu list is extended, you can type your way to the font you want to use. Type the first letter of the font you want, and the list scrolls to this letter. If you quickly continue to type the letters of the font's name, the list continues to scroll until you land on—or very near—the font you need.

Choosing from Categories of Fonts

When deciding on a typeface to use, there are categories of fonts, each with their own ideal use. You have display (headline) and body text choices. Traditionally bold *sans serif* fonts such as Arial, Helvetica, and Futura are a poor choice for setting body text, except for web pages, where research has proven that sans serif fonts are more easily read onscreen. Conversely, *serif* fonts such as Times, Garamond, Clarendon, and Bookman are too spindly to use as headline text, but rather are used for body paragraphs.

A *serif* is an embellishment added to the end of a stem (a stroke) in an individual character. Serifs come in many styles: for example, ITC's Latino family is recognizable by the triangular shape of the serif, while Linotype's Charlemagne (a variation of Charlemagne is used for the Harry Potter signatures) uses a squared-off serif with a slight dimple. A character without a serif is *sans* (without) serif. Sans serif typefaces can be commanding in tone: you'd probably use Helvetica Condensed, for example, to warn consumers not to drop a hair drier in the bathtub.

To divide the category of typefaces further, there are Roman and Gothic styles, and a font can be Roman in structure with or without serifs. A Roman font is composed of both thick and thin strokes in the character's structure, while a Gothic typeface uses either identical stroke widths or *nearly* identical.

Then there are typefaces that depart from Roman/Gothic categorization:

- **Handwriting fonts**   These typefaces can look like script or cursive handwriting, ranging from the elegant and expressive to Okay Crayon (by OkayCat), which looks like a child's handwriting rendered in textured crayon.

- **Script fonts**   You'll definitely want to install at least one or two script fonts if you're designing wedding invitations, logos for dress shops, or other signage that is supposed to look classy. Brussels (AKA Brush Script) is a nice blend between script and handwriting, and Muriel (Murray Hill) comes on the Xara install CD; however, if you want extremely elegant scripts with characters that have swashes that interlink, you'll need to invest in one or two. At the inexpensive and serviceable end, Cursive is available at BuyFonts.com for $2, and if you're willing to forgo a Happy Meal or two, Sloop Script is remarkably fresh, legible, and elegant (available in three styles for $40 each).

- **Blackletter fonts**   Blackletter typefaces are not easy to read, but if you have a funeral or Hallowe'en party to advertise, or a logo for a Mega-Destruction rock group T-shirt, blackletter fonts cast the tone of anything you type.

- **Pi (picture) fonts**   A digital font is composed of a runtime program that Windows executes, instruction sets for kerning and metrics, but beyond this, the characters in a font don't have to be English, and they don't even have to be text in any language. Pi fonts—also called dingbats and extras when the picture font offers embellishments to an accompanying text font—are collections of little vector drawings. Pi fonts are especially welcome to add a distinctive element when you're designing a logo. You already own a few Pi fonts: Windows Wingdings and Web Dings come preinstalled with your operating system.

Finally, designer typefaces don't belong to any class of typeface. Grunge fonts (deliberate degraded typefaces), typewriter-style fonts, Retro (good for creating fast-food and novelty logos), fonts whose characters are mirrored to simulate DaVinci's secret manuscript writing … are all examples of highly recognizable styles. Here is a compendium of typeface specimens discussed in this section.

Sans serif — Headline fonts

Serif — Paragraph text fonts

Designer and novelty fonts

Pi (picture) fonts

Although we use the terms synonymously today, a *font* refers to a specific set of glyphs or files you install on your system. A *typeface* refers to a style of character set and can have many different styles, such as Bold, Bold-Italic, Condensed, Old Style (which has numbers whose baselines alternate for legibility), Expanded, and others. Clipboard (a font that ships on the Xtreme CD) is a font because it has no family members (nor deserves any). On the other hand, Bodoni is a typeface and has quite a large family.

Starting Places to Add to Your Font Collection

BuyFonts (www.buyfonts.com/) offers a diverse range of typefaces, priced from an incredible $2 and up. The collection includes reasonably priced typefaces, covering handwritten and script styles in addition to good typefaces for the basis of a logo. Mr. Curtis has also graciously allowed The Xara Group and McGraw-Hill the use of six of his typefaces for our readers; be altruistic if you like his work and buy a commercial font of Nick's or two. Nick's styles are reminiscent of the 1940s and the Art Deco 1920s text used in advertisements, product labels, and other signage. Nick's Fonts is at http://new.myfonts.com/foundry/Nicks_Fonts/. Also check out the largest online clearing house for commercial and independent typefaces at www.myfonts.com.

A *glyph* is often the term used to describe a font character. Picture fonts don't often have legible characters.

Setting a Tone for Your Text Message

Authoritative, Clean, and Cold

Impact—Gothic sans serif

Bastion (Britannic)— Roman Sans serif

Stymie (AKA Lubalin Graph, Rockwell, Roland)—Gothic serif

Hamlet (Handel Gothic)— Semi-Roman sans serif

Serif Gothic— Gothic serif

Goudy OldStyle— Roman serif

Inviting, Informal, and Warm

You've often seen text cast in a typeface that screams at you or that so softly whispers that you ignore the message. The *tone* of a message using a specific typeface needs to be appropriate to what the text is telling the reader. For example, a company that manufactures pharmaceuticals would shake the confidence of the consumers if their logo used Microsoft's Comic Sans—you take the font lightly, so you take the company's logo lightly.

Consider the range of available font styles as a "font thermometer" running from cold, authoritative typefaces at top to warm and casual fonts at the bottom. When designing a logo, the right or wrong choice of typeface depends entirely on the tone of the product or service. Informal typefaces are appropriate for leisure services, games, and certain food items, while sans serif fonts tend to lend impact and seriousness to companies that offer electricity, legal advice, and products that the potential buyer needs to consider carefully. See how the typefaces you own run in degrees from casual to no-nonsense.

Logos and Logotypes

Two similar types of corporate identification are used today:

- **The Logo** A logo is an identifying graphic that may or may not require additional text to make clear who the company is and what it does. For example, Apple, Inc., uses the highly recognizable stencil of an apple with a bite missing. Apple is often confident enough of their logo that they don't need to "spell it out" and no text accompanies the logo. McDonald's hedges (but might not need to) by integrating the company name with the golden arch silhouette logo; Dolby Systems and Arm & Hammer use distinguishing graphics as their logos.

- **The Logotype** A logotype spells out the name of a company or product by customizing text with a simple graphic, or occasionally not using a graphic at all but commissioning a typeface for exclusive use. Google is a perfect example of a corporate logotype: Catull, a Roman serif font from the Berthold type foundry is used to identify the Web giant. Microsoft used Helvetica Black Italic for almost two decades as their logotype, with that tiny notch missing from the first *o*. Perhaps the most highly recognizable logotype is Walter E. Disney Enterprises; the hand script opens Disney films. Alternatively, Disney uses the mouse-ear silhouette as a logo on several of their retail items.

If you can say it with a picture, text becomes subordinate and you need to ask yourself whether the text is necessary. Today we live by icons: icons are internationally understood, and if a product or company lends itself to the visual gestalt of depicting exactly what a company does instead of using text, you're well on your way to designing a terrific logo. Figure 8-2 shows examples of fictitious company logos and logotypes. The wedding photography logo doesn't really need the text—the visual message is internationally understood; this logo might work better with the photographer's name next to the logo.

FIGURE 8-2 Logos and logotypes depend heavily on a visual that stands for the type of good or type of company advertised.

Different Approaches to Logos and Logotypes

The following sections comprise a mixed bag of Xara Xtreme techniques, all producing different looks through different approaches to designing identifying graphics. You'll be sure to find a specific treatment to suit just about any logo need. By working through the tutorials, you'll be able to produce many variations on a basic theme.

Logotypes and Using Varying Font Weights

A typeface family such as Futura lends itself to a logo treatment because of its simplicity, which is a key rule in creating logotypes. As an artist, you evaluate how far you can twist, distort, overlap, or generally create text art and still maintain legibility of the typed word or phrase.

One way to create a logo from pure text is to mix weights of the same typeface. For example, an all-night eyeglass and contact lens store, Night Vision, could get a logotype in about five seconds by using all caps (to maintain legibility) and then using Futura Light for the first word and Futura Black for the second, with no space between the words because the weight difference graphically puts a separation between the words. Alternatively, you could use two different colors for the two words and make a striking yet simple logotype.

The Punctuate font on the Xara installation disk (also known as Bauhaus) is good for a logo because it's very heavy, yet its spirit is light and a little playful. This font can be effectively used for food product logotypes, bold but appealing in a way. A second approach here to make this particular font into a logotype is to kern the characters so tightly together that they overlap; by coloring the overlapping areas a different color than the main text, you have a logotype. Here's how to do this:

1. Using Punctuate as the typeface, with the Text Tool, type **Marmalade**—130 points is a good working size. You can simply use the Selector Tool to move the text into position on the page.

2. Highlight the text and then apply an orange color (the color visually reinforces the text message).

3. With the text still highlighted, set the Tracking on the Infobar to about –90. Click the Decrease button several times instead of entering the value in the number box

so you can experience visual feedback on the page, an important human designer skill.

4. Select the text with the Selector Tool—you cannot convert text to shapes while the Text Tool is the active tool.

5. Press CTRL-SHIFT-S with the text selected, and you have text shapes that are no longer editable as text (using the keyboard) but completely editable as shape objects.

6. Press CTRL-U; Xara groups converted shapes automatically. Press CTRL-U a second time to ungroup to individual characters.

7. Press ESC to deselect all the letters. Hold SHIFT to select the first two letters—the *m* and *a* in "marmalade"—and then press CTRL-K to duplicate these letters. You do this because the Combine Shapes operation in the next step will delete the parts of the letters you don't need, but you'll still need the original letters under the duplicates.

8. Press CTRL-3 to perform Arrange | Combine Shapes | Intersect Shapes. The result is a little wedge—apply a deeper shade of orange or even brown to this shape.

9. Repeat steps 7 and 8, working from left to right, character by character (for example select the *a* and *r*, followed by the *r* and *m*, and so on), until all the new intersect shapes are in place. The clone shapes will temporarily hide the previous wedge shape, but you'll resolve their invisibility once you perform the Intersect Shapes operation.

This playing-with-characters section would be incomplete if you didn't play with the orientation of text characters. For example, text is still legible if highly recognizable characters such as *S* and *U* are flipped vertically and horizontally. "Topsy-Turvy" is a good example. The text is still legible, and the logotype can look fresh and original, even though flipping characters might not sound like an undiscovered idea. It's all in the *treatment* and how you bring text together graphically to make a visual idea in addition to what the text literally says.

Use Wide Character Tracking

It's fashionable to create wider spacing between characters than the font creator meant for you to use. However, large tracking values *also* provide the designer with a logotype possibility—you can fill in the gaps between characters with a second word or phrase.

A fictitious company called Modern Furniture wants to stress the fact that they sell furniture, and the fact that it's modern is of subordinate importance. First, you choose a very narrow typeface—Runymede is a good choice that you installed. Then, with "Furniture" highlighted, set the Tracking to about 900%, three times the width of the character to allow some breadth plus space to insert alternating characters in "MODERN."

Choose a bold sans serif typeface next to make the visual distinction between it and the narrow "Furniture text"—Fustian is a good typeface you have on the install CD (and can download using the Fonts Gallery). Make the point size about one-third that of the "Furniture" text and set the tracking to about 2000%. Then with the Selector Tool, move the "MODERN" text into place, alternating characters with "Furniture." You might need to adjust the tracking of "Modern" a little more, and consider bracketing the text with a text ornament to visually balance the composition.

With different text colors, sizes, and font choices, you've created a logotype effect that's eye-catching and reads fairly quickly. As with all logo treatments, you'll want to use this interleaving text trick no more than once or twice for paying gigs;

there's nothing worse than two clients getting together and singing the praises of nearly identical logotypes.

The Heraldic Logo Treatment

You've seen initials that appear to interlock; stems go behind and in front of each other, similar to the initials on wax seals and college sports teams and recently on designer colognes and apparel. The following tutorial shows you how to create such an interlocking character effect for an imaginary cologne. Goudy, Garamond, Bookman, and Clearface are all good alternatives for a Roman serif typeface, but you can use the system font Times if you don't have a stockpile of Roman fonts.

Here's how to create an almost regal logo for a company that sells the intangibles of elegance, exclusivity, and style:

1. With the Text Tool, type an uppercase *B*, using a Roman serif font you access from the Fonts menu list. Make the character about 330 points in height, about 3 ¼ inches, just to give you some working room. The fictitious cologne is designed by Barbara Bouton; you can use different characters in your own work after you learn the technique and choose a name for your fragrance.

2. Apply a unique color (any color aside from black) so you can easily refer to this character on the page. Switch to the Selector Tool, press CTRL-K to duplicate the character, and then click the Flip Horizontally button on the Infobar.

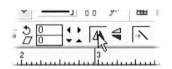

3. Give this duplicate a different color than the original, and then use the Selector Tool to move the reversed character around until it aesthetically fits over the original. Make sure the stems are visible and the character almost appears to embrace the original character while still maintaining legibility.

4. Choose the Contour Tool. With the original character selected, drag a contour outward from the character, using the control handles, until the meter on the Infobar tells you the Contour Width value is about 9 pixels. Type **1** in the Number Of Steps field to the left of the Infobar; you only need one outline of the character.

5. Perform step 4 on the duplicate.

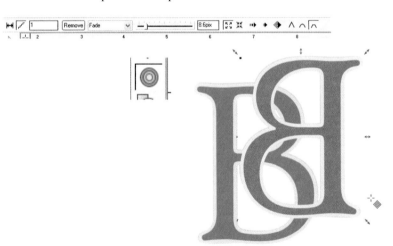

6. Select both text objects with the Selector Tool and then press CTRL-SHIFT-S to convert the text to simple shapes. Then ungroup the shapes by pressing CTRL-U three times.

7. With the Pen Tool, carefully draw a closed shape around the bottom (original) B's center horizontal stem, where both bowls join.

Subtract shape from top B's contour

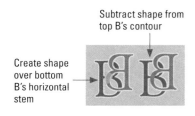

Create shape over bottom B's horizontal stem

Subtract contour from bottom B

Create shape over first B's contour

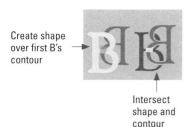

Intersect shape and contour

Subtract result shape from top B

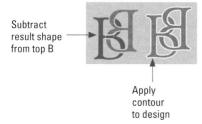

Apply contour to design

8. Select the shape and the contour shape that belongs to the backwards B, and press CTRL-2 to subtract the top shape from the contour shape.

9. Select the contour you just subtracted from, hold SHIFT and click on the bottom B, and then press CTRL-2 to subtract the contour shape from the original B.

10. Select the original B's contour and then press CTRL-F to put it at the top of the stack of shapes.

11. Create a shape by using the Pen Tool that covers the area where the reversed B's bottom bowl intersects the original B. With the shape and the contour selected, press CTRL-3 to get a shape that's the intersection of both shapes.

12. With the intersection shape and the backwards B selected, press CTRL-2 to subtract the shape from the backwards B. You now have interlinked initials.

13. Optionally, group the resulting shapes and put a one-step contour around them. Just click OK to any warning dialog boxes that state a contour item cannot be ungrouped until the contour is removed.

Let's put the logo in context now: import Perfume bottle.jpg to a blank page. Copy and paste the double-B logo and position it on the bottle. Use the Mould Tool in Default Perspective mode to distort your new logo to match the perspective of the bottle image. You can apply a Mould to a shape that has a contour, but you must select the shape and not the contour, or the Mould Option buttons on the Infobar will appear dimmed. See Chapter 6 on working with the Mould Tool.

Mould Tool
Default perspective

Adding 3D Text to a Logo

If you're lucky in your career, at least once you'll be asked to do a knockout, full-color, highly visible logo for a restaurant or night club. For an assignment like this, you want to pull out all the stops, and extruded text might fit the bill. Your success with extruded text depends on using the right typeface. In the steps to follow, assume you have a green light on 3D text, and you have an idea font, *Greek Diner Inline* (based on Linotype's Lithos); you installed it at the beginning of this chapter. You also use Nick Curtis' Copasetic typeface in the steps to follow; it's harmonious with Greek Diner Inline and you'll need it for subordinate text in the design.

Tone is important when designing a logo that features a bitmap image, as Club Vesuvius.xar does. Greek Diner Inline supports and does not detract from the graphic of the Polynesian drink mug—it works because the tone of the logo is neo-primitive. Follow these steps to get the assignment going:

1. Open Club Vesuvius.xar. The text is set in Arial (so there are no font mismatch alerts when you open the file) on one layer, and the image is on its own layer under the Text layer.

2. Double-click the "CLUB" text to change from the Selector Tool to the Text Tool, and then double-click within the text to highlight it. Choose Copasetic NF from the Fonts menu list on the Infobar. The size of the text is fine as is.

3. With the Text Tool, double-click in the word "VESUVIUS" to highlight the whole word. Apply Greek Diner Inline to it from the Font menu list. The point size is good as is.

4. Choose the Fill Tool, with VESUVIUS selected. Hold CTRL to constrain the direction for a liner gradient, and then drag from just below the bottom of the text up to slightly above the top, making the top portion default black.

5. Click the bottom gradient handle and then click on a yellow swatch on the color line.

6. Double-click on the gradient control line a little below midway to set an additional gradient color point. With this new point selected, click a red color on the color line.

Good Times•Strong Drink
Occasional Sacrifices

7. Hold SHIFT and click a red color to make the outline of the text red. You're doing this to predetermine the edge color of the text when you extrude it. 3D text gets its color from the outline color.

Using a Unique 3D Text Effect

The attraction of 3D text to a consumer can lose its shine after they've seen extruded text on every other package in the grocery store. Therefore, let's do the 3D text a little differently. You've probably seen how playful text looks when every other character is rotated in a different direction; follow these steps to see a 3D treatment of rotated alternating characters:

1. With the VESUVIUS text selected with the Selector Tool (*not* highlighted with the Text Tool), press CTRL-SHIFT-S to make the text into editable shapes. Then press CTRL-U twice to ungroup the shapes to individual characters.

2. Press ESC to deselect the objects. While holding SHIFT, select every other character (V, S, V, and then U).

3. Choose the Extrude Tool, and click the 3D button at top left (Apply Extrusion) on the Infobar to set an initial extrude value for the four selected shapes. Then drag up and to the right on any of the shapes to point the extrusion up and right, click the Show Lights icon so you can see which way the three lights are pointing, and then set the Extrusion Parameter drop-down list to show Extrude Depth and crank up the Extrude Depth to about 66 as shown in Figure 8-3. The four characters aren't grouped in any way and you can edit them independently in case the lighting isn't perfect. *Don't* deselect anything yet; *lighting* is next.

4. If necessary, drag any one of the white lights toward the front of the shapes; the other three lights will automatically behave identically.

5. The green light might not look so good casting on a reddish character. Click the Color Editor button next to the Color Line and then pick Light 2 Colour from the

FIGURE 8-3 You can extrude individual shapes to the same direction and extrusion depth if you select them before using the Extrude Tool.

drop-down list at the top of the Color Editor box. In the Color Field, drag the marker to white, and then adjust the Green Light 2 pointer on the page to bring it to point at the bottom right of the four character shapes.

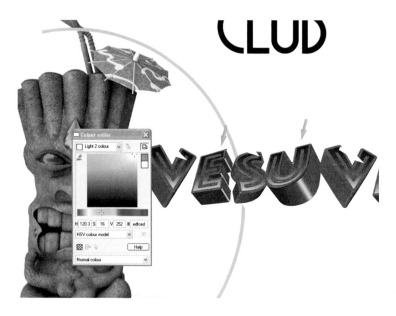

6. Repeat steps 2–5 with the remaining unextruded characters, except direct them up and to the *left*. Save your work now; don't close the document.

Fitting the 3D Text

The green outline circle is in this document for two reasons: to align the 3D text around the top of the mug and to use as a base for fitting the remaining text along the bottom of the logo.

Tackle the first part first:

1. Drag a horizontal guide down to about the eye level of the mug.

2. One character at a time, with the Selector Tool, reposition the characters until their horizontal centers are aligned with the green circle outline.

3. Using your artist's eye, space the characters until the first and last characters intersect the guide. The text is on a layer on top of the mug, but a nice design element might be to eclipse the first *U* and the *I* by the straws and the umbrella; because the characters are very simple and bold, legibility won't be an issue. To put these characters behind the image, open the Object Gallery, click on a shape (it's named "Extrusion"), and then drag it to the bottom layer, below the Photo Mug.png title.

4. Because you more or less performed a batch extrusion with the characters, the extrude depth, lighting, and angle of rotation might not be what you'd consider polished. Select a character in question by using the Extrude Tool, increase or decrease the extrusion depth either manually or by using the slider on the Infobar, and then adjust any light if needed.

5. With the Selector Tool, click a selected character. Then click it to put it into Rotate/Skew transformation mode, and drag a control handle to place the character(s) more randomly and also to close a gap between characters. Feel free to scale a character up or down, too; volcanoes beg a little chaos.

Creating Curves for Logo Embellishments

Much of the work in the following steps has to do with setting up two curves to apply two lines of text. Xara Xtreme doesn't automatically fit a second line of text to an imaginary outer curve, so you need to build one from the circle in the document, using the Contour Tool.

 Chapter 9 contains extensive documentation on the Arrange | Fit Text to Curve command, used in this assignment.

1. Choose the Contour Tool from the Toolbar, and then select the green outline circle. Drag the circle inward until the Infobar tells you the Contour Width is about 42 pixels.

2. Type **2** in the steps box at the left of the Infobar, and then press ENTER. This generates two additional circles plus the original, and you'll use all three in this example.

3. With the Selector Tool, either hold SHIFT and drag a corner control handle outward until the Scale field on the Infobar tells you you've reach 110%, or type **110** directly into the field and then press ENTER. To be legible, the text you'll run along the bottom curve of the circle needs a little wider arc than for the circle's original purpose.

4. Press CTRL-SHIFT-S to convert the contour group into editable shapes, and then press CTRL-U twice to create three shapes you can now edit with the Shape Editor Tool.

5. On the Object Gallery, click the Guides title to work on a non-printing layer.

6. With the Pen Tool, draw a diagonal line that bisects the mug and extends from outside the outermost circle (next to the first V), down and right to just outside of the same circle, running at about 10 o'clock to 4 o'clock. Peek ahead to Figure 8-4; it's not cheating.

7. Press CTRL-K to duplicate the line, and then click the Flip Horizontally button on the Infobar. Create a new horizontal guide at the base of the mug by dragging a guide from the ruler (press CTRL-L to toggle the rulers on if they are hidden).

8. Lock the Guides layer now—click the arrow icon to the right of its title (in the Object Gallery) so the status icon now looks like a lock. Click any other layer title now so you can do some editing and you're not working on the locked Guides layer.

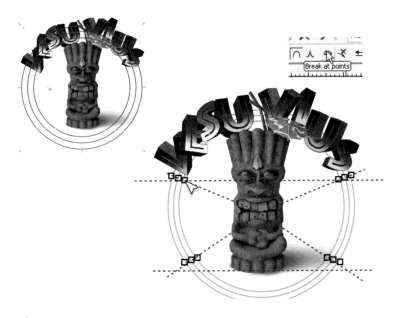

Break at points

FIGURE 8-4 Create arcs from the contour circles to use as text paths.

9. With the Shape Editor Tool, click at the intersection of the outside circle and the X guide you drew in step 6. After the control point has been created, right-click and then choose Break At Points from the pop-up menu or click the Break At Points button on the Infobar. Now click to add a control point on the opposite side, on the opposite intersection. Click the Break At Points button.

10. Repeat step 9 with the other two circles. When you have created the breaks as shown in Figure 8-4, switch to the Selector Tool and delete the top arcs and then the very bottom middle arc. Consider coloring the two remaining bottom arcs a different color for reference. You can hold SHIFT and click orange on the Color Line, for example, to color the outline. You'll use these two lines fit text to. Don't delete the six left and right arcs—you'll use them as a logo embellishment.

Work with Text Fitted to a Curve

In the following steps, you can copy the text and then paste it onto the arcs with the Text Tool selected, or type any description of the night club you like. Here's how to add that snappy slogan beneath the mug:

1. Copy the first line of text, or if you have a better slogan, proceed to step 2.

2. With the Selector Tool, select the uppermost arc at the base of the mug.

3. Choose the Text Tool, and then hover above the selected arc until the cursor is just an I-beam, with no cross hair at the center. This is your visual indicator that the cursor is in position for making text fit to the curve.

4. Type something; or alternatively, press CTRL-V to paste the Clipboard text.

5. Highlight the text and then choose Copasetic NF from the Fonts menu list. The font size should be okay as is; if needed, adjust Tracking until the text looks visually appealing.

6. If the text is on the bottom side of the arc, with the Selector Tool, choose the arc and the bound text, right-click, and then choose Reverse Text On Curve from the pop-up menu. This happens if you don't *precisely* click *slightly above* the curve before pasting and/or typing.

7. Center the text on the line: with the text highlighted, with the Text Tool, find the little red dot on the line that indicates the beginning of the text fitted to the curve and then drag the dot left or right until the text looks visually centered along a horizon.

8. Repeat steps 1–7 with the second line of text. Congratulate yourself and take a mini-break. You might not be aware of how difficult it is to put two consecutive lines of text along concentric arcs, centered, when using programs other than Xara. You have achieved a sophisticated look for the client in record time and should hit them up for a bonus when the logo is finished.

Use a Stroke Shape for an Embellishment

The six remaining lines suggest a finishing touch as a design element: they force the viewer's eye to complete the circle outside of the mug. But they should be ornamental lines, and here's where the Line Gallery proves indispensable:

1. Open the Line Gallery, and then open the Stroke Shapes/ Pressure Profiles folder.

2. With any of the six lines selected, double-click the Saw Tooth preset and then set the width to about 16 points.

3. With the line selected, press CTRL-C to copy it. Select the remaining five arcs, and then press CTRL-SHIFT-A to paste the *attribute* (the property) of the sawtooth line to the remaining lines.

4. Find some nice colors that complement the logo. Select the lines one at a time, hold SHIFT, and click on the Color Line to apply the outline color. Figure 8-5 shows the logo nearing completion.

FIGURE 8-5 They're more than funny little line presets: Stroke shapes can make great ornaments for logos, certificates, and wash-off tattoos.

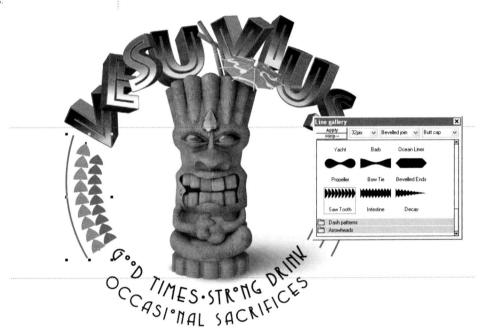

abc

Finishing the Logo

You need to hide the lines that support the text and add the word "CLUB" to the logo now. Not difficult stuff, following these short steps.

1. With the Selector Tool, click both lines of text and then set Line Width on the Standard Bar to None.

2. With the Shape Editor Tool, click a point just above and to the left of the first *V* in "Vesuvius"; then click a second point above the second *V*. If necessary, double-click the Constant stroke in the Line Gallery to remove the Saw Tooth setting.

3. While the line is selected, put your cursor at the center of the line and then drag up and to the left until the line becomes a curve and approximates the curvature of the VESUVIUS lettering. Because the 3D text is all over the place (not aligned), it would be impossible for a viewer to tell whether this curve is perfectly concentric compared to the other arcs in the logo. You *could* fuss over this step, build a new circle, convert it to curves, and then break it at points, but this would be fussy.

4. With the Selector Tool, hold SHIFT and select the CLUB text and the newly created curve. Go to Arrange | Fit Text to Curve. Adjust the tracking and positioning of text as needed and set the curve line width to None.

5. Patronize the club. They have a soft rock group, **Pumice**, live on Friday nights.

9

Desktop Publishing with Xara Xtreme

Although Desktop Publishing (DTP) seems today to have been supplanted by Website creation (HTML), the two arts share a core trait—the designer takes text and graphics and organizes them into an understandable presentation. Happily, Xara Xtreme has publishing features that accommodate both printed and virtual pages; often, a page layout can be re-purposed to use as a Web page. This chapter takes you through the art of good page design—how to arrange elements in a way that graphics don't fight the text and everything has a level of visual importance so the most important things strike the reader first, as you intend it. First, you'll lay out a small restaurant booklet-style standing menu intended for personal printer output, and then you'll move on to the more ambitious task of designing a page layout for a magazine. You'll learn invaluable tricks through the course of the tutorials, and with what you gain through experience, you'll be able to adapt the steps to just about any assignment of your own.

 Download and extract the contents of Chapter09.zip, which contains everything you need to work through this chapter's tutorial steps. Install the fonts on your system.

What's on the Menu Today?

Whether it's a 4-star restaurant, or a Mom and Pop roadside eatery, presentation is everything: the staff uniforms, the way the food is arranged on the plate, and especially the menu—the first thing a customer notices after being seated. Let's suppose in this section that you have a client (or you are the client) who runs a small, limited-menu restaurant, and the restaurant is bound for larger things, perhaps a franchise or more expensive location in the future.

A booklet style layout for the menu is the ticket here. Open a new file in Xara, press CTRL-SHIFT-O for Options, click the Page Size tab, choose U.S. Legal from the Paper Size drop-down list, and then click Portrait. This gives you 14 inches in height by 8 ½ inches in width. This paper size is supported by inkjet paper manufacturers and even most moderately-priced inkjet printers. If you fold this paper in half each way, you have a booklet that's 7 inches by 4 ¼ inches, which in turn you can trim down to 6 inches by 4 inches, a good size to rest on tables. This also means that the standing menu can be bled; graphics can run right to the edge of the crops.

In the following sections, you'll set up a template, including guides for margins, and then play DTP professional, designing the cover, adding graphics, building a logo, and formatting text provided for you to make a neat, convenient arrangement of the restaurant's *bill de faire*.

Setting Up Guides

Guides on this U.S. Legal-sized page serve two important functions: to show where the printable area is, thus avoiding text and images unintentionally falling off the printable page, and also to serve as snapping points—Xara's guides can magnetically attract objects in proximity to them, so perfect alignment is a snap. The orientation of objects on the page is not intuitive when you're making a booklet: top left is the cover (upside-down, which rectifies itself after you fold the page), top right is the back (also upside-down), and then the interior pages are right-side-up from bottom left to bottom right.

In the steps to follow you'll add guides to break the page into four sides when folded, and then add the face page's graphic to get the ball rolling.

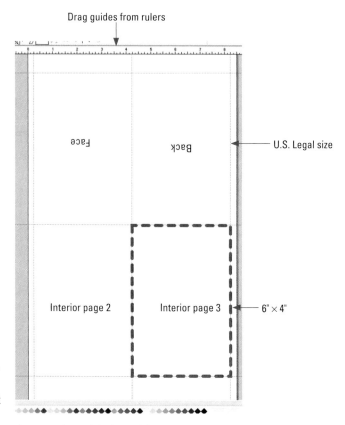

Drag guides from rulers

Face

Back

U.S. Legal size

Interior page 2

Interior page 3

6" × 4"

Here's how to set up a U.S. Legal paper size with the guides you need and then place the image for the front:

1. Press CTRL-L to display rulers, if they aren't visible. If the rulers aren't set up for inches, press CTRL-SHIFT-O

for Options. On the Grid and Ruler tab, set Major Spacing to **1in** (no space) and Number Of Subdivisions to **8**. Zoom into the vertical ruler, and then drag a guide from the horizontal ruler at exactly the 7" mark on the vertical.

2. Drag a vertical guide from the vertical ruler and place it exactly at the 4 ¼" mark on the horizontal ruler.

3. Drag a vertical guide to the ¼" mark on the horizontal ruler, and then create another vertical guide at exactly 8 ¼" on the horizontal ruler.

4. Finally, put a horizontal guide at 1" and another at 13".

5. Choose File | Save Template: why waste this setup work when you can open a new file with these guides all set to go for future assignments? Save the file to (wherever you installed Xara)\Templates\ENG (or other language). Choose the name carefully; it will appear under File | New in every new session of Xara.

6. Press CTRL-SHIFT-O for Options. Click the View tab, click Import At DPI Specified In The Image File, and click OK. JPEG, TIF, Photoshop PSD, and certain PNG files can retain image resolution information when saved; the image you'll import in the next step has resolution information, and if you didn't perform this step here, you'd be obliged to do manual resizing of the image.

7. Press CTRL-ALT-I to import The Quiet Spot.jpg; locate the file and choose it.

8. With the Selector Tool, drag the image until its upper-left corner snaps to the center of the two guides in the middle of the page at 4 ¼" width and 7" height. Notice that the image runs outside of the cropping guides—the image was created deliberately this way (and you should do the same when cropping images) so that some "unimportant" image area bleeds outside where you'll crop. Bleed prints, particularly in desktop publishing, create a sophisticated, polished, savvy presentation.

9. Save the file with a name you'll remember. Don't close the file. You saved this file as a template in step 5; because you've named the file, it's now no longer the template file, but the template is indeed saved for future use.

Trim for bleed

Fitting Text Along a Curve

As described in other chapters, a nice banner-envelope mould effect can turn a phrase rendered in an ornamental typeface into a serviceable logo. However, the Fit Text to Curve command (shown in interactive mode in the following steps) can be effective, too, for "embracing" the graphic of the coffee cup with "Quiet Spot," the name of this fictitious diner. You'll not only see how to add and move text along an arc but also how to visually integrate the text by using a shadow to visually separate light text from a similarly light background image area.

 If you purchased the download version of Xara Xtreme, you won't have the fonts you need for the tutorials. With an Internet connection going, in Xara, click to open the Fonts Gallery and then click Get Fonts.

1. BANGLE__.TTF in the Fonts folder in the Xara folder is a very nice typeface to express the idea of "quiet." If it's not available on your system, install it by dragging the file into the Fonts folder in the Control Panel.

2. With the Ellipse Tool, drag an ellipse so the top of the arc can represent the curve of the "Quiet Spot" text you'll add to it (peek ahead to Figure 9-1). Give the shape an outline width (any color will do), and no fill. Choose the Selector Tool and reposition and scale the oval as necessary.

3. With the Selector Tool, right-click over the shape and then choose Convert To Editable Shapes from the pop-up menu. Text cannot be fitted to a QuickShape (a shape that has special editing properties), and ellipses and rectangles belong to the QuickShapes category in Xara Xtreme.

4. With the object selected, choose the Shape Editor Tool, and then marquee-select the left and right control points. Then right-click and choose Break At Points from the pop-up menu. This two-step editing process is shown in Figure 9-1.

5. Press ESC to deselect and then click the lower half of the circle. Press the DELETE key on your keyboard to delete the bottom half of the oval; the top arc is used now for text. Select the top arc and then choose the Text Tool.

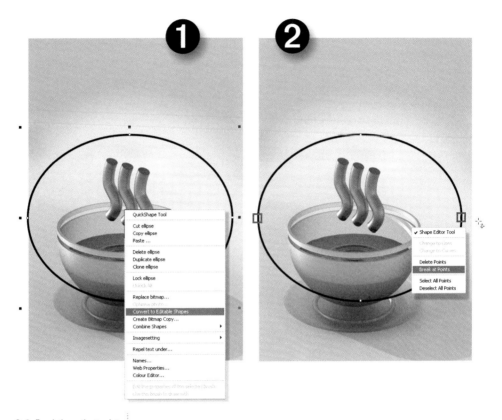

FIGURE 9-1 Break the path at points after simplifying the QuickShape to a regular path.

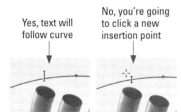

6. Watch what your cursor looks like as you hover it near the top of the arc. If there are cross hairs on the cursor, you're not in position to click an insertion point for text that will follow the arc's path. If the cursor only has an I-beam and no cross hair, click and then type **Quiet Spot**.

7. Press CTRL-A to select all the text, and then on the Infobar, choose Bangle from the Fonts drop-down list. Then click the Center Justification button.

8. While the text is highlighted, type **72** in the Point Size field and then press ENTER.

9. The text probably is not visually centered above the wavy image objects, and this is quickly fixed. Look for a red justification mark on the line the text is bound to. With the Text Tool cursor, drag this mark to the left or right; the cursor might not be on the dot after you start dragging, but the text will move anyway.

10. The spacing between characters that fitted to a curved path might be too loose or too tight—in this case, they're too loose. You can use the Tracking arrows on the Infobar to correct this: with the text highlighted, click the left arrow to tighten the tracking to about –80 (or whatever you feel looks good). Then highlight the space between the two words and tighten the tracking to about –250. The text has a polished look now.

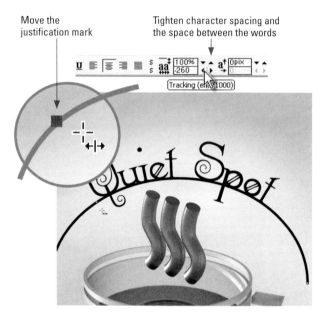

Move the justification mark

Tighten character spacing and the space between the words

Curves you fit text to have a top side and a bottom side. If you want the text, bound to a curve on the opposite side of the path, right-click over it and then choose Reverse Text On Curve from the pop-up menu.

Turning Fancy Text into a Logo

We're missing the word "The" in "The Quiet Spot," and one or two other modifications are needed to finish the front of the booklet menu. A heavy version of Bodoni can complement the treatment of the text cast in "Bangle." Install BodoniHeavy (BODONHE__.TTF) from the Fonts gallery if you installed from the physical CD; click Get Fonts if you bought the download version. Here's the deal: The "Quiet Spot" text could be more subtle if you make the color similar to the background of the coffee cup. To make it separate, you add a Wall Shadow with a high Blur value. When cast in Bodoni Heavy, the word "THE" has such high character recognition due to its weighty strokes that if you partially hide it behind the "Quiet Spot" text, it is still legible as the word "THE" and truly integrates to make the text a handsome logo.

1. Zoom in. Then with the Selector Tool, CTRL-click on the arc outline, and then SHIFT-click the Set No Color icon to the left of the Color Line to remove its appearance from the composition. The arc is still there, but the path has

Wall shadow

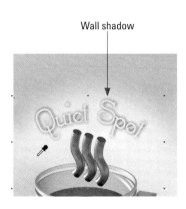

FIGURE 9-2 Play with text as though it is a graphic object to make a logo that's elegant and legible.

no visible attributes. This means in the future you could even retype the diner name or choose a different font and the text will still be bound to the curve.

2. Select the text with the Text Tool. With the color sampler eyedropper, drag over the image, very close to the text, to apply the sampled background color to the text.

3. Choose the Shadow Tool. Click the Wall Shadow button, and then drag the sliders to about 40 pixels Shadow Blur and 38% Shadow Transparency. Then drag with the Shadow Tool to move the shadow until it's just about centered relative to the text. If you feel the text doesn't quite separate enough now, highlight the text with the Text Tool, open the Color Editor, and make the text just 4–5% brighter without increasing its saturation.

4. With the Type Tool, click an insertion point near the center of the Quiet Spot text. Type **THE** (all caps). Then highlight the text, and choose Bodoni Heavy from the Fonts drop-down list.

5. Drag the color picker close to the text while it's selected. Fill the text with the background color, a little darker than the "Quiet Spot" text.

6. SHIFT-click the Color Editor icon to set the Line Color. Drag the Color Editor eyedropper to a position over the "Quiet Spot" text to set the line color. Set line width of the outline to about 4 points on the Infobar.

7. With the Selector Tool, select "THE" and then press CTRL-SHIFT-B to put the text behind "Quiet Spot."

8. Drag the bottom control handle for the text object down, stretching the text, as shown in Figure 9-2. A nice logo in only a handful of steps.

9. This is optional: A nice slogan would add a professional touch. You can use Premier Railway.otf (an author-created typeface based on Premiere) to type **Fine Food & Atmosphere** over the bottom of the coffee cup. The font has rails on the top and bottom of the characters, and instead of using a space between words, type the = character to put rails between words. You can sample a pale ivy color from the coffee cup image to fill the text; approximately 26 points will work well.

Putting the Front Page in the Right Place

Before you import the text for the menu, the front page doesn't
go where you've been working on it—not if the booklet is going
to print correctly. Here's how to position the front page text and
graphics:

Rotate
180 degrees

1. Press CTRL-A to select all, and then press CTRL-G
   to group the text and objects.

2. With the Selector Tool, move the group to the
   upper left of the page layout.

3. Click the selected group to put it into Rotate/
   Skew transformation mode.

4. Hold CTRL and then drag a rotation handle
   until the group rotates 180 degrees. CTRL
   constrains the rotation to the default
   constraint angle of 45 degrees, so four
   "stops" do the trick.

5. Click the group to put it back into the normal
   transformation mode and then move it until the
   right and bottom sides align with the central
   guides on the page.

Pouring Text into the Layout

The Rich Text Format (RTF) is almost as capable as Microsoft
Word's DOC file format. It retains text color, font choice, and
point size, and Xara Xtreme version 5 has an import/export
filter for RTF text. Let's begin formatting the text by first
importing it and then putting it in a paragraph frame in Xtreme:

1. On the Standard Bar, click the Zoom Factor drop-down
   list and choose Document so you can see the whole
   layout, and the text after it's imported. You don't place
   imported text in a frame—it sort of has a mind of its
   own and flows all over the page and pasteboard area.
   Then, you corral the text into paragraph blocks.

2. Press CTRL-ALT-I (File | Import), and then choose the
   Quiet spot menu.rtf you downloaded earlier. A query
   box appears that asks you whether you want to Merge,
   Insert (the text), or Cancel the operation. Click Merge;
   when you choose Insert, Xara automatically adds pages
   to a document to handle text that won't fit on the page.

You don't want an additional page, and the text will simply overflow onto the document pasteboard. Fortunately, your view was zoomed way out to see (and cut and paste) the entire text block.

3. With the Text Tool, click and drag (marquee-drag) a rectangle that fits inside the guides of what is page 2 in the booklet. This is an empty paragraph block you'll shortly paste the imported text into.

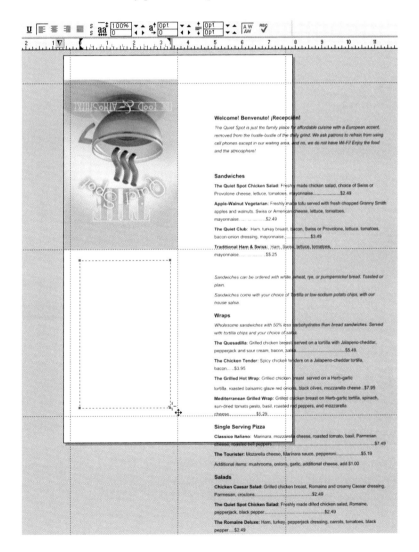

4. Put the Text Tool cursor in the imported text, click, and then press CTRL-A to select all. Now press CTRL-X to cut the text.

5. With the Text Tool, click your cursor inside the green outline paragraph text frame; the four corners of the frame light up in red and the border becomes a dashed outline. Press CTRL-V to paste the text.

6. Your view has apparently gone to Mars; Xara is tracking the pasted text to the very last paragraph line. Fortunately, all you need to do to return to the view of the page is choose Document from the Set Zoom Factor box on the Standard Bar. Note that the text that overflows the frame is dimmed to a light gray. Save the file again, and the next stop is some heavy-duty DTP text formatting.

Performing Spel-Chekking

New to Xtreme 5 is a built-in multilingual spell checker: use it regardless of who promised you that the copy you were given was proofed. It takes very little time to do a second proof.

To run spell checking as you type, click the ABC button on the Infobar when the Text Tool is active. Select the language that applies to the language in your text and click to toggle on the Check Spelling As You Type option. Whether you type or import text, the checking utility underscores in red any word it doesn't recognize. You then have the option to replace the word, ignore it, or add it to your personal dictionary.

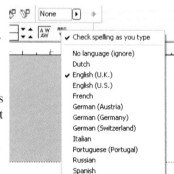

You do not have the Webster's Unabridged Dictionary, 475th Edition, under the hood in Xara Xtreme, and you'll undoubtedly run into false flags, particularly with proper names and regional phrases—and spell checking doesn't guard against grammar errors. *Homonyms* can be troublesome, and no spell checker on Earth will flag you if you type "Their is going to be some fun tonight" or "They're is going to be …"

If you spell-check the imported text, you'll notice the checker will flag "Wi-Fi," a few other regional spellings, and "Provolone." Provolone is spelled and capitalized properly, but Xara's spell checker has an incomplete list of imported cheeses. The remedy is a simple one: you right-click over an underscored word and then choose Add To User Dictionary from the pop-up menu. If a word is indeed misspelled, you choose the correct one from the possible suggestions on the pop-up list and Xara auto-corrects the word in place. This is why you should spell-check *before* you

format text—a long misspelled word replaced with the shorter correct one can cause a line break where you don't want it in a paragraph.

Using Fonts and Font Sizes

To be fair, you were given a worst-case scenario in this chapter; a thoughtful copywriter could have formatted the text with the necessary fonts, font sizes, and you'd be home by now. Let's get real, and get to work with Xtreme's DTP features; often, you're lucky you didn't get the text for an assignment handwritten on a brown paper bag, right?

It's time to pull the headline for the booklet spread out of the menu part of the imported text and apply a better typeface than Arial to the menu.

1. All the text before the subhead "Sandwiches" is introductory text. It doesn't belong in the body of the menu, and because this booklet is folded, straddling the facing pages 2 and 3 with the text is no problem. Put your Text Tool in front of "Sandwiches" and then SHIFT-click in front of the word "Welcome!" to highlight (select) the top text section (click and SHIFT-click as a quick method to select a block of text between the two clicks); then press CTRL-X.

2. Switch to the Selector Tool and move the paragraph block down to accommodate space needed for the new text above it. Press ESC or click on an empty space to deselect all items.

3. Back to the Text Tool. Create a headline area across both pages by marquee-dragging the cursor to make a new paragraph frame. Press CTRL-V to paste the text into the frame.

4. Anyone who is running Windows XP has a nice sans serif family of typefaces called Century Gothic (similar to Avant Garde in look) already installed, and let's use it for its clean look here. Press CTRL-A to select all the text within the paragraph frame; click the Center Justify

button on the Infobar to set the text apart from the columns of menu items, which will be justified flush left.

5. Choose Century Gothic from the Fonts drop-down list.

6. Highlight the "Welcome! Benvenuto! ¡Recepción!" text and then assign it about 30 points in font size. While it's highlighted, give it a 70 or 80% black fill by clicking the swatch on the Color Line. This softens the text for the reader, making a "cold" typeface a little warmer in the message's presentation.

7. Highlight the blurb after the headline text. Drag down on a bottom corner of the text box if needed to make all the text visible. Click the Italic property button to suggest someone is talking to the reader. *Softly.* Give this highlighted text 10 points in font size. Usually, 10 points is on the small size, especially for older readers, but Century Gothic is a sans serif typeface, making it acceptable at small point sizes.

8. With the text highlighted, increase its line spacing (*leading*) to 110% of the typeface's size from the default of 100% (adding a little air without significantly increasing the header's overall size) by clicking the up arrow next to the value field on the Infobar.

9. Because there is a hard return between the headline and the blurb (it was put there in the RTF file), Xara treats each section as a paragraph. This means you can add a space between the headline and the blurb by adding space after the first paragraph. Highlight the whole paragraph frame by pressing CTRL-A while the Text cursor is in the frame. Type **0** in the Space Before Paragraph to remove any previous formatting, type **6** in the Space After Paragraph field, and then press ENTER.

Line Spacing   Space Before/After Paragraph

Highlight; then cut text from here

Marquee-drag a new paragraph frame; then paste here

Formatting the Menu Items

You're going to return to one of Windows' default fonts again in the following steps: Book Antiqua is an attractive and highly legible typeface that will serve the menu's item list quite nicely. Also, you'll find a feature in Xara's Fonts drop-down to be an invaluable time-saver. You might have noticed that text you select with the Text Tool immediately changes to a preview of any font name you hover over on the Fonts drop-down list: this is called Live Preview. Only when you click on the font name does the selected text change. But *family members* of a typeface (bold, italic, condensed)—when a typeface has members—are listed on a flyout from the font name; you choose them and apply that "style" (family member) to the entire selected text.

In this example… no, no, you don't want to apply a family member to the selected menu text. The RTF file was carefully formatted so each entry is in bold, followed by a description in Normal of each savory item. To keep this formatting, you select the main font from the list, not a member of the family. Let's work through this one:

1. Highlight the menu items with the Text Tool; you don't want to select all because the name of the entrée category should be in a different font.

2. Drop the Fonts list down, and then hover over Book Antiqua but don't click yet. Look at the preview on your page. If you think you can do better from your list of installed fonts, go for it. If not, click the font name, but don't click any of the family member names.

Click the main font name; *don't* click
a family member on the flyout

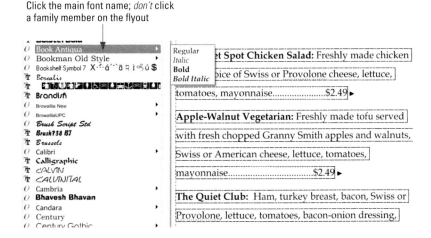

3. Choose 10 points from the Font Size drop-down list.

4. Highlight the word "Sandwiches." Choose Bodoni Heavy and give it a 14-point font size.

5. Save, but don't close the file. You're closer to finishing the layout than you might think.

Setting Tabs

By default, Xara puts tabs every half-inch in paragraph text. You can change this by applying a new tab to the text; if, for example, you put a new tab at .333 inches, all subsequent tabs are .333 inches apart. Something fancy restaurant menus feature is a tab alignment of prices—customers can scan the menu quickly, and having all prices justified against the decimal in the dollar (or yen, or peso) value gives a clean look.

Follow these steps to remove the ill-executed dot leader in the RTF imported text and put a decimal leader in a good paragraph place.

1. Highlight the text with the Text Tool.

2. On the ruler, to the left of the column markers, is a Tab button that toggles to different justification types when you click on it. By default, it's a left-justified tab. Click this button to change the proposed type of tab you'll create to Center, then Left, and a final click gets you to Decimal Tab. Hover over the marker, and a Tool Tip tells you when you have the correct tab.

3. Scan the highlighted text for the longest line of text— with attention only to the lines *before* the price.

4. Click on the ruler just a little after the longest line of text to add a decimal tab.

5. Remove the dot leaders by highlighting them and then pressing BACKSPACE.

6. One at a time, put your cursor directly after the last word and before the price, and then press TAB. If you need to adjust and fine-tune the position, keep the menu text selected and drag the decimal tab within the rule.

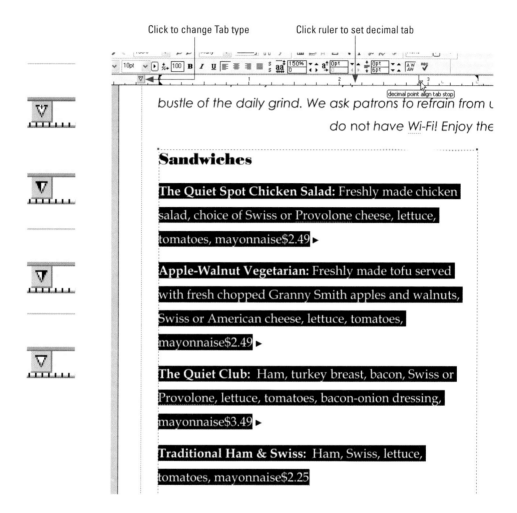

Typefaces that offer the closest match in compatibility with Web-safe fonts—typefaces used on HTML pages—are at the top of the list on the Fonts drop-down, above the horizontal divider. See Chapter 11 for details on building Web pages.

With the exception of the word "Provolone" underscored (you can turn spell checking off to hide the flags), the menu is looking fairly awesome. In the following section, you'll address the rest of the hidden, unformatted text for the menu in short order.

Do you remember Paste Attributes from other chapters? This
command works for text as well as for fills and effects.

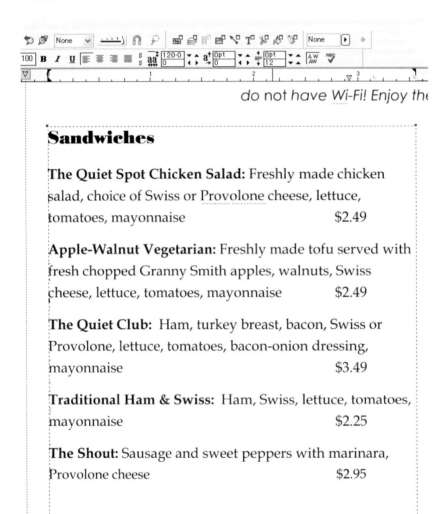

Use Linked Paragraph Frames

When you insert your cursor into the menu block of text, you'll
see a red down-arrow toward the bottom right of the frame. This
is the button for loading your cursor with the overflow text, the
faint gray text falling outside of the box—the text that currently
won't fit in the paragraph frame because of the frame size or the
point size of the text.

You still have panels 3 and 4 to fill in this booklet layout. Fortunately, you have the text. Here are the steps for creating linked paragraph blocks, linking the text in each frame so that if you resize the frame, the overflow goes to the next frame dynamically. You'll also see that the hidden text is not formatted. If you copy formatted text in the lower-left panel, highlight the unformatted text after it's in a new linked frame, and then press CTRL-SHIFT-A, you paste the *attributes* of the formatted text. The unformatted text takes on the font, the point size, the alignment, the color, and even the decimal tab you created in the previous steps. Make sure you highlight *only* text that should take the new attributes; if the Fonts drop-down says <Multiple>, you've highlighted text that has two different typefaces, and shouldn't.

1. Zoom out if necessary until you can see the bottom two panels.

2. With the Text Tool, click the red down-arrow button on the text frame.

Welcome! Benvenuto! ¡Recepción!

The Quiet Spot is just the family place for affordable cuisine with a European accent, removed from the hustle-bustle of the daily grind. We ask patrons to refrain from using cell phones except in our waiting area, and no, we do not have Wi-Fi. Enjoy the food and the atmosphere!

Sandwiches

The Quiet Spot Chicken Salad: Freshly made chicken salad, choice of Swiss or Provolone cheese, lettuce, tomatoes, mayonnaise $2.49

Apple-Walnut Vegetarian: Freshly made tofu served with fresh chopped Granny Smith apples, walnuts, Swiss cheese, lettuce, tomatoes, mayonnaise $2.49

The Quiet Club: Ham, turkey breast, bacon, Swiss or Provolone, lettuce, tomatoes, bacon-onion dressing, mayonnaise $3.49

Traditional Ham & Swiss: Ham, Swiss, lettuce, tomatoes, mayonnaise $2.25

The Shout: Sausage and sweet peppers with marinara and provolone $2.95

Click to load the
Text Tool cursor

3. Marquee-drag to create a new paragraph frame in the lower-right panel; try to keep inside the guides on the page layout—if you don't, this is okay. You can resize a paragraph frame by dragging a corner handle with the Text Tool at any time.

4. Highlight the word "Sandwiches" and then press CTRL-C.

5. Highlight the word "Wraps" and then press CTRL-SHIFT-A.

6. Highlight the formatted menu items in the lower-left panel and then press CTRL-C.

7. Highlight the unformatted menu items in the new paragraph frame and then press CTRL-SHIFT-A.

8. Insert your cursor in the newer menu items, remove the dot leaders one at a time, and then press the TAB key to put a tab between the last word and the beginning of the price. You'll see that the decimal leader tab is in place and the prices neatly align.

9. Highlight the blurb at the top of the two-page spread and press CTRL-C.

10. Highlight the descriptions of the meal categories (one at a time, such as "Wholesome sandwiches with…") and then press CTRL-SHIFT-A. Click the Left Justify button on the Infobar to remove the center justification. You'll notice the new formatted paragraph frame, with a gray line that shows you which paragraph frame has linked text and where it's linked to on the page.

Marquee-drag a new paragraph frame

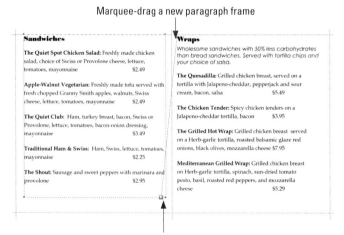

Frames are linked

Create Hanging Indents

Learning to make hanging indents is valuable, although not really necessary for this booklet layout. A hanging indent is also called an *outdent*—the first line in a paragraph starts flush left, and every subsequent line is indented. It's a useful trick for making numbered lists in Xara and also for bulleting items—such as you'd find on a menu. Let's suppose you want to add some color to the layout here, but colored text is hard on the eyes. Instead, you add bullets to the menu items with a symbol font and then highlight the symbol and apply a color fill.

The lowercase glyph *m* in Geotype.ttf is a nice coffee cup symbol that can visually reinforce this booklet's cover image. Follow these steps to create a hanging indent bulleted list with paragraph text:

1. Highlight the menu items to make the tabs visible on the ruler.

2. Drag the left margin marker to the right, where you want the paragraph text to begin. Half an inch at most is good.

3. Set the type of tab to left align, as you did with the decimal tab, by clicking as many times as needed to toggle the Tab icon to left justify.

4. Click anywhere on the ruler, close to but not directly on the new location of the left indent marker.

5. Drag the new tab marker to the zero point, where the left indent marker was in step 1.

6. Put the I-beam cursor at the far left of the first line, click, and then type **m**.

7. Press TAB to tab the first line of text to align with the following lines. You might need to press TAB twice to scoot over the first (default) tab if you created your new tab after any of the default tabs.

8. With *m* highlighted, choose Geotype from the Fonts drop-down on the Infobar. Set the point size now to about 18 points so the intricate little drawing is visible.

9. With the glyph selected, click a fill color on the Color Line. The bulleted list is looking good now, but you'll notice that the bullets aren't centered relative to the text;

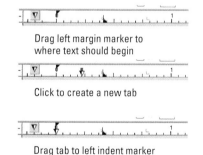

Drag left margin marker to where text should begin

Click to create a new tab

Drag tab to left indent marker

they need to be dropped a little. Don't stop at mere bullets for bulleted lists; use a fun picture font character.

10. With the bullet still highlighted, on the Infobar, click the Baseline Shift down-arrow until the bullets look a little more planned and less haphazardly placed. Press CTRL-C and then highlight the remaining bullets and press CTRL-SHIFT-A to paste all the formatted attributes.

Finishing the Booklet

You've done some work here, however, consider how many parts of this booklet you can reuse in future assignments. You have a template, and you can easily copy the formatting of the text and then use the Paste Attributes command to do a jiffy format of similar text.

What remains is to create a new linked paragraph frame for the remainder of the text, format it, and rotate it until it's in the correct orientation for page 4 at top right.

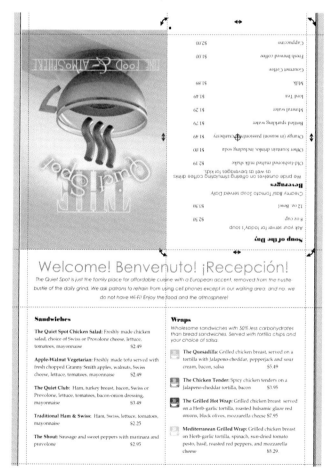

FIGURE 9-3 Turn the page upside-down so when you fold the menu, it will read right side up.

1. With the Text Tool, click the red arrow on the lower-right paragraph frame, and then marquee-drag an area to its right, on the page's pasteboard area.

2. Format the text by copying and pasting the already formatted attributes, exactly as you did while building page 3.

3. With the Selector Tool, drag the paragraph frame to the top right of the page.

4. Click the selected frame to put it into Rotate/Skew mode. Alternatively, if you're very careful, you can put your cursor just inside the object's selection handles to rotate it. Hold CTRL and then drag the handle until the text block is upside-down, as shown in Figure 9-3.

5. If your restaurant accepts credit cards, credit cards.xar contains scalable vector reproductions of The Big Three in the United States. Copy and scale them, and put them at a small size in a conspicuous place in the layout. These guys are hard to find and are a gift to our readers; use them to your benefit in future assignments.

6. Put hairline crop marks at the outside guides. You can do this easily by using the Pen Tool because the control points snap to the guides by default. Use the .25-point width on the Infobar, and make 'em black. Now you can print to an inkjet and also export the file to PDF format and send to a commercial printer when this business grows and can afford commercial printing.

7. Save the file. You can go back at any time, adjust the menu items and the prices, and even replace the bitmap image on the front page in no time. Also consider making a copy of this booklet file and deleting all the menu text. This booklet you created would also make a nice holder for a gift certificate or a thank you note from the restaurant to the customer who helped put out last week's fondue fire.

Magazine Page Layout

Page layout requires a little more imagination than making a menu. The elements are practically the same—headline, graphics, body text—and imagination is what makes the difference between a boring layout and an inspired one, so consider the freedom to design in between nervous gulps. The following tutorials walk you through the design aspect, not the content creation, of first a one-page and then a two-page magazine spread. The subject of the article is a fairly boring one: an ode to the toppings on a hamburger, so your mission— should you decide to accept it, Jim—is to add interest to ennui through *layout* skills.

Learn to Love the Grid

A grid, in page layout (frequently called *The Swiss Grid*), is essentially a set of graphical rules. You don't even have to lay down guides on a Xara Xtreme page if you can mentally picture a grid when you lay out the elements.

When laying out a page, you need structure, specifically a sort of scheme for element alignment, to lead the reader from an important element to a less important one, and so on. The cohesiveness of the page layout depends on the relationship between elements and their proximity to one another; a grid, on the page or imagined, is key to this goal. Professionals have been using a grid system for publications before computers as we know them now even existed, and there's no reason to ditch a working methodology simply because we work on a screen and not a drafting table nowadays.

A page grid:

- Can have any number of cells. However, more than three columns or rows, and you have visual confetti and not a grid.

- Doesn't have to feature content in every cell (some can be vacant), and cells in a grid don't have to be of equal size.

- Can float the elements within the cells at any alignment. Your own eye is going to tell you when elements in neighboring cells should be aligned next to each other or aligned identically relative to the cells they occupy.

- Being a rule-based system, like all rules, once you thoroughly understand them, you can successfully bend and break the rules as a designer. This means your objects don't have to perfectly fit in a cell and elements can span cells; a page grid is a structure from which you hang stuff. It's your support, it's your playground, but it's not a pair of handcuffs.

FIGURE 9-4 Create a grid on a page or in your mind as the structure for the page's elements.

Figure 9-4 shows a few examples of classic page layout grids. The structure of each grid defines the page layout.

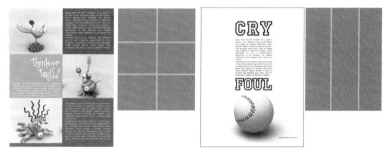

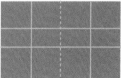

Open Just try to top this.xar now to work the steps:

Using a Headline as a Graphical Element

The headline to this magazine article is "Just try to top this!" It's a designer's privilege to fancy-up a headline by making it a graphic (a logo in a certain sense), and this is the first stop in this page layout. You'll see after opening the file that the text has not been formatted and that the word "This!" is not text at all, but a group of shapes; it was necessary to convert the text to a shape so a contour could be applied to both the word "This" and the exclamation mark, which is not part of the Team Spirit character set.

Follow these steps to get a handle on how Team Spirit works; the font includes special characters to complete the underscore swash for words and phrases:

1. Highlight the top line of text by using the Text Tool.

2. On the Fonts drop-down list, choose Team Spirit NF. You'll see some unattractive gaps between words because a special character needs to replace the spaces between the words.

3. Insert the Text Tool between "Just" and "try" and then press BACKSPACE to remove the space. Type an

underscore here (SHIFT-HYPHEN)—this is the character Nick assigned to complete the underscore swash.

4. Repeat step 3 for the other spaces, and then after the *p* in "Top," type a right parenthesis (SHIFT-0) to add the character that rounds and returns the underscore swash.

5. With the Selector Tool, move the grouped graphic of the word "This" until it overlaps the text, but just a little so the headline is an integrated graphic with all the words legible.

6. Select both the text and the group, and then press CTRL-G to group the two.

7. Click on the selected group to put it into Rotate/ Skew transformation mode, and then rotate the group counterclockwise until the stems in the text (the vertical components) look perfectly vertical, another design embellishment. Save the file now, but don't close it.

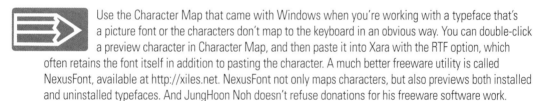

Use the Character Map that came with Windows when you're working with a typeface that's a picture font or the characters don't map to the keyboard in an obvious way. You can double-click a preview character in Character Map, and then paste it into Xara with the RTF option, which often retains the font itself in addition to pasting the character. A much better freeware utility is called NexusFont, available at http://xiles.net. NexusFont not only maps characters, but also previews both installed and uninstalled typefaces. And JungHoon Noh doesn't refuse donations for his freeware software work.

Create a Grid, Import, and Repel Text

The Repel Text feature in Xara Xtreme is dynamic and the best implementation of DTP text wrapping in any program to date. Looking at this layout and the elements you have, repelling the text you'll soon import will give you a wonderful design opportunity to flow the paragraph around part of the burger. Let's get to laying out the grid and then bringing in the text:

1. A number of grids can be used with this page, but you'll begin with a simple one: Drag two vertical guides from the rulers to create three even columns, and then one horizontal guide to *unevenly* divide the page at about the 5" mark on the vertical ruler. Drag two vertical guides from the horizontal ruler—put them at 2 ¾" and 5 ½".

2. Put the burger at the lower right of the page, and then move the headline to the left, just above the burger, so it occupies the two left columns. There is absolutely no professional decree that says a headline needs to go at the top of a page.

3. Press CTRL-ALT-I and then go get the Burger text.rtf file. Choose to merge the file when asked.

4. Make certain the current editing layer is the Text layer; click it to highlight it on the Object Gallery if it's not already selected.

5. With the Text Tool, marquee-drag a paragraph frame from the second grid column at top to the bottom right of the layout, staying inside the guides that were originally created in this file.

6. Put the Text Tool cursor in the imported text, press CTRL-A to select all, and then press CTRL-X to cut the text to the Clipboard.

7. Click the cursor inside the paragraph frame and then press CTRL-V to paste the text into the frame. Use white space by leaving unfilled cells in your grid to push the reader's eye toward the content on the page.

The margin on this page is wider at right than at left because it is to go in a magazine, and magazines have gutters. Therefore, this is a left-facing page.

8. Select all the text, and try Palatino Linotype on the Fonts drop-down list for the text; it came with windows XP and it's a nice departure from using Times New Roman all the time. Specify 12 points for the text.

9. With the Selector Tool, select the burger and the grouped headline, and then choose Arrange | Apply Soft Group—CTRL-ALT-G is a very good keyboard shortcut to commit to memory. What you have done is to create a group from the grouped headline and the burger (which itself is a soft group of grouped objects), without moving anything to a common layer. All the burger elements are on different layers, as is the headline, but it's still a (soft) group that you can move as a single entity.

10. Showtime for the Repel Text feature: the text is beneath the Soft Group on its own layer. With the Selector Tool, right-click over the burger and then choose Repel Text under from the pop-up menu.

11. Type **14pt** (a little more than the height of the text is good spacing) in the Extra Repel Margin field and then click Repel.

12. This is *really* cool stuff (for desktop publishing people). Try dragging the soft group around the page and watch how the repelled body text rearranges itself. Unfortunately, there appears to be too much text for the layout. Dimmed text is overflow text… and ultimately it has to go somewhere on the page. Or you'd ask the copywriter to cut a paragraph or two. No, strike that thought, and continue to the next section.

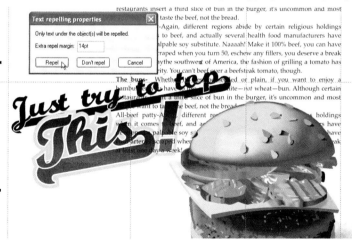

Some might consider it excess to ingest one of these now world-adored meals with all the topping, but anything and everything from a garden, plus stuff that definitely doesn't come from a garden, has become an Eating Way of Life.

Processed cheese-Usually American, occasionally the "designer color" blend goes on top of the burger, always rectangular, but placed beneath the other toppings—order in important for the maximum taste experience. Substitute jalapeño cheese for a Western burger, and use Bleu for a unique fare and charge 20% more for the meal.

Dill pickles-The dill variety of the pickled cucumber is a hard and fast rule; sweet pickles tend to influence the overall taste and conflict with other condiments. Gherkins rule, and they rule above both the lettuce and the cheese.

Lettuce-Iceberg is almost universally used; Romaine is for salads, not burgers. The lettuce should be added after the burger is cooked—warm lettuce is like cold *soup* is!

The Onion (*Allium cepa*)- Although regional differences support different onion types, red onions and Vidalia are not used as often as the plain old cooking onion. If you want to get fancy like that famous Scottish restaurant, you chop and cook the onions.

Tomato-A Grade A tomato is commonly used. Occasionally in the southwest of America, the fashion of grilling a tomato

Overflow text

 Text itself can be used to repel text. Just make sure the text that is going to push the other text around is either on a layer on top of the repelled text or just above the text on a single layer.

Creating a Lead-in Paragraph

Because your grid has white space, you can use it to pull the introductory paragraph from the body text and create what you see in magazines as a lead-in paragraph. Lead-ins are frequently of a larger point size, and the "air" between the characters helps the layout by allowing some of the white area to serve as a design element. Follow these steps to finesse the page layout:

1. With the Text Tool, highlight the first paragraph and then press CTRL-X. Press ESC to make sure you have the current text frame deselected.

2. Marquee-drag a new paragraph frame to the left of the original, make it the width of the left column, and then press CTRL-V to paste the Clipboard text. This text is still associated with the other frame, but now it's the first paragraph frame as far as reading the text goes.

3. Press CTRL-A to select all, and then increase the point size on the Infobar to 18 points.

4. Click the Right Justify button on the Infobar. Most times, right-aligned text is hard to read in English publications, but this text is large and there are few words per line, so it's acceptable here, and you've added another design element.

5. Play with the paragraph frames, using the Text Tool to drag frame-corner control handles until the text looks neatly aligned and the repelled text doesn't break in the middle of a line. You can resize the lead-in paragraph frame, reposition it, and drag the bottom control corners down to get the flow you need.

A Variation on the Page Layout

You can quickly make a new layout by using the existing grid; you can create an equally interesting and legitimate treatment of the article's elements by reworking the elements in the grid or envisioning a *different* underlying grid. You can use a lot of line spacing (leading) to leave white space on the page; this treatment is fashionable in magazines today for lead-in paragraphs.

Follow these steps to create an alternative layout:

1. Select all the lead-in text, and then increase the line spacing to 160%; you can click on the Increase button next to the number field on the Infobar, or type this value in and then press ENTER. Move the paragraph frame up by using the Selector Tool, and then with the

Text Tool, drag one of the bottom frame control points down until none of the text is hidden.

2. With the Selector Tool, choose the soft group, and then press CTRL-ALT-U to remove the soft group.

3. On the Object gallery, drag the Headline layer to beneath the Bottom Bun layer but above the Text layer.

4. Move the headline until it looks like it does in the illustration here. Select the burger along with the headline and then apply the Soft Group again (CTRL-ALT-G).

5. Move the Soft Group around just a little so the repelled text can update itself.

6. With the Text Tool, cut from "Processed cheese" to "The Onion," create a new paragraph frame by marquee-dragging with the Text Tool in the left column below the lead-in text, and then press CTRL-V to paste it.

Create a Two-Page Spread

Let's dream on for a moment and believe that this story is important enough to merit a full two-page spread in *The Quarter-Pounder Quarterly*. Here's the deal: Because this burger is an illustration, and the talented fellow who drew it was thoughtful enough to group all the foodstuffs and put them on individual layers, you can change the illustration to suit your page layout. Think about this one: Vector artwork is scalable, vector data is sent to a printer at the maximum value the printer can output, and the sort of dramatic layout rearrangement you'll do in a moment is extremely hard to do when you're handed a bunch of bitmap photos.

Here's how to add a facing page to the existing document, have it your way, and go to town rearranging the illustration's group:

1. Hide the Text layer by clicking its eye icon on the Object gallery.

2. Ungroup the headline and then delete the text, but not the "This!" graphic. You'll need to retype this headline because this layout will feature it unrotated, and it's not worth your time trying to precisely align the text's baseline to a perfect horizon.

3. Click on the burger and then choose Arrange | Remove Soft Group (CTRL-ALT-U).

4. One object at a time, pull the onions, pickles—all that good stuff—apart vertically but keep them horizontally centered. Take care that some of the shadow objects don't come unaligned—there's a shadow on the cheese and one casting from the onion, and these are all partially transparent feathered objects. You'll put them where they are appropriate, according to how you decompile the burger.

5. With the Text Tool, type the headline on the Bottom Bun layer, and then arrange the object icons on the Object gallery so that the headline is below the drawing of the bottom bun. This is for a design look.

6. Press CTRL-SHIFT-O to open the Options box. Click the Page Size tab.

7. Click the Double-Page Spread button. Then click Apply and then OK to dismiss the box. It's *that* easy to make a two-page spread.

8. Marquee-select all the burger elements by using the Selector Tool, apply the Soft Group arrangement to the elements, and then put the illustration right in the gutter of the spread. This might dampen the effect of the illustration a little when it's bound into a magazine, but designers crop unessential visual elements to the gutter and page borders all the time. And you *cannot* run text across a publication border unless you're certain it's the center spread.

9. Move the headline to the top of the page. With the Text Tool, add some underscores between "try" and "to" so the headline straddles the gutter.

10. Move the "This!" graphic until it sits on the right facing page, to the left of the sesame seed bun and below the headline text.

11. Unhide the text and arrange it so there are two equal columns on the left and the right pages.

12. The soft group should still have the Repel Text property, but to make sure, right-click over the burger—if Repel Text Under is not checked, click this item on the pop-up menu and then reapply the feature.

13. Move the burger around a little to wake up the repelled text.

14. Put your lead-in opposite the "This!" graphic on the left page. You'll wind up with a fresh, new two-page layout.

Export to PDF for Commercial Printing

It would be criminal to conclude a chapter on desktop publishing without the *publishing* part. Unlike even a decade ago, getting your layouts to a commercial printer does not involve making your own separations (although *you* can with Xara), deciding on a color space, and remembering to include your fonts with the job lest your layout come back printed in Courier New.

The PDF file format has been almost universally embraced by commercial printers today; it's almost 100% goof-proof (*bullet-proof* in printing "pre-flight" lingo) and Xara will embed (when a font is coded to permit it) a subset of the typeface, the characters used, so there are no font files you can forget to include.

To export your work, specifically a page layout, to PDF file format:

1. Press CTRL-SHIFT-E to export the file.

2. Choose PDF or PDF/X (*.PDF) from the Save As Type drop-down list. Name the file in the File Name box and click Export.

3. In the Xara Xtreme PDF Preset dialog box, you have your choice of High Quality or Commercial Printing if you want to send this layout to a commercial printer. If you choose Commercial Printing, you'll be exporting to PDF/X, which is a highly optimized and proprietary sort of PDF file. All fonts will be embedded; however, the file format presumes your work is all set to go in CMYK mode. These examples are *not*, and therefore this is *not* the best export option unless you thoroughly know the physical printing characteristics of the print press that will render this job. A better choice for the beginner is High Quality. Color mode is maintained with this option, and a good commercial printer knows how to do RGB-to-CMYK color conversions for you so the print will look its best. Click High Quality, and then click Advanced Options.

4. In the Advanced Options box, on the General tab, make sure Embed Fonts When Permitted and Font Subset Only are checked. Optimized For Fast Web Viewing is not necessary unless you want to use this layout for both the Web and commercial printing. Check View PDF when finished if you have Adobe Acrobat Reader or other 3rd party reader installed (or nothing will happen; there's no native Windows program to open a PDF).

5. Click the Objects tab. Bitmap Compression can stay at its default of Native; choose None if you're nervous about bitmap quality and don't mind larger files. Certain objects in the burger layout cannot be expressed as Xara vector art when exported to a PDF page; feathered objects and transparency call for rendering the object as a bitmap. Therefore, you want to make any bitmap areas of high printing quality, so leave the Rasterization Resolution at its default of 300 dpi.

6. In your free time, browse the other tabs: Security settings will only result in accidentally locking your commercial printer out of the document, and the other settings aren't relevant to simply pulling a PDF for commercial printing. Click Export, and in a moment you'll see your work as a PDF. Figure 9-5 shows the dialog boxes you'll see when you export.

FIGURE 9-5 Exporting to PDF file format creates a copy of your work that can be edited later to a minor extent and imported back to Xara, and can serve both commercial printing and online documentation purposes.

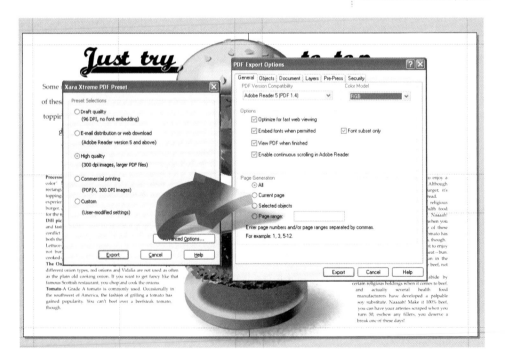

10

Creating Web Animations

When you go online and land on a web page, any animations on the page attract your attention. This is reason enough to dig into the animation features in Xara Xtreme; the Web is one big marketplace today, and those who don't provide the latest type of content lose to more glamorous sites. But a *bigger* reason to become proficient with the Frame Gallery and other animation features is that as a designer, you don't have to limit yourself to blinking buttons— once you've mastered Xara's drawing tools, you can put *your artwork* into motion. This chapter takes you through how to animate vector art; how the qualities of timing, concept, and mini-story-telling add a dimension to drawings; and how to export your moving pictures to GIF and Flash Shockwave file formats.

Download and extract the contents of Chapter10.zip, which contains everything you need to work through this chapter's tutorial steps. Additionally, there are Flash files and the Xara documents used to build them included in the archive. They are simply for you to check out and analyze. Although the techniques for creating these animations are covered in this chapter, there are no tutorial steps for them.

Understanding the Capabilities (and Limits) of Web Animation

Xara animation features produce small gems; Xara Xtreme is not a nonlinear video editing suite, and it's not Adobe Flash. However, if you get your head and creative skills around drawing and editing something on a page in Xara, chances are excellent that you can then *animate* it. Animated GIF files are a piece of cake to produce once you understand how Xara handles bitmaps, references images, and defines durations. The sections to follow explain a little about the nature of animation and what transformations are valid to export to the Flash SWF (Shockwave) file format.

Remember that Xara's implementation of Flash is strictly for animation; Xara is a *drawing* program that can help you create animations. It does not support Flash features such as audio, embedded movies, and scripting for interactivity.

Your Director's Options for the Script and Casting

The more captivating animations you see on the Web were created by gifted individuals who treat web animations very much like traditional film. Let's pare any good motion picture down to its essentials before covering what you can do in Xara with your "actors" and the "story."

- **Completeness** Cliffhangers can sometimes intrigue an audience, but usually an incomplete story irritates us. Before you do anything in Xara, think of something interesting to present that has a beginning, a middle, and an end, like any good story. The concept can be exceedingly simple, yet make a creative point. Animation without a complete idea behind it lacks artistic soul and doesn't keep your audience with you. We're not talking about keeping your audience riveted to their seats for two hours. A bouncing ball, for example, is a very simple story; it's complete within its own idea. If you further animate the ball so it has some spin, wiggle, and stretching, the story is developed through its actor, and your audience will view it for perhaps 10 seconds—far more of their time given to your work than a sign that says "Sale" and merely blinks on and off.

- **Timing** Xara Xtreme builds animations using the keyframe paradigm: You set a key pose for a shape, define a duration it occupies a frame, and then create a different keyframe. Xara does the 'tweening—the frames that make up the animation in between keyframes. As the director, it's your call how long a scene persists onscreen, how fast the animation plays, where it might pause, and how the animation completes itself. Flash and GIF animations can loop, and it's usually a good idea to allow them to loop; there's nothing worse for your ego than to allow your animation to stop after playing once … and your audience wasn't watching your web page yet. Therefore, take into consideration the devices used in Hollywood to conclude a scene or an animation. You can create *cycles* (where the last frame plays into the first frame), you can fade in at the beginning and fade out at the end, or you can simply fade to black if there's a different animation somewhere else on the web page. The quality of *time* is a nonintuitive thing to add to the mix when you design something, but once you get a handle on all the dimensions of a presentation, you can produce work many other folks can't.

- **Vector versus bitmap**   When considering your audience, and also what you can do to animate an idea, the structure of your animation can be bitmap, vector, or a combination of both. Bitmap animations are very large when compared to vector Flash format, but on the other hand, some things (such as animating photos) cannot be achieved with vector artwork. A Flash slide show of photos, for example, can be created by placing a number of photos in a Xara document, and then over time, you increase the transparency of one slide to reveal the following photo. Bear in mind that Xara can reference vector artwork in an extremely compact way. If, for example, only the *changes* in a path are recorded to Flash file format, you could in reality make a lasso twirl about for several minutes and the file size would be less than 1K! This is because the path is only written once to the Flash data file, along with the changes as it animates. Conversely, bitmap animations usually have to be written to a Flash and GIF file *one complete frame* at a time, exactly as motion pictures are sequenced. Although you can occasionally make GIF files smaller by reusing parts of a frame, the rule is that bitmap animations are larger than vector animations of the same visual quality. If you think your audience is mostly composed of users with dial-up connections, it would be *deadly* to cobble only bitmap animations for the website no one will have the patience to wait to see.

Object Properties You Can Animate

Xara has features that Flash does not support, but if you're careful in planning, the workarounds covered in this chapter will get your idea where it wants to go. The following is a list of actions supported in Flash as pure vector animation.

- **Move, scale, disproportionately scale, skew**   Any shape you draw can be moved on the page and distorted (transformed) by using the Selector Tool and by nudging. You cannot change a path's control points and have

Xara perform tweening automatically for you. This means yes, you can change control points and curves, and add and delete curves, but the result might look like a choppy slide show with no auto-created transitions between keyframes.

 You can animate text traveling along a curve and export it as a Flash movie. See Chapter 8 for the steps on how to use the Arrange | Fit Text To Curve command.

- **Rotate objects**   You can rotate shapes and also rotate them after you've moved a shape's transformation center outside of the object (terrific for making waving flags).

- **Transparency**   As long as you use the Mix transparency type, you can animate the percentage of *flat* transparency over time, and Xara does the tweening. However, you can achieve a fairly smooth *manual* tweening of linear and some other gradient transparencies, as you'll see later in this chapter. It's *not* hard.

- **Flat fills**   You can do some exciting color modulations when you change the flat color (solid color) of shapes over time. Imagine how interesting you can build an animation when you have several different objects changing colors *at different rates* over time. Or different shapes of the same color, changing to the same alternate color, at different rates over time.

Objects and Fills that Flash Supports

You can create certain shapes and fills in Xara that Flash animation can't handle, and Xara warns you of this before you export an animation. The good news is that everything that Flash can handle, Xara can create. The following list describes what you should and shouldn't use when making a scene for animation:

- **Outline properties**   Standard Flash export supports outline width and color but only the rounded line caps and joins. If you choose to export to Flash version 8, it supports Xara's other types of control point properties. Flash does not support Pressure Profiles/ Stroke Shapes, dashed lines, or other categories in the Line Gallery. However, if your design calls for a fancy outline stroke, you can convert the line to a shape—choose Arrange | Convert Line to Shape.

▦ **Fill properties**   Flash will render flat fill-color types, plus linear, circular, and elliptical gradients. A gradient can contain up to eight color transitions (color stops). Fill tiling is limited to Simple, and the Fade Fill effect is the only option on the Infobar that Flash will understand.

▦ **Transparency**   If you apply transparency to a gradient-filled shape, you are limited to the Mix transparency type. However, when you fill a shape with a flat (solid) color, you can use linear, circular, and elliptical transparency shapes.

▦ **Text**   The Flash rendering engine in Xara can accept any typeface you have installed. You can also animate inter-character spacing (kerning) values.

▦ **Bitmaps**   Photos and digital paintings can be exported to a Flash animation, but they cannot be as efficiently compressed as vector shapes. A good idea is to make a copy of high-resolution images at the size you intend to use, in JPEG file format. To do this, you first import a bitmap to a page, scale it to the required size, and then press CTRL-SHIFT-C (Arrange | Create Bitmap Copy). After scaling the picture, open the Bitmap Gallery, click the copy of the image, and then click Save. Then import the copy to your animation file. If you don't care about optimizing the saved image size, you can leave the bitmap image in the animation file and successfully export a Flash animation. You can export colorized images, saturation, temperature color, and blurring with the Photo Tool without making a copy. However, brightness and contrast changes need to be exported and then imported. Fractal cloud and plasma fills export without making a copy; they are automatically converted to bitmaps, so expect a larger Flash file as a result.

▦ **Effects**   All effects—Contours, Blends, and Moulds applied to shapes—can be exported, and the parent shape can be moved, scaled, and so on. The effect itself can be changed over time, but Xara will not automatically 'tween frame changes and the animation might look a little choppy. Soft shadows and bevels will be written out as bitmaps.

✉ 3D extruded shapes can be written to a Flash file, but you have to hand-animate frames; Xara will not perform tweening on this sort of object. The good news is that if you're into 3D animation, Xara 3D is available for less than $30. It accepts shapes you've designed with Xara Xtreme, and Xara 3D does indeed export complex 3D animations flawlessly to Flash file format.

The Animation Jump-Start Tutorial

This chapter discusses some very entertaining animation examples. For the moment, it's a good preparation to simply create your first animation to get your bearings within an animation page (which is not the same as a default XAR document) and discover which control bars and galleries do what.

Open Billiards.xar; the file has been a little pre-processed for you. The big idea in this chapter is to learn how to animate, so the drawings have been done for you. Therefore, because Set Design and Central Casting are tucked away, you'll just learn to be the Director. Let's suppose you opened Xara today and clicked the New Animation icon, and then did this Billiards.xar drawing. And you want the ball to bounce off the cushions and finally sink in the corner pocket. Here's what you do:

1. Open the Frame Gallery. By default, you have the first frame already entered, and its default frame duration is 0.5 seconds. This might seem like a long time for this frame to play, but bear in mind that Xara will perform tweening on the 5 ball wherever you move it in the drawing. So you can use this duration and make a big, dramatic move in Frame 2.

2. Open the Name Gallery from the Galleries Control bar. The rule is if you don't name an object (or group of objects), Xara can't perform the tweening—it can't reference an unnamed object for future frames.

3. All the shapes in this composition have been named for you. If you had created this XAR file from scratch (a billiards term), you select the 5 ball group of shapes with the Selector Tool. On the Name Gallery, click New. In the Names dialog box, type a name for the 5 ball (**5 ball** is good), and then click Add. With the Names box still open, you click the shadow object and type **0.5 ball shadow** in the Apply Name field; the dialog box resets

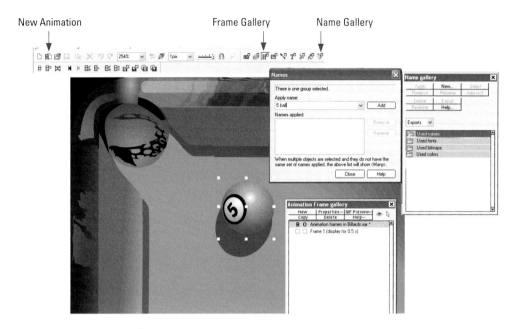

FIGURE 10-1 After you've drawn and named objects that need to be tweened, you're ready to animate the scene.

when a new shape is selected. Click Add, and then close the box. You have your actors named and Xara can now tween movements and other transformations. You don't need to name the pool table because it doesn't animate in this film. Figure 10-1 shows the action of naming the ball and shows you where the galleries are.

4. On the Animation Frame Gallery, click Copy. Doing this makes a duplicate of the content and positions in Frame 1. By default, the same duration is entered for Frame 2.

5. With the Selector Tool, click on the 5 ball to select it and SHIFT-click the shadow to add to the selection. Move the 5 ball and shadow to the top center of the cushion. SHIFT-click the shadow to deselect the shadow object.

6. Click on the 5 ball while it's selected to enter Rotate/Skew mode. Rotate the ball about 150 degrees clockwise (alternately, you can type **–150** in the Angle Of Selection field on the Infobar and press ENTER). Here's another of this book's Big Time Tricks: While rotating—the shadow was deliberately *not* grouped with

the ball shapes—if you rotated all the shapes as a group, the shadow would rotate, and shouldn't.

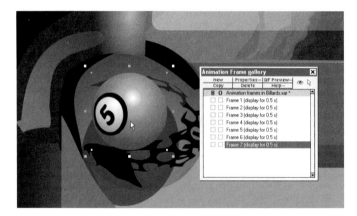

7. Click Copy on the Frame Gallery, and then repeat steps 5 and 6 to move the ball and shadow to a new location and rotate the ball only. Do this about five times or until the amusement wears thin. Because this will become a Flash vector movie, the saved Flash file size has little bearing on how many frames are in the animation.

8. Click Copy and then move the ball to the corner pocket. Move the shadow, too; it's time to conclude the animation.

9. Click Copy. SHIFT-click the ball and the shadow. Hold SHIFT and drag a corner selection handle toward the center of the selections until the Infobar reports that the group is about 70% of its original size; then release.

10. Click Copy. Move the selected group up and left until they disappear behind the cushion and wood railing. A lot of the magic you'll soon see is due to careful planning of object order on the page—the railing is a top object, above the ball on the page, so it's a convenient way to make the ball disappear.

It's time to preview the animation and, if it looks good, export it to Flash file format.

1. Click the Preview Flash Animation In Browser button on the Infobar.

2. Your default web browser is called, it pops up, and you can see the animation. This file is being played

locally from a temp folder on your system; no Internet connection is required to preview Flash files. Close the browser now.

3. Let's assume the animation looks great. Click the Export Animated Flash button on the Infobar. Choose a folder for your animation's destination and click Save; in a moment, Xara writes an unbelievable 20K (or smaller) animation that can be scaled to full-screen size and still play back smoothly. A dialog box may appear, offering instruction on how to use the file in web pages; you can close the box or click Help to learn more.

 If your browser plays back Flash animations, the chances are 90% that you also have a desktop Flash Player installed. If a SWF file is represented by a white page icon with a big *F* in the center, you're all set to play a Flash file at any time. Double-click the icon and Adobe Flash Player appears and plays the file.

 When you export Flash animations that contain imported bitmaps, the Options button when you export does not change the JPEG quality of any images. The JPEG quality slider is for adding compression to Xara effects such as bevels and soft shadows. If you need smaller JPEG images in your animations, you export and then import the copy.

Making a GIF Web Emoticon

Emoticons are a method members on web forums use to emphasize a comment; it's hard to tell whether someone is being serious or sarcastic when a written statement is ambiguous. Animated emoticons are more fun than still images, andyou only need to produce a limited number of frames.

Open Emoticon.xar in Xara now. The GIF file in the zip archive you unpacked is the finished animation—the Xara file has a single frame with an emoticon representing a stunned expression.

GIF animations are written to file as bitmaps, so you are not constrained in any way by the use of gradients, fills, or fancy outlines. One thing, however, to bear in mind when making emoticons is the size. Depending on your forum software, emoticons should be no more than 42 pixels on a side. Therefore, as you design an emoticon, periodically zoom out to 100% viewing resolution to see what your audience will see at actual size. One pitfall in icon and emoticon design is that the ambitious designer puts too much detail into the art or uses line widths that just won't resolve when the vector art is translated to bitmap format.

Let's tackle an emoticon now that spins its eyes and appears to be saying "Oh, wow!"

1. Open emoticon.xar, press CTRL-A to select all, and then click the Zoom To Drawing icon on the Standard Bar for a good look at what you need to animate. Press ESC to deselect.

2. Open the Animation Frame Gallery and make sure the duration of the first frame is set to 0.2 seconds on the Frame tab in the Animation Properties dialog box. Usually 0.1 or 0.2 seconds is good for GIF animations, taking into account the Internet connection speed of most users and the size of the GIF file. This duration basically plays frames in real time with no pause. If you need to add a pause to a specific GIF animation, anywhere from 0.5 seconds to 2 seconds works. Anything longer and you bore your audience. GIF animations are 100% bitmaps; therefore, tweening of vectors isn't used, so you don't need to name objects.

3. To begin, this emoticon needs a transparent background—everywhere outside the emoticon should allow the forum's default page color to show through. Click the Properties button on the Animation Frame Gallery, and then click on the GIF Options tab.

4. Check the Make Background Transparent box if it's not already checked; the non-transparent areas of the emoticon will blend to the page color.

5. Set the Number Of Colors In Palette to 32 and then click the Preview Frame button on the Infobar. You do this to save on exported file size. The GIF file format is capable of 256 maximum unique colors. This emoticon doesn't contain nearly this many colors, and 32 is a guess based on experience. If the frame preview looks good, 32 was the lucky number. For tiny emoticons, anywhere between 18 and 128 unique colors in its palette usually works. Every frame is a new bitmap in GIF animations so they add up in saved file size; limiting the palette to exclude unnecessary colors is a wise first step. Click OK to close Animation Properties.

Preview Frame

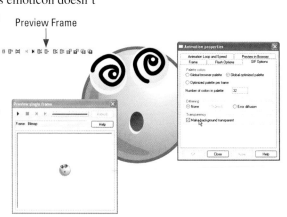

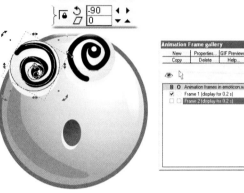

6. Click the Copy button on the Animation Frame Gallery. The eyes need rotating; this will be a four-step animation, so 90 degrees clockwise for Frames 2, 3, and 4 will return the degree of rotation to Frame 1. Click one eye, type **–90** in the rotation (Angle Of Selection) field on the Infobar, and then press ENTER. Do the same with the other eye.

7. Select the fellow's mouth and make it slightly larger by holding SHIFT while you drag a corner handle (SHIFT keeps the object's position centered). Then round it more by holding SHIFT and dragging outward on a middle bounds handle.

8. Click Copy. Rotate each eye by –90 degrees (clockwise), and then hold down the SHIFT key to increase the fellow's mouth to animate the unspoken word "Wow!"

9. Click the Frame 2 title on the Frame Gallery and then click Copy. Although the mouth expression is correct and will cycle back to Frame 1 smoothly, the eyes need rotating to bring the spirals back full-circle. Rotate them by –90 degrees each (clockwise).

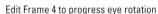

Edit Frame 4 to progress eye rotation

10. Click the Export Animated GIF button. The Options button in the Export Animated GIF box is your "last chance" to redefine the palette options, the length of the animation loops, and other options you have in the Preferences box accessed from the Animation Frame Gallery. If you're game, choose a destination folder and then click Save.

Manually Keying a Flash Animation

Here's where you pull out all the stops and make a visually rich drawing that moves through time. Actually, you won't be doing any drawing, but by following these steps you'll learn how to do just about anything with a drawing of your own and then set keys yourself. When you copy frames that are of a duration of 0.2 seconds, the animation is a little coarse but of acceptable quality for the Web. What you lose by adding complex gradients and transparency to an animation is Xara's help in tweening frames, which speeds up work and keeps it smooth. But you might find this loss offset by the capability to perform just about any edits, using any type of fill, in your artwork.

Load Pencil countdown.xar; the SWF file in the zip archive you unpacked is the completed tutorial.

What you are going to do is have the cartoon pencil come into frame, write "321," and then exit. You accomplish this by progressively revealing the numbers by using a gradient transparency. Figure 10-2 shows the setup; you can see the transparency control handles on the number 3, and outlines have been drawn in this figure to show you the two other, completely hidden numbers.

The pencil is a group of objects and the pencil's shadow is one shape. This was done for the same reason as the separate 5-ball shadow in the earlier tutorial: you rotate the pencil as you move it, while keeping the shadow from rotating all over the place. You'll also see a creative reason why the pencil is cartoonishly bent—this is an old animator's trick. If you keep the frame transitions fast and rotate the pencil occasionally, the pencil takes on more of a perceived cartoonishness than what you actually animate—it will look soft and almost floppy.

Here's how to animate the scene by hand:

FIGURE 10-2 Hide Flash elements by using transparency you can diminish over time to make a fade-in.

Gradient positioned so entire character is transparent

Linear gradient, Mix type

1. With the Animation Frame Gallery open, click Copy. The second frame contains the same drawings, and the playtime is the same 0.2 seconds. None of the objects are named, because Xara's tweening power isn't called on in this example.

2. Zoom out as necessary and, with the Selector Tool, SHIFT-click the pencil and the shadow. Drag the Set View Quality slider all the way to the left so you can see the outlines of the shapes. Drag the selected two shapes to the beginning of the 3, the top left.

3. Click Copy. Move the pencil and its shadow to the top right of the 3, select the 3's outline, and then go back to High Quality view—drag the Quality slider all the way to the right.

4. Choose the Transparency Tool, and then drag the entire gradient line (both control points) to the right until the opaque part of top of the 3 meets the pencil point.

5. Click Copy to create the next frame. Select the pencil and shadow. Lower the view quality setting on the Standard Bar to aid positioning as needed. Move the pencil and its shadow, and then repeat step 4 to extend the transparency until the 3 stroke meets the pencil point. Finish the 3 using 2 or 3 more frames; consider rotating the pencil once in a while, as you would do if you were drawing a large *3* on a physical sheet of paper. You'll want to put the transformation center of the pencil at its point; you don't want the pencil rotating from its center but instead from its fulcrum, the graphite that meets the paper in the drawing.

6. After you've dragged the start and end transparency control points on the 3 until it's completely opaque, move on to making the pencil "draw" the number *2*. The steps and technique are the same as in steps 2–5.

7. Perform the same steps to reveal the 1; don't forget that after you edit a frame, you *must* click Copy on the Animation Frame Gallery.

8. Click Copy once all three numbers have been "drawn," and then add two more frames to move the pencil out of frame, stage left (your right).

9. Preview the animation, and then export it to Flash file format. And pat yourself on the back for doing something that breaks the animation rules but works, nonetheless.

Gradient directions

An After-Class Special

You are not obliged to do anything with the Judy JumpRope. xar file, but if you think you're going to get seriously into animation, this is what's called a *cycle* animation, very much like the emoticon example. The actions in the last frame are one frame short of completing the beginning, so it loops perfectly.

This ZIP file includes a few other animation projects and the completed Flash animations; after you contemplate for a few moments what can be done with Xara's animation engine, you'll find yourself as hooked on it as on that fresh-baked bread they serve at restaurants so you can't finish your meal.

This completed animation was built by hand-animating the first four frames, as shown in Figure 10-3. The little cartoon girl's head and body were moved and scaled just a little between Frames 1 and 4. Each frame is a copy of the previous one, and the only things stopping Xara from tweening this animation are the legs and the rope; their paths change and path alterations cannot be tweened. Because auto-tweening was out of the question, this made using Pressure Profile outlines for most of the body possible; they were converted to shapes (CTRL-SHIFT-S or Arrange | Convert to Editable Shapes) and thus made legit to use in a Flash animation.

Frame 3 was copied by using the Copy button on the Animation Frame Gallery, and finally Frame 2 was copied to the last position in the collection of frames. It would be a good practice exercise on your own to delete all but the first frame in this file and then hand-key it to create the animation.

FIGURE 10-3 An example of how 6 drawings—two of them duplicates—can make up an *animation cycle.*

When you work on an animation document, the Infobar provides you with context-sensitive options. However, most of these options are also available on the Animation Frame Gallery. Except for export options and the capability to review frames sequentially, you have everything you need on the Animation Frame Gallery for editing between frames. A good idea is to have the Animation Frame and Name Galleries open onscreen at all times while you animate.

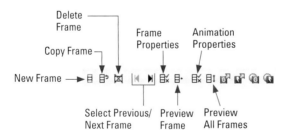

11

Building Interactive Web Pages

For the artist and designer, even with little or no HTML coding experience, you can use Xara Xtreme 5 to build a visually rich website, almost effortlessly. Xtreme has developed a different approach to website building as you'll learn in this chapter; it's *object-oriented*, there is very little code to fuss with and break, and the creation process is only marginally more involved than drawing your page design in Xara and then exporting it. You can take existing documents you've created in Xara, such as newsletters or flyers, and export them as web pages. Xara writes out your work in XHTML and CSS-compliant format that validates as correct using any of the validation services. You can even use Xara to upload your completed website to the Web.

 Download and extract the contents of Chapter11.zip, which contains everything you need to work through this chapter's tutorial steps. Put all the files in a new folder you create, and for this chapter's tutorials, it might be best to name the folder *BLS website* for future reference.

What Do You Want to Broadcast Today?

Because the Web is so diverse today, Xara accommodates several of the common needs to communicate visually, with many avenues of approach:

- **Build an entire site**   You can use all of Xara's design and text tools to create your own layout, rollover buttons, text panels, headers, and banners. You can sprinkle a few of Xara's pre-built page elements into your composition if you like. And adding YouTube videos, games, RSS feeds, and web widgets and gadgets to your pages is also as simple as copying and pasting.

- **Export existing Xara documents as web page(s)**   You can take any document you've created for print, and with a nip and tuck here and there, turn it into a fully-functioning web page, complete with navigation from page to page.

- **Create web graphics** You can create web-ready graphics, buttons, banners, and other elements to be used with blogs such as WordPress and Blogger, social networking sites such as Facebook, and websites built with conventional, code-based, HTML editors such as CoffeeCup HTML Editor and Adobe Dreamweaver.

- **Customize an existing template** Xara comes with a full complement of professionally designed templates that you can customize by changing the color scheme and replacing the stock photos, illustrations, and text with your own.

Creating a Website from Scratch

You'll learn in this section how to create a website for a band. All you need is an example band: *Bang Shang A Lang*, a real pub group headquartered in Sydney, Australia, have graciously allowed us to use their name, photos, and other online content in this example. The website you'll create needs to have an unconventional look and feel to reflect the informal character of The Bangers, yet requires easy audience navigation. Xara Xtreme's unique design-centric web creation tools are well suited for this task.

Setting Up the Workspace for Web Creation

The monitor sizes and screen resolutions users run are increasing yearly. As of 2008, http://3schools.com reported that 86% of web users are using a screen resolution of 1024 × 768 pixels or larger. To keep ahead of the curve, you begin by defining a page for The Bangers' website accordingly. You do *not*, however, set the width of your web pages to 1024px or greater. Browser elements such as toolbars and scroll bars take up screen space, and audiences don't always navigate with a maximized window. Xara offers a preset for a 955px XGA wide page, a good default size for a web page, which you'll use in the steps to follow:

1. Choose the 955 Pix Web Page (XGA) template from the File | New menu. In your own work, you can use the Paper section of the Page Size tab in Options (CRTL-SHIFT-O) to set a custom width or height for your page. For Bang Shang A Lang's site, stick to this default template size.

Advanced Website
docked below Toolbar

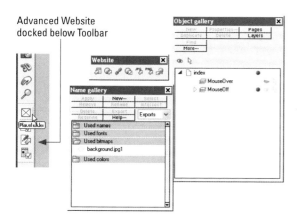

2. Choose Window | Control Bars to display the Control Bars dialog box. Check the Website and Advanced Website check boxes to open those Control Bars if they are not already open.

3. Click to open the Object Gallery and the Name Gallery. You will be using these galleries a lot; they should be open and handy. By default, these Control Bars dock above the Standard Bar, but you can hold ALT and then drag the bars to dock beneath the Toolbar for the sake of convenience.

When you choose a Xara web page template, two named layers—*MouseOver* and *MouseOff*—are automatically created for each page in the document, and the first page is automatically named index. *Don't* change the names or spelling of the layers and don't rearrange the stack order of *MouseOver* and *MouseOff*. Xara uses this naming and structure to generate Rollover buttons and you'll mess up the code Xara generates by changing these.

Xara also automatically sets the ruler unit to pixels and the ruler origin (the 0, 0 point) to the upper-left corner to conform to HTML specifications.

Build Elements and Add the Folder to the Designs Gallery

The elements that go into Bang Shang A Lang's example website should be in a folder (as recommended at the beginning of this chapter) called BLS Website; the graphics and photos for the website have been created for you.This is a *website* creation adventure—you are not expected to draw all the elements.

1. Toggle the Designs Gallery open and then click Disc Designs.

2. Locate the BSL website folder, and then double-click to open it.

3. Click Add, and click Create if greeted with a dialog box to create a new index. You now have the elements you need for the website.

Set Options Before You Begin

Press CTRL-SHIFT-O to access Options. When you import a graphic, whether in your own work or in the example content provided for you, you'll want to maintain its layer name. The Imported Layers drop-down list on the General tab should be set to Maintain Imported Layers Names; if you don't do this, organizing elements and *finding* them can ruin your website composition. Click OK to exit the Options box.

Plan a Website's Topology

Unless you intend to post a single web page—as a brochure or a Coming Soon placeholder for a future elaborate site—it's best to plan on how many pages you're going to post before adding anything to the index page, your top page.

Web pages are made up of a lot of graphical and text elements, so after you make them, you'll be wise to organize them for easy import to the web document. Bang Shang A Lang's website in this example will consist of a top page and three linking pages

- **The Tour Map**   This page features a large graphic of the world, with interactive buttons that viewers can click on to pop up a map, directions, and concert dates.

- **The Gallery**   A page that shows thumbnails of the group's members. On this page you can learn how to make thumbnails pop up to display full-size photos.

- **The Video page**   A page dedicated to music videos the boys have posted on YouTube.

When you build a website, you don't have to work linearly, designing the index and then the next page and so on. You can leave a page blank and simply name it. By doing this, you now have targets for links you create on the index page. To get you into generating HTML code Xara Xtreme-style—without taking a break for hours to draw shapes—the bare-bones content of these three pages has been provided for you. In the following steps, you'll add these three pages to your index page… so you can then get right down to layout and linking:

1. Open the Designs Gallery to the resource folder you added to it earlier.

2. Drag the Link pages.xar file into the current index page.

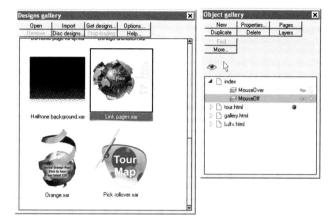

Done! Look at the Object Gallery; you'll see that you have three pages following your index page. Now you can proceed to add elements that will be featured on every page and create links from the index to the other three pages. Remember, you don't have to fill in a page to link to it from the index; the page just needs to exist in the Xara document.

Multi-page documents can have layers unique to a specific page; my2ndpage.html, for example, can have five layers, while index.html only has one. However, if you intend to have common graphics on several pages, for the sake of organization and your own sanity, it's best to keep a layer that contains common graphics and text on a layer with the same name and stacking order throughout the document.

Adding the Background

Because this template will be smaller in pixel dimensions that a lot of the audience's screen resolution, you need to specify a background color or a bitmap for the document. If nothing is coded into the HTML, the high-res audience will see white padding around the pages, which looks like My First Website.

- To set a solid background color, hold CTRL, drag a swatch from the Color Line, and then drop it onto the page. If you want a custom color, mix it up by using the Color Editor and name it by clicking the Tag button. After you add the color to the Color Line, hold CTRL, and drag it onto the page.

■ To specify a bitmap for the areas that extend beyond
the page dimensions, import a bitmap. Then on the
Bitmap Gallery, right-click over the file and choose
Set Page Background. You'll see that a new special
layer is created for you on the Object Gallery—Page
Background—the title is in blue text for easy reference
and is locked for good reason.

For BSL's website, go with a bitmap background. Because
this file is in your Designs Gallery folder, the steps are short and
simple:

1. Open the folder
on the Designs
Gallery, and then
drag the thumbnail
of background.jpg
onto the page. It's
now added to your
document.

2. Open the Bitmap
Gallery. Right-
click over
background.
jpg and then
choose Set Page
Background from
the pop-up menu.

3. Delete the bitmap
you dropped onto
the page.

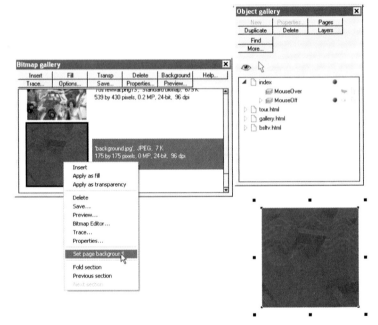

Chapters 2 and 5 show you the way to make seamless tiling bitmaps and vector graphics. There
is no sense in using a bitmap for a web page background if it doesn't tile. Full-page bitmaps
are usually too large in file size to display a web page quickly. You are best off creating the
bitmap and saving it as a JPEG at 65 to 80% Quality, at a pixel size no larger than 300 pixels at its greater
dimension. Ideally, the saved JPEG should be no more than 3 to 5K.

Repeating Elements

If you're building a website one page at a time instead of
importing the three link pages as you did in the previous section,

the page background will automatically continue on each successive page. However, because the three link pages were imported and not created in this Xara document, they do not feature the tiling background.jpg purple notes. Adding the backgrounds is easier than you might think; additionally, you'll see how to create a *panel* in the steps to follow. Web designers frequently use a panel, also called an *overlay*: a background that is laid over the background. The visual appearance is quite interesting and professional in appearance.

1. Add the background.jpg to the index page as a background. To add the purple bitmap background to *all* the pages, expand the index.html Page Background layer so you can see what's in there. Unlock the page by clicking the Lock button.

2. You can see the purple bitmap as a mini-thumbnail; click it to make it the active layer on the Object Gallery, and then choose Arrange | Repeat On All Pages.

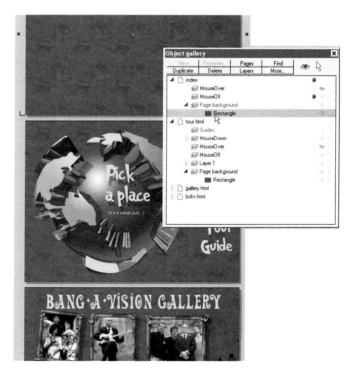

Now to add an overlay:

1. On the Object Gallery, click Layers to let Xara know your intended operation is to create a new layer, and then click New. Type a new name for this layer's title; **Panel** is fine. If necessary, drag this layer's position on the Object gallery list until it's above the Background layer but below MouseOff.

2. On the Designs Gallery, right-click over halftone background.xar, and then choose Import from the pop-up menu.

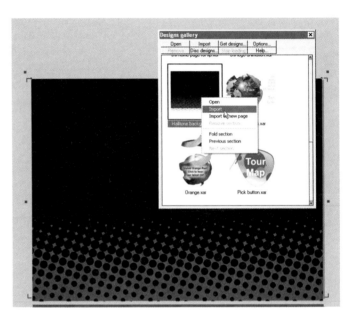

3. This halftone design will probably not land *precisely* to line up with the page, because it's not exactly the same size as the web document page. With the black halftone and purple solid rectangle group selected, type **0** in the X field on the Infobar, type **0** in the Y field, and then press ENTER. It's aligned to the page now.

4. On the Object Gallery, drag the title for the halftone graphic to the Panel layer.

5. With the halftone graphic selected, choose Arrange | Repeat On All Pages.

Repeated items are unique to each page. You can remove one from one page but keep the rest. Repeated items will dynamically update if, for example, you change some text and then use Arrange | Update Repeating Objects.

Add a Static Graphic

There's nothing special about the graphics in the Resources folder; they were drawn in Xara, and you import graphics you've drawn that were for any purpose into a web page

Repeating Objects and Updates

Repeating objects are terrific for quickly cobbling elements common to multiple pages. However, a good question is: What if I need to *change* that common element? What if you spelled "Moran Accounting Services" with two "o" s?

Under the Arrange main menu, you'll find Update A Repeating Element. With the element selected, press SHIFT-ALT-R (Arrange | Update Repeating Objects). The object updates on *all* pages where it already appears. The repeating element is added or updated on all the pages that exist at that moment. Note that when you add a new page to the Xara document, the repeating element is *not* automatically added to the new page. To add the element to the new page, you must use the Repeat On All Pages command (SHIFT-CTRL-ALT-R). The Update Repeating Objects command (SHIFT-ALT-R) only updates objects that are already in place.

To change the position or attributes of a repeating object on one or *a few* of the pages, it's best to go to each page and manually make the edit. Be aware that you will have to *redo* these changes and edits each time you update the repeating object; this command undoes any custom changes you've made.

and repeat it—or not. You don't have to have MouseOff or MouseOver as a layer label, but it helps for the sake of organization to name the layer, or the object itself, something you'll spot in a jiffy later (by using the Names Gallery).

This index page is crying for a large central identifying graphic. Guitar.xar is in the Resources folder and in the next few steps you'll add a copy to the index page:

1. On the Designs Gallery, either right-click over Guitar.xar and choose Import from the pop-up menu—or drag the thumbnail onto the page.

2. While the guitar drawing is selected, with the Selector Tool, hold SHIFT and then click on the halftone shape.

3. Press CTRL-SHIFT-L, and then in the Align Proxy box at top, click at 12 o'clock to align the guitar to the top of the page. Click Apply.

4. Because imported layers are placed at the top of the Object Gallery list, you now need to drag the imported layer down until it's beneath the MouseOff and MouseOver layers—these rollover layers cannot serve

their special purpose when objects are above them, hiding button shapes.

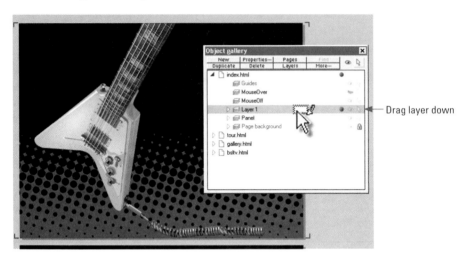

Drag layer down

 Tidiness is always important when designing anything, but if an area of a shape falls off the web page in Xara, areas outside the page are clipped when the file is written as a PNG or JPEG resource for the Web. Therefore, the halftone graphic, for example, will not extend beyond the defined limits of the web page.

GIF Animations and Web Page Placeholders

Chapter 10 shows the steps to making animations and then exporting them to GIF or Flash, or to *both* formats from the same Xara design. Pretend here that you created BSL logo animation. xar. The graphic is a headline for the top of the index page and was animated by creating moulds on each word that bulge and pucker in successive frames.

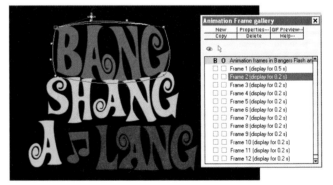

GIF and Flash animations do not reside directly within a Xara document you want to export as a website. Rather, they exist as GIF and SWF files that display on a web page because they're copied to a specific folder on the web server, and then they are called by reference from the page you work on in Xara. To declare this reference, you create a placeholder that you put on the page—a shape of the same dimensions as the animation file. Actually, you can work either of two ways when building a website with animation elements:

- Create the placeholder first, make note of its height and width, and then build the animation, using a page size of the same dimensions as the placeholder.

- Create the animation first, note its size, and then make a placeholder in the web document that matches its size.

If you create a Flash animation, the dimensions are usually of no concern if you animate shapes that are all vectors. However, when designing an animation to export as a GIF, this is a bitmap animation, and unless you scale it to meet the dimensions of the placeholder exactly, it will stretch or shrink when your audience views it, and it won't look too good.

Although Flash animations will look clean and smooth at any size in a web page and are typically smaller in file size than an equivalent GIF animation, Flash is not automatically installed on computer systems nor does it come as part of web browsers. This means that some members of your web audience won't be able to see your Flash animation until they download the plug-in for their browser from Adobe Systems. On the other hand, 99.9% of all commercial web browsers—Internet Explorer, Firefox, Chrome—play GIF animations as part of their native capability to display graphics.

Here's how to put a placeholder on the index page for the animating logo and make the association between the page and the GIF file:

1. Open the BSL logo animation.xar file as a separate document. The most convenient way to make the placeholder is to make a copy of one of the frames in the BSL logo animation.xar file so you have an idea of what is on the index page instead of guessing in the future at a solid-filled rectangle. With the animation file open, choose the Rectangle Tool, and then drag a rectangle that more or less fits over the entire page. The background in this animation is a background fill and not a shape, so Xara cannot make a copy of it.

2. Give the rectangle no fill. Then with the rectangle selected, press CTRL-SHIFT-C to make a bitmap copy. In the Create Bitmap options box, choose True Color from the Color Depth drop-down list, and then click Create.

3. Press CTRL-C to copy the bitmap, and then close the document without saving.

4. In the website document, make sure the Panel layer you created earlier is the current layer; click its title on the Object Gallery to highlight this layer if it's not.

5. Press CTRL-V to paste the bitmap into the document, and then move it to the upper right of the page.

6. With the bitmap selected, on the Advanced Website Control Bar, click the Placeholder button.

7. Choose Replace With Graphic File; then click Browse and choose Bangers logo animation.gif from the folder you are using for resources in this chapter. Figure 11-1 shows the process. Click the Open button to make the selection and then click OK to close the Web Properties box.

Placing Text

Xara can import Microsoft's Rich Text Format (RTF), so there's no problem creating flyers from an RTF file a friend typed, for example, and then converting the flyer to a web page. Also—and this is what you'll do next—you can import a text file that has all the blog information, headlines, and personnel

FIGURE 11-1 Use a placeholder in your document, and then link the placeholder to the GIF animation.

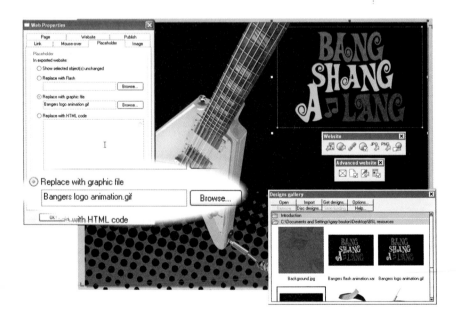

listing for Bang Shang A Lang's website. The band was kind enough to allow us to copy the text from their current website; it was pasted into WordPad, and clearly this is the fast, easy, and accurate method for adding text to a site you need to update.

Text can exist in two states on a website:

- **Editable text anyone can copy**   You are limited to certain typefaces when you use live text on a web page; Xara lists them on the Fonts drop-down list at the top of the list. The World Wide Web does not support every font you own, sadly.

- **Text that's legible but is a bitmap**   If Xara detects a noncompliant typeface in your document destined for the Web, it renders a bitmap version of the text. This means that if you want to use any typeface you've purchased and installed, it will have to display as a bitmap. The downside to this is that computer reading machines can't read such text to disabled viewers, and search engines cannot provide any details in the text for Google, Bing, and other search services.

Therefore, you can get creative and see what typefaces are compatible with your website. The following steps take you through the addition of text to the index page:

1. Hold the mouse wheel down to access the Push Tool, and then move your view to Xara's gray pasteboard area. When Xara imports the RTF text file, the text goes to the center of the window. Things will get messy, and the text is black and will be hard to find on the web page.

2. On the Object Gallery, click to select the layer the guitar is on. Press CTRL-ALT-I, and then in the Import File box, click the Files Of Type drop-down to choose Rich Text Format. Choose Banger text.rtf; click Open.

3. Choose to merge the text to the current page.

4. The text is already formatted for you in the proper font, font size, and alignment; this is one of the advantages to document collaborators using the RTF file format. However, if the text didn't have formatting, you'd highlight the desired text by using the Text Tool, and then pick a font from the drop-down list at the top of the list, the ones that fall under the heading Web Safe Fonts. Highlight the headline text, "Sydney's Premier...,"

click the white swatch on the Color Line, and then press CTRL-X to cut it to the Clipboard.

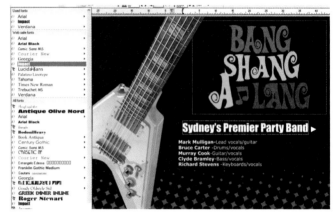

5. Click to create a text insertion point below the GIF animation placeholder, and then press CTRL-V. With the Selector Tool, reposition the text if necessary. You'll see when you preview the page that the text and graphics are positioned 99% accurately compared to your layout. HTML is tricky and nonintuitive; you might need to adjust the text occasionally so it is positioned correctly in Web Preview but looks a little off in the Xara document.

6. Perform steps 4 and 5 with the text for the personnel in the band. Make it white and place it directly below the headline. You'll add a Flash animation below it shortly.

7. Finally, the remaining text is a dynamic area of BSL's website: a blog that needs updating several times a week. Therefore, this needs to be editable text, so you must use a web-safe font. Part of the beauty of the Repel Text feature is that not only can you fit text in a casual style into a layout, but Xara also writes the text in its repelled position *to a web page*. So let's *do* this: Select the text and then cut it to the Clipboard (CTRL-X). With the Text Tool, drag a text frame at the upper left of the page, somewhat overlapping the guitar's neck. Press CTRL-V to paste the text, and then press CTRL-A to select all and apply white to the text.

8. With the Selector Tool, select the guitar, and then press CTRL-F to put it to the front of the layer.

9. Right-click over the guitar, and then choose Repel Text Under from the pop-up menu. Type **9pix** in the Extra Repel Margin field and then click Repel.

10. Select the text and move it around just a little until the line breaks look good. The future blogs can now be pasted into this text frame, overwriting last week's blog, and the text will retain its repulsiveness.

Create a Placeholder for Flash Content

Creating an internal link on this page for a Flash movie is almost exactly like linking up the GIF animation you performed earlier. Follow these steps to add a movie of the lads at the bottom right of the index page:

1. Create a placeholder rectangle that is exactly 395 pixels wide and 186 pixels high; with the Rectangle Tool, drag a rectangle of close dimensions, and then type **395** in the Infobar's W field, press TAB to move to the next field, type **186**, and then press ENTER. While you're creating a rectangle, these fields are not locked

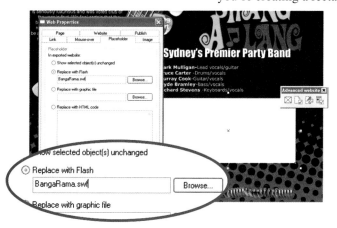

to scale proportionately. If you create a placeholder of exactly the same dimensions as the Flash file, browsers don't scale the bitmap Flash file—so it looks smooth, and they display the content a little more quickly.

2. Click the Placeholder icon on the Advanced Website Control Bar, click Replace With Flash, and click Browse. Choose BangaRama. swf, and then click Open.

As covered in Chapter 10, Xara can create SWF animations that are vector and bitmap in content. The BangaRama.swf was not created in Xara; a movie editor was used, and the SWF is a little larger in file size than is wise to put on a top page of a website. Fortunately, the Bangers don't care.

Previewing a Website

Xara Xtreme has an internal engine that displays your work as you'd see it in a web browser; you don't need an active Internet connection to regularly preview how your site is shaping up. It's a good idea to check periodically to see any potential snags before you get too deeply into the layout of the pages.

Click the Export & Preview Website button on the Web Control Bar—you're not really exporting anything yet, so don't feel reluctant.

Creating Navigation Bars and Rollover Buttons

Website navigation buttons, internal and external link buttons, can look like anything you choose, and you can create the links by using one of two methods:

- You assign a link to a shape on the page.
- You create a rectangle that has no fill and no outline around the shape and then assign a link to the rectangle.

Rollover buttons are link buttons that change appearance depending on the audience's cursor action and position. A rollover button is just a link button, and its capability to apparently change shape or color has nothing to do with how you link the button to an external or internal page. The following sections walk you through how to create a rollover button and navigation control for BSL's website, and how to use the Website Control Bar to specify the links.

Xara Resources for Web Preset Elements

The Designs Gallery and the Xara installation CD contain some sample buttons and navigation bars you can drag into your page. You can change the shape, the color, the fill, the text, and of course where they link to suit your needs. The sample buttons are two-state rollover buttons, which means that when you hover the mouse over the button, the look of the button changes, and when you move the mouse away, the button changes back to the original look.

If you purchased the downloadable version of Xtreme 5 and not the physical CD, you haven't missed out on all the templates on the CD if you have an Internet connection. Open the Designs Gallery, and then click the Get Designs button. In moments, your Designs Gallery will be populated with several folders of templates and other pre-built web elements such as Flash animation examples. You add them to a website you're building by dragging the thumbnail onto your page, and then customize the element if needed. The Xara Group continually updates new templates and other material, so even if you bought the physical CD, you'll be surprised in the future at the new goods you receive by clicking Get Designs.

Making a Three-State Rollover Button

Buttons can be any shape you want, and if you make the buttons yourself, you can make a *three*-state button:

- The default look (MouseOff)
- A new look when the mouse hovers over the button (MouseOver)
- A *third* look for when viewers click down on the button (MouseDown)

Adding a clicked view for a button is a nice usability enhancement because it helps visitors confirm that they have clicked on a link.

To make a rollover button, you need to create as many buttons as you assign states (down, over, off), but the visitor perceives only one button. You can simulate a rotating effect in response to the visitor's cursor actions, you can make a button glow, you can get really creative with rollovers. However, the buttons must overlap by at least 50% as you view them on their unique layers, or the generated HTML code won't work.

The page-link rollover buttons for BSL's index page are guitar picks, fitted to the neck of the guitar; the artwork has already been created for you to import later, so you can focus on creating the button states, not drawing shapes. The following steps show how to assign buttons of your own the proper action and how to create the link to the page visitors go to when they click on the pick:

1. Choose File | New | 640 Pix Web Page (VGA) because the page dimensions don't need to be huge to build rollover buttons. In this example, the buttons should be about 78 pixels in width and 73 pixels high. The web page preset is key to this example; it has layers named properly for the HTML code.

2. Press CTRL-SHIFT-O to open Options. Set the Nudge Size to 125pix and then press ENTER, which both applies the new value and closes the Options box.

3. Draw a guitar pick or any button shape you feel will serve the BSL index page well for linking to a tour map page (which you'll import later in this chapter).

4. With the Text Tool, set the justification to Center Justify on the Infobar, and then type **Tour**. Press ENTER to start a new line, and then type **Map**. Make the button and the text contrasting colors (a red pick with pale yellow text works with the page design well). Center the text within the button, scale it as necessary, and choose a web-safe font for the text. Arial, the Xara default typeface, is web-legal.

5. Open the Object Gallery if it's not open. You can see that the button you created is on the MouseOff layer as it should be.

6. With both objects selected (CTRL-A), press CTRL-K to clone (duplicate) both shapes, and then press the LEFT ARROW key on the keyboard to nudge the duplicates so you can see them.

7. Choose a different color for the duplicate button; consider in your own work leaving the text the same color so you don't irritate or disorient the audience. This is the button visitors will see when they hover their cursor over the button.

8. Select the duplicate button and text, and then on the Object Gallery, drag the titles for these shapes up to the MouseOver layer. Make this layer visible by clicking its closed-eye icon on the Object Gallery.

9. With the MouseOver layer selected on the Object Gallery (it should be highlighted with the black dot to the right of the title), click New. A new layer appears and its title is open for you to type in a unique name. Type **MouseDown** exactly as you see it here, in "camel case" text.

10. Select either the original button and its text, or the duplicate, and then press CTRL-K.

11. Press any ARROW key to move the button into visibility on the page. Then drag the text and button shape titles up to the MouseDown layer title on the Object Gallery.

12. Give the button on the MouseDown layer a unique color or effect such as the Shadow Tool's Glow.

13. Select and then nudge the MouseDown button and text back to precisely over the MouseOff layer's contents, and then do the same with the MouseOver layer's contents so you see only one button.

14. Select all (CTRL-A) and then choose Arrange | Apply Soft Group. You might want to commit to memory CTRL-ALT-G, the keyboard shortcut for this command. Soft grouping is a new feature in Xara that groups objects on different layers but keeps them on their original layers. Hide the MouseDown and MouseOver layers to work with a better preview of the graphic.

15. Copy the soft-grouped button to the index page of the Banger's site. Save the website document and keep it open; you can save but close the button rollover file.

You can delete the button now; it was an exercise and you have finished buttons in the Resources folder.

Assigning a Link to the Button

The Link tab of the Web Properties dialog box is the place to go to assign links to elements of your web page. The kind of link and the destination of the link are stored as part of the individual object's properties and not the document's properties. Here's how to add the pick buttons to this index page:

1. Drag the All 3 pick rollovers.xar file from the Designs Gallery onto the page.

2. Take your time and position each button. The soft groups have an additional Strings layer so the picks appear to be stuck under the strings. These shapes should guide you to the correct position of the buttons. Make sure Show Selection Bounds Handles is toggled on (on the Infobar), and keep the bounds of each pick from overlapping one another. Hotspots on the page work erratically if at all when hotspots (link areas) coincide on the page.

3. Select the Soft Grouped graphic that makes up the button; begin with the Tour Map pick.

4. Click the Link button on the Website Control Bar.

5. Click the Link To Page button, and then choose tour. html. Click Apply.

6. Link the Gallery pick to gallery.html by repeating steps 3–5.

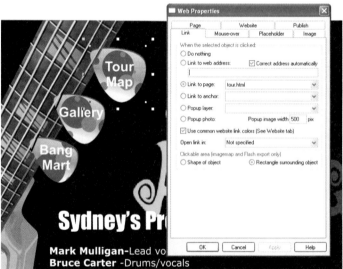

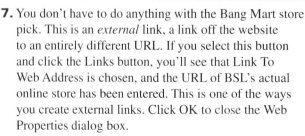

7. You don't have to do anything with the Bang Mart store pick. This is an *external* link, a link off the website to an entirely different URL. If you select this button and click the Links button, you'll see that Link To Web Address is chosen, and the URL of BSL's actual online store has been entered. This is one of the ways you create external links. Click OK to close the Web Properties dialog box.

That's it. If you choose to preview the website now, you can interact with the Rollover button. Clicking down on it will take you to the (hardly completed) Tour Map page.

 You can store link buttons in separate Xara files as long as the links specified are external. If you create internally linked buttons (by creating dummy pages in the link button file), it's very hard to import the buttons, because a new page is created with the buttons—they cannot be placed without then cutting and pasting.

External Links for Sales and Publicity

http://www.youtube.com/watch?v=89w9c2RlGxk&e
http://www.myspace.com/bangshangalangtheband
http://www.facebook.com/pages/Bang-Shang-a-Lang/21133708120

Bands and other groups frequently set up spaces on social networks, multiplying their efforts to publicize events. BSL is no exception; open social network links.xar and copy the appropriate text to the Clipboard. Then one at a time, click a graphic, click the Link button, click the Link To Web Address button, and paste the copied address into the space. Click Apply. Once you've linked all three buttons, copy them to the index page file and position them in a row below the Flash movie placeholder.

There is also a two-state button of an orange that peels itself when the visitor hovers over it. From the Designs Gallery, drag the orange.xar thumbnail onto the index page and position it below the guitar. The link to BSL's store to listen to the CD they offer (and to buy it) has already been made for this graphic. The index page is complete; it's time to move on to finishing the Tour Map page.

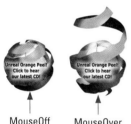

MouseOff   MouseOver

The Tour Guide Google Map Page

In the following sections you'll see how to display outside content on your website. The content comes up in-place, and visitors don't move off your web page. You'll learn how to find, copy, and place Widget code and create a Popup layer in Xara so the background of the page remains persistent.

Google Maps on your Website

Google has done extensive mapping of our world and has collected satellite photography which:

1. Should scare private citizens with good reason.

2. Can be used on a website page via a link that contains some code.

In this example, The Bangers want to provide explicit directions to where they're playing around the world. The following steps show you how to find the map, copy the code, and then have Xara display a map on the tour page in a pop-up window when visitors hover their cursor over a marked area on the layer below the map.

1. On the Object Gallery, click the tour.html page title to move your view to the map page.

2. On the Designs Gallery, drag the Green tour button.xar thumbnail into the page. In this instance, it's okay that the button imports to the top of the layer stack on the Object Gallery for the Tour page; it doesn't interfere with any other objects' links. Leave the layer order as is.

3. Position the Pick button toward the lower east of the Australia continent; accuracy obviously is not critical with this stylized globe. On the Object Gallery, open the Tour Button layer and click on the Shadow Group to make it the active object layer. With the Text Tool, type **The Unity Hotel, Balmain** on three lines at 10 to 12 points in Arial, center justified, so the text fits within the Pick button. Make the text a light yellow.

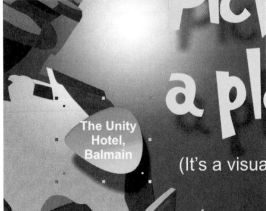

4. Learn where in the world you want to display a map. Bang Shang A Lang frequently plays at the Unity Hall Hotel, Balmain, in New South Wales. Open a web browser window and type **http://maps.google.com/**.

5. In the search field at top, type **Unity Hall, Balmain, Australia** and then press ENTER.

Google Map offers you the option of showing a conventional map, a geological survey-type map, or a satellite photo of the destination. You can use any of these on your website. Be sure to click Map, Satellite, or Terrain before clicking the Link button. Also, you can set the size of the map as displayed on your web page by clicking the Customize link text in the Link pop-up box.

6. When the map appears in the window, you'll see above it that you have a Link option; click the underscored word and a box appears where the code is listed for embedding the HTML code into a placeholder on the website you're building. Insert your cursor into the bottom of the two fields; the text is automatically highlighted. Press CTRL-C and you can close the browser now and return to the tour page.

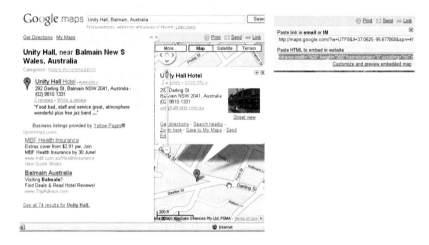

7. You won't use the code just yet; create a text frame with the Text Tool (diagonal-drag with the tool) on the page's pasteboard and then press CTRL-V.

8. On the Object Gallery, click the top layer title (for the tour.html page) to let Xara know you want to create a new layer (and not a new page); then click New.

9. The name field is open for editing. Type, *exactly*, **MouseOverPopup1**. This new layer needs to be directly above the Tour Button layer. If it isn't, move the Popup Layer up or down (as needed) in the list by dragging it until it's above the Tour Button layer.

10. Create a rectangle on this layer over the Pick button, hiding it—this is the position of the pop-up window. Although the rectangle is a placeholder for the map, you can put anything you like behind the rectangle to add an embellishment when the map pops up. You can even add text explaining what the visitor is looking at.

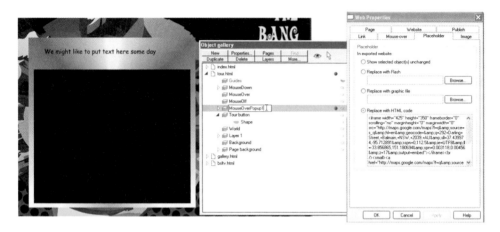

11. Select all the text on the pasteboard (CTRL-A) and copy the code (CTRL-C). Select the rectangle object you created and click the Placeholder button and then click the Replace With HTML Code option. Paste (CTRL-V) the code into the field below the Replace button. Click Apply. Keep the tabbed window open.

12. Hide the Popup Layer by clicking its eye icon on the Object Gallery. With the Selector Tool, select the pick. Click the Link tab, click the Popup Layer option, and then choose MouseOverPopup1 from the drop-down list. Click Apply and you're good to go. Click OK to close the box. Figure 11-2 shows what the preview looks like.

If you want to get into this Google Map pop-up technique on your own, add tour dates all over the world for The Bangers until they get jet lag. You know the technique now, and you can also use the MouseDownPopup1 attribute so a map doesn't pop up until the visitor actually clicks the location guitar pick button. Successive pop-up windows can be declared by adding the following number in the sequence after the last *p* in MouseOverPopup.

FIGURE 11-2 Use data and graphics from other sites, played on *your* site with a pop-up window.

Adding a Schedule Widget

The Bangers have provided the world with a tour date guide in the form of ReverbNation's Show Schedule Widget. A widget usually is driven by JavaScript, and in this example, you add a pop-up to the tour page that lists the band's schedule similarly to snagging the code from Google Map, as follows:

1. Create a Popup Layer named MouseOverPopup2—or whatever the next number in your pop-up sequence is— to display the widget above a button on the page. You can use the guitar pick; give it a text label that clearly states what hovering over the button does. Make sure the Popup Layer is directly above the layer containing the button, as you did with the Google Map pop-up.

2. Go to www.reverbnation.com/controller/widget_code/ blog_shows_widgets_popup/artist_22492.

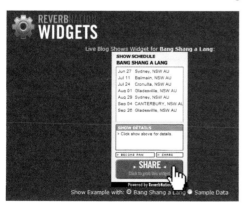

3. Click the Share button, and then click the Copy button to copy the code to the Clipboard.

4. Select the shape on the Popup Layer you'll link to the button. Click the Placeholder button on the Control Bar. Click the Replace With HTML Code button and then paste the code into the field below. Click Apply.

5. Click the Link tab in the Web Properties box. Click the Popup Layer option and then choose the MouseOverPopup (the number after your previous pop-up number) layer name, click Apply, and then treat yourself to an interactive preview.

Create a Photo Gallery

Galleries of drawing and photographs are a staple on the Web. You have at least two methods of building BSL's photo gallery that shows a thumbnail, and then a visitor's cursor action displays a larger image.

- **Use a Popup Layer** The image thumbnail on the page links to a layer containing the larger image.

- **Use a link** This takes less steps than creating a pop-up and provides a "look" for the page that's fashionable on the Web as of 9AM this morning.

You already know how to set up a Popup Layer and link to it, exactly as you did earlier with the Google Map links. The next steps show you how to use the Xara Popup Photo one-click feature in the Web Properties box and also how to work around a possibly uncomfortable reality that pop-ups do their thing with the image but do not display a *background*.

1. Press PAGEDOWN to go to the Gallery page, and then delete the halftone pattern group of shapes—the gallery is intricate enough without the fancy overlay element. From the Designs Gallery, import the Banger framed gallery pics.xar.

2. One by one, with the Selector Tool, scale each grouped object to a thumbnail size that will accommodate the addition of five pictures and the BSLTV link button at lower right on the page layout.

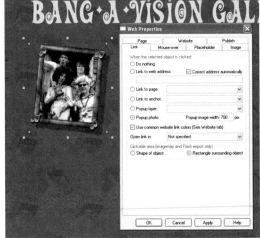

3. Click the Link button on the Control Bar, and then click the Popup Photo option. Your only option is the Popup Image Width, measured in pixels. The images are medium-sized JPEGs (the frames are vector art), so you can specify a width as great as 700 pixels by typing this value in the box. Then press Apply.

4. Here comes the not-so-good news. In the creative need to make this photo a little wacky (okay, wack*ier*), the

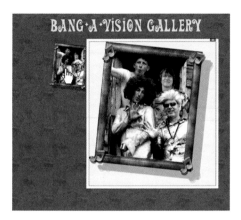

rotated frame in combination with the fact that the vector notes at the corners are protruding from a perfect rectangle forces Xara to write a rectangle around the frame. Specifically, the rectangle for the pop-up box is larger in four areas than the content and the background shows; rather, *nothing* shows in these areas. This looks unprofessional, but there is a simple way to remedy this.

5. First, create a rectangle that touches the outer corners of the grouped objects.

6. Put it behind the framed photo (CTRL-SHIFT-B), and then choose the Fill Tool.

7. On the Infobar, choose Bitmap as the Fill type and Repeating Tile from the Fill Tiling drop-down list. From the Bitmap Name drop-down list, choose the thumbnail of the background.jpg image you used to cover the background of all pages. Any bitmap you use as a fill in a Xara document can be accessed and used on a different shape. The object should have no outline.

8. Hold CTRL (to keep the scaling of the bitmap from rotating) and then drag the outer fill control handle until the pattern in the purple bitmap looks about the same size as the pattern in the background. Then drag the center fill control handle just a little at a time until the fill in the rectangle mostly aligns with the pattern background.

FIGURE 11-3 Pop-up photos need a background if the content isn't perfectly rectangular.

9. Group the framed photo and the filled rectangle, and then declare the group as the Popup Photo link on the Link tab of the Web Properties box, exactly as you did in step 3. Figure 11-3 shows the process and the resulting pop-up photo window. You can repeat the process for the remaining images on the Gallery page.

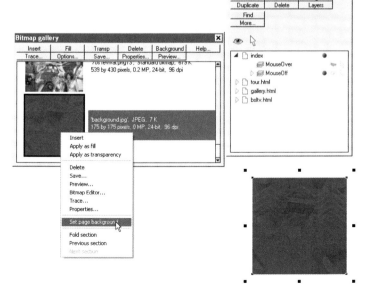

Create a Video Page

As far as the topology goes for this website, we traveled a little off the beaten path. Instead of listing the BSLTV video gallery as a button on the top page (there wasn't enough room on the guitar neck for a fourth pick), the TV cartoon drawing on the Gallery page links to the video page. This is okay for a free-form website, reflecting the band's aesthetic sensibilities. You'll offer navigation controls, demonstrated a little later in this chapter.

There's a potential problem with listing four of the Banger music videos: as played in a YouTube linked window on the page, the default size of the video windows is too large to feature four on the page. You could create Popup Layers for the videos, but extending the BSLTV page is much simpler:

1. Press CTRL-L, if needed, to display page rulers for a better reference to this procedure.

2. The next goal is to extend the bottom edge of the BSLTV page. However, the background objects will obstruct your view of the bottom edge of the page. To make the process easier, in the Objects Gallery, locate the bsltv.html page, and then turn the visibility off for the Panel and Page Background layers. You'll restore their visibility after completing this procedure. Hover your cursor near the bottom edge (zoom in if necessary).

   When the cursor turns to a two-headed arrow at the bottom edge of the page, drag the page down until you reach about 85 pixels on the vertical ruler. When this task is completed, you can toggle the Panel and Page background layer visibility back on in the Object Gallery by clicking the eye icons.

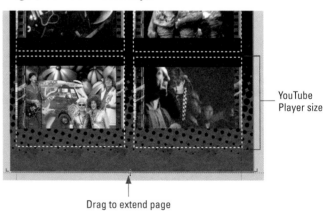

YouTube Player size

Drag to extend page

Embedding YouTube videos to play on a page requires that you find the video on YouTube, but you copy the embed code exactly as you did earlier with the Google Map code.

1. Open Video embed codes for YouTube.txt in a text editor; copy the code after the "First video" comment

line, but before the next pound sign remarked text (comments in HTML code such as this are ignored by Xara's editor and web browsers).

2. Select the video placeholder in the upper-left corner—not the photo, but the dashed yellow outline. SHIFT-click the Set 'No Color' swatch to the left of the Color Line so the placeholder is invisible. The photos will not appear on your page; they're merely a visual reference—YouTube producers determine the start screen for uploaded videos.

3. Click the Placeholder button, click the Replace With HTML Code button, insert your cursor in the text field, and then paste the Clipboard code. Click Apply.

4. Repeat steps 1–3 to create links for the placeholders for the third and fourth videos, but not the upper right.

Use a Widget to Play a Video

Many web designers add a JavaScript widget to play a video locally—the FLV movie is stored on your provider's server and a widget such as the JW Player handles the playback. The JW Player can also play MP3 files and other content, so this widget is worth a little discussion here; Xara does not play back content other than graphics, text, and GIF and Flash animations. Download the JW FLV Player. It is free for non-commercial use, and under $50 for a commercial license.

www.longtailvideo.com/players/jw-flv-player/

If you're wondering how on earth you create a movie in FLV file format, you begin with an AVI, QuickTime, or other standard movie file. FLV is a Flash video, unlike a Flash Shockwave file (SWF) that Xara Xtreme can write. NCHsoftware.com offers a converter to turn AVI, QuickTime, and WMV movies to FLV file format. It's about $30 U.S. and the trial version lets you make a few FLVs for free before it times out.

Here is how you deploy the JW FLV Player on the site you build in Xara:

1. Directions are provided for installing the JW FLV Player in the files you download from www.longtailvideo. After you've published your website (covered at the end of this chapter), you put *yt.swf, swfobject.js,* and *player-viral.swf* files in the *index_html_files* folder that contains the files for the Xara-created site. Also put the video or audio file you want to play in this folder. In this example, you'd put *metoo.flv,* the video file, and *metoo.jpg,* a preview file for the video in the folder.

2. Use the JW FLV Player Setup Wizard: www.longtailvideo.com/support/jw-player-setup-wizard?example=1. Click the Embed Parameters section and in the *source* field change /jw/embed/player.swf to **/index_html_files/player-viral.swf** or **/index_html_files/player.swf** depending on the version of the JW FLV media player you downloaded. This is the correct path if your website is installed into the root of the web server. In the Height field, enter **344**, and in the Width field, enter **425**, or any other dimensions you want.

3. Click the File Properties section of the Setup Wizard, enter the full web address from which the video (file) will load and also for the preview bitmap (image) you are using, if any. In this example, enter **http://your_website.com/index_html_files/metoo.flv** and **http://your_website.com/index_html_files/metoo.jpg**. Remember to substitute your actual website address for the *your_website* part of the address.

4. Click the Update Preview & Code button and copy the code from the Copy Your Code text box. Paste this code into a text editor such as Notepad.

In the text editor, edit the first script tag to path the swfobject.js script to your web server. Change it from:

```
<script type="text/javascript" src="http://
www.jeroenwijering.com/embed/swfobject
.js"></script>
```

to

```
<script type="text/javascript" src="http://
your_website.com/index_html_files/
swfobject.js"></script>
```

5. With the upper-right placeholder on the video page selected, open the Placeholder tab of the Web Properties box.

6. Copy the code you edited in Notepad, and then click the Replace With HTML Code option and paste the

copied code into the Replace With HTML Code field. Click Apply.

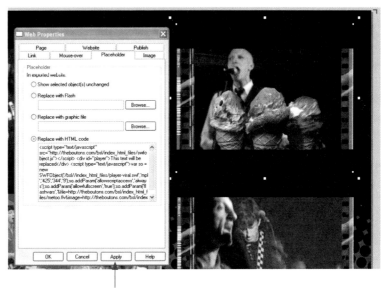

Anyway to make this look unclicked!

This might sound mind-boggling, but you really only need to edit three areas in the HTML text and copy three files to your web server. You can copy them to the folder Xara generates when you publish the site, and then there is only one folder that contains the content for your site.

Linking Pages

Forget about image slices: you can apply link areas to a single graphic with Xara Xtreme by drawing no fill and no outline rectangles, and then link the rectangles in about the same time it takes to sneeze. The pages need navigation controls so visitors can get from one page to the next easily; the following steps show you how to use the Navigation.xar file and how to hook things up:

1. Click the Gallery page on the Object Gallery to let Xara scoot you to the view of this page. Zoom into the lower-right corner, below the cartoon TV set.

2. On the Design Gallery, in the Resources folder for this website, drag Navigation.xar onto the page and position it below the arrow on the TV graphic.

3. Choose Arrange | Repeat On All Pages.

4. With the Rectangle Tool, first drag a rectangle around the compass rose in the center (the graphical device used in this example for "home"). Give it no outline width and no fill, but keep it selected or you'll lose it on the page.

5. Click the Link button on the Control Bar to open the Link tab. Click the Link To Page option, and then choose Index from the drop-down list. Click Apply.

6. Repeat steps 4 and 5 on the left- and right-pointing hands, linking them to the previous page and next page, respectively.

7. On the Control Bar, move the Set View Quality slider all the way to the left until you can easily see the rectangles you recently created around the three graphics. With the Selector Tool, SHIFT-click the three rectangles and then choose Arrange | Repeat On All Pages (to apply the links for all the pages). Return the Set View Quality slider toward the right again. You can then delete this navigation graphic from the top index page, and because the video page is longer than the other pages, you'll want to move the navigation graphic down on this page a little.

8. Finally, link the cartoon TV set to the BSLTV page.

Adding Contact Info

The Contact Us footer on many professional sites is the final touch in this website. Instead of a hypertext link, you use the Mailto protocol to get the visitor's e-mail reader to pop up. Finish the site by following these steps:

Copyright symbols are valid HTML code and the shortcut for creating a © symbol is CTRL-ALT-C.

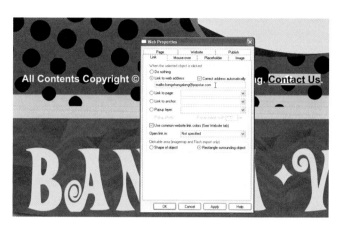

1. On the index page, at the bottom, in about 11-point Arial (in white), type **All Contents Copyright © 2009, Bang Shang A Lang. Contact Us**.

2. Highlight the words "Contact Us."

3. Open the Link tab page, click the Link To Web Address option, and then type **mailto:bangshangalang@ popstar.com** exactly as you see it—no capitalization and no spaces. Click Apply.

4. Select the text with the Selector Tool, and then choose Arrange | Repeat On All Pages. Because the web address always uses the same Mailto protocol, this linked text will remain linked on every page.

5. Go to the video page and adjust the position if needed to move the text down or up. Press CTRL-S.

Publishing or Uploading Your Site

You have two choices to upload the website now and go live.

1. You can use Xara's built-in Publish Website feature.

2. You can use a third-party standalone FTP program.

Publishing a website by using Xara's Publish feature is easy, but one or two pitfalls exist for the inexperienced web manager. Using a third-party program FTP program takes a few more steps, but offers much more control over which files are uploaded and *where* they are uploaded.

Xara's FTP publishing settings are *global* settings; they are *not* unique to each Xara file. This means that the settings apply to every page you publish from Xara Xtreme every time you publish to the Web from Xara. The Publish module was designed for personal use and makes the assumption that *you* are going to upload *your* site, not for a possible client of yours. If this is what you intend, Xara's Publish feature works as intended.

If you're going into the Websites Are Us business—and Xtreme is more than up to the task as you've seen in this chapter—a standalone FTP program is best to get your client's or friend's website onto a server and online. *FileZilla* (http:// filezilla-project.org/), for example, is a free, open-source, and easy-to-use FTP program.

To manually publish your completed website, follow these steps:

1. Click the Export Website button on the Website Control Bar.

2. Choose a target folder on your hard disk for the exported files. Use Windows' Create New Folder button in the Export File dialog box if you don't have a new folder all set up. Double-click this folder to open it and then click EXPORT.

3. The result is that you now have several HTML files in the root of the folder, and a folder that contains all the content for the site, index_html_files. If you have a third-party widget such as JW Player referenced on the website, you must copy its files to this folder or the website will generate errors in a web browser.

4. Check with your ISP to see exactly where the index_ html_files folder should go. Theboutons.com is hosting the completed example website in this chapter so you can see the finished project. We put the files in a public_html folder, and if you type **http://www.theboutons.com/bsl/** in your browser, evidently the site plays as well as Bang Shang A Lang does on a Friday night.

Remote Site: /public_html/bsl/		
Filename ∧	Filesize	Filetype
..		
index_html_files		File Folder
bsltv.html	8393	Firefox Doc...
gallery.html	7856	Firefox Doc...
index.html	11582	Firefox Doc...
tour.html	12879	Firefox Doc...

Do not manually change the names of the files or the name or location of the index_html_files folder or you will create broken links on the website. Let Xara name the files.

12

Tracing for Commerce and Fine Art

If you check out the Utilities menu in Xara, you'll find an invaluable assistant for tracing images to vector format: the Bitmap Tracer is your key to problem-solving and creating captivating artwork. This chapter leads you through the options and techniques you use in the Bitmap Tracer with several examples of speeding up your workflow, from replicating a low-quality GIF logo a client needs to update, to some pretty surreal, photorealistic artwork.

Download and extract the contents of Chapter12.zip, which contains everything you need to work through this chapter's tutorial steps.

Understanding How Auto-Tracing Works

Usually we can ignore anything "magical" a computer application does and simply appreciate the result of such magic. However, if you understand how Xara and other programs create vector-shape versions of bitmap images, you'll be better informed to make good option choices and better prepared to do a little (if any) manual editing of the results.

Figure 12-1 shows a simple bitmap graphic at left. At right is a 3D visualization of how the bitmap is interpreted to vector shapes by using Bitmap Tracer. There is an order of objects created from the bitmap visual data, and the tracing utility usually works outward-in to find edges between the various colors in the bitmap original. If an image area is an "island"—if it is completely surrounded by a different color—a discrete shape is placed above the background color. If a color area is not completely surrounded, you'll receive various shapes butted against one another.

In the sections to follow, you'll work with a number of bitmaps, all for different types of assignments; in the process you'll gain some manual skills and work *with* the Bitmap Tracer to produce complex compositions that would take days to trace entirely by hand.

 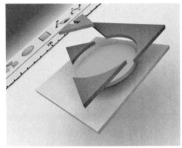

Your Options in Bitmap Tracer

If you have a bitmap graphic handy, import it to a new Xara document now, just to get a handle on the options and features in the Bitmap Tracer.

Choose Utilities | Bitmap Tracer. The illustration below shows the utility's options and features.

FIGURE 12-1 The Bitmap Tracer utility creates objects whose outlines are based on the difference in color in the original bitmap.

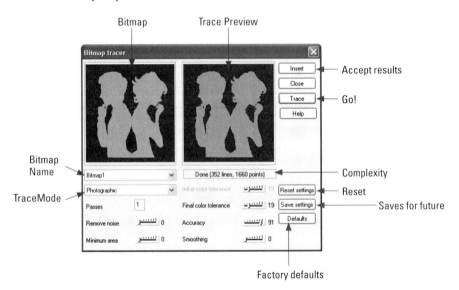

- ▨ **Original Bitmap and Trace Preview**   The main preview windows provide a side-by-side comparison of the original bitmap and what the vector version might look like; you click Trace to commence the tracing process. You are not committed to this version of the trace. If you don't approve of the rendering, change some of the options and then click Trace again. It is only when you click Insert that the vector version is placed in your document and the Bitmap Tracer box closes. These windows do not zoom or pan—the Preview always shows the entire image.

▓ **Complexity**   After you've clicked Trace, a legend just below the Trace Preview box at right tells you how many shapes will be created and how many control points are going to be generated. Expect a lot if you're tracing a photo, but if the legend tells you 900 lines (closed paths, shapes) and a bazillion control points have been calculated—for a two-color logo—rethink your settings.

▓ **Reset Settings**   This button undoes all changes in Bitmap Tracer, restoring all settings to those defined when you first opened the utility.

▓ **Save Settings**   Bitmap Tracer saves your current settings when you click this button. There are not unlimited undoes nor is there an option to save a preset. Therefore, it's a good idea to always click Save Settings before clicking Insert. Then, if you're close but not quite there with a setting for a specific bitmap, you can refine the saved setting an hour—or a week—later.

▓ **Bitmap Name**   You don't have to have a bitmap image selected on the page to have Xara trace it. In fact, you don't even have to have the bitmap onscreen; any bitmap imported to a page can be displayed in the preview and traced. All you need to do is use the drop-down list to specify which of the bitmaps you've imported should be auto-traced.

▓ **Trace Mode**   In the world of bitmaps, you have color depths. Digital photographs usually accept the Photographic tracing mode the best, although there will be exceptions, based on the quality of the bitmap image and your intended creative use for a tracing. The 256 Colors (Limited color) tracing mode is generally a good one for imported GIF images such as the logo you'll trace in the following section. The Bitmap Tracer will add vector shapes to your document in this mode, with a maximum search performed on the bitmap of 256 or fewer unique color values. The Grayscale mode ignores color in a bitmap entirely and traces objects whose colors correspond to 256 levels of black. The Monochrome trace mode is best suited for what scanner manufacturers call line art. The Bitmap Tracer assigns black or white to shapes it creates, moving color values to either black or white based on the bitmap's original brightness levels.

▓ **Passes**   Only available in Photographic mode, you can specify from 1 to 5 evaluation passes. Higher settings

produce a phenomenally large number of shapes and
processing can go slowly, but the resulting trace is often
mistaken for a photograph in richness and detail.

 If you accidentally get caught up in an overly complex trace, press ESC to stop the process.

- **Remove Noise**   This slider commands the Bitmap
  Tracer to ignore very small random pixels you probably
  don't want to trace anyway. Use this slider when auto-
  tracing heavily dithered GIFs a client or friend might
  have sent you from a web page, asking "Can you do
  something with this?" And you don't have the heart to
  ask them for a lighter.

- **Minimum Area**   Use this slider in combination with
  the Remove Noise slider. Minimum Area determines
  which fine details might be ignored in the trace, such
  as large noisy areas, grains of sand in a photo of the
  beach, fringing caused by chromatic aberration with
  inexpensive digital cameras, and so on.

- **Color Tolerance**   When you define more than one
  pass, you have the option to choose both an initial and a
  final color tolerance for the utility to evaluate similarity
  of colors in the bitmap, thus reducing or increasing the
  number of vector objects created based on the bitmap's
  colors. Always set the initial tolerance higher than the
  final color tolerance to force the tracing utility to make a
  coarse pass and then a finer one, so it is *you* who decides
  to create objects you might never use or need.

- **Accuracy**   This slider controls the fitting of the vector
  outline to the edge of contrasting colors in the original
  bitmap image. A tighter fit requires a little more system
  memory and the result shapes will have more control
  handles. Use Accuracy in combination with Smoothing—If
  you have a low-resolution bitmap and want high accuracy,
  consider increasing Smoothing to avoid auto-tracing the
  rectangular pixels themselves in the image. Accuracy has
  no impact on how tightly a corner is rendered—if you need
  sharp corners on a photo of furniture, for example, you set
  the Smoothing slider to a low value.

- **Smoothing**   This slider has an effect on accuracy,
  particularly sharp corners in the original bitmap.

Cleaning Up a Logo

Import Globe Partners.gif to a new Xara document. Let's suppose you were given this GIF logo and your client needs you to update the logo to reflect artwork of the 21st century (the choice of typefaces is pretty bush-league) and to create the graphic as vector artwork at different sizes for all sorts of display.

A cursory examination of the logo shows that significant dithering has been introduced to the shading on the Earth. This dithering has only a minor impact on the auto-trace of the Earth; however, you'll probably need to replace the colors in the bitmap before finishing the job.

Whenever you receive a low-resolution, low-quality bitmap you're asked to rework, your workflow should go like this:

1. Unless the logo features a distinctive handwritten or other custom typeface, you're usually best off discarding (not tracing) the text. Instead, recast the text portion, using the fonts you have, or charge the client to buy the same font. In this example, a variation on Novel Gothic and Bank Gothic are used; however, the client mentioned a new font so the point is moot.

If you can't discern a typeface, What The Font (http://new.myfonts.com/WhatTheFont/) is an excellent Web resource for visual identification of a typeface based on a screen-captured sample of the font in question. You press PrintScreen, paste the graphic into a Xara document, and crop the screen capture down to the text only. Then select the graphic, press CTRL-SHIFT-E to export it, and choose BMP, JPEG, or any other format MyFonts.com supports. In seconds you'll have the font, availability, and pricing at your fingertips.

2. You crop down to only the elements you need to have Bitmap Tracer auto-trace. Simple logos such as a sphere or a cube are usually best hand-traced by putting the original on a locked layer and then using the Shape Editor or Pen Tool to manually trace the shape.

3. You put shapes over areas you don't want to trace, and then make a bitmap copy of the shapes and the original bitmap for tracing. Doing this simplifies the trace procedure—you'll see how this trick works later in this chapter.

Optimizing a Copy of the Graphic for Tracing

You need to optimize and massage the original bitmap data a little to allow the Bitmap Tracer utility to do its best work. Let's prepare the graphic, the Earth, for a proper auto-trace:

1. Create a shape that surrounds the globe graphic only. The quickest way to do this is a single-click technique with the Pen Tool.

2. With both objects selected, press CTRL-3 (Arrange | Combine Shapes | Intersect Shapes). There is also a button on the Arrange Toolbar you can access from Window | Control Bars.

3. You need to edit the edge where the ligature of the *L* in "Globe" intrudes on the globe so the graphic will be traced as desired. Put a rectangle behind the cropped bitmap of the same color as the original background. Use the Eyedropper next to the Color Line to sample and then apply the original bitmap background color.

4. The image is now cropped, but the Bitmap Tracer disregards cropping (crops in Xara aren't permanent). You need to make a copy of the cropped image to make Bitmap Tracer evaluate only the pixels that represent the globe; press CTRL-SHIFT-C to make a bitmap copy of the selection.

5. In the Create Bitmap options box, choose True Color from the Color Depth drop-down list on the Palette Options tab. This step is not mandatory when you're creating a bitmap copy for tracing, but by default "True Color+Alpha" is selected, and alpha masking will cause Bitmap Tracer to produce an extra (unnecessary) background object.

6. Click the Bitmap Size tab, and then type about **280** in the DPI field to generate a bitmap copy that's about 480 pixels in height. What you are doing here is up-sampling the original image. Some loss of image quality is inevitable, but you're creating artificially enlarged details that will help guide the auto-tracing process, giving it more data (albeit fake data), and original image quality is not the goal in this preparation process. Click Create.

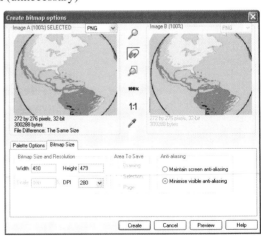

7. If you zoom way into this bitmap copy, you'll see color pixels that the Bitmap Tracer will notice but really shouldn't notice. Some color-dithered areas in the land masses and in the ocean parts should be moved in color value to the rest of the desired colors in the graphic. This is a job for one of the Live Effects that ships with

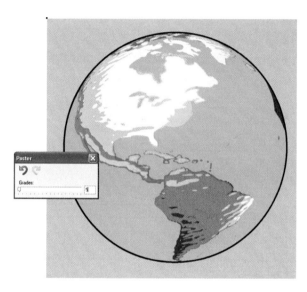

Xara Xtreme. With the bitmap copy selected, choose the Live Effect Tool—the icon with the plug on it (live effects are plug-ins)—from the Toolbar.

8. On the Infobar, click New to access the drop-down list of available filters. Choose Color Filter | Poster.

9. Drag the Grades slider down from its default of 256 maximum possible colors to 5. This action moves certain values in the globe image to more frequent ones, makes the edges well defined, and in general makes the image better suited for a very clean auto-trace. Click the Close button at the upper-right corner of the slider box.

10. By default (which you can change in Utilities | Options), Live Effects bitmaps are rendered to screen resolution (96ppi), but you want to maintain the 280ppi resolution you specified for the copy in step 6. Click in the field to the right of the Edit button on the Infobar (it should say Automatic). Type **280** in the field and then press ENTER.

11. Because this is a Live Effects object, it doesn't count as a new bitmap that Bitmap Tracer can trace, so you need to make a copy now and, in the process, reduce the unique number of colors still farther. Press CTRL-SHIFT-C, and then in the Create Bitmap Options box on the Palette Options tab, choose 256 Colors from the Color Depth drop-down list, choose the Optimized Palette, and set Dithering to None. Then on the Bitmap Size tab, make the resolution the same as the current image (280 dpi) and click Create. You can delete the original and the copy now, leaving this recent copy on the page. Save and keep the file open.

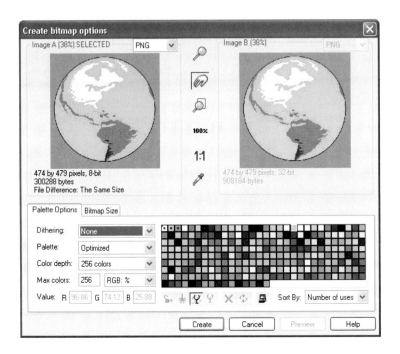

Bitmap Tracing

The tracing part of this example might seem anticlimactic after all this documentation. However, you still have some creative manual work to accomplish after the tracing, and the next steps explain what settings to use for this image and why you should choose them.

1. Choose Utilities | Bitmap Tracer.

2. Choose the image from the top drop-down list and then choose Limited Color from the Trace Mode drop-down list. The bitmap has a maximum of 256 colors, so the Limited Color option is the right choice.

3. Drag the Remove Noise slider to about 12 in this example and then click Trace to preview the proposed trace in the box at top right. You want to play with the Remove Noise amount on a case-by-case basis; images that you've enlarged can take a higher value.

4. Drag the Minimum Area slider to about 19. Then click Trace to preview. You want to watch for white gaps between objects in the preview window at right. Higher values will produce greater gaps, but a small or no value in minimum area will result in a billion trash objects you don't want traced.

5. Drag the Final Color Tolerance slider to about 25. Because this bitmap has very few colors, a fair degree of *in*tolerance causes similarly colored areas to be evaluated as identical, reducing the number of shapes created.

6. Use a value of about 434 for Accuracy. Greater Accuracy in this example will produce unwanted edges in the trace, showing the pattern of the component pixels themselves. There is a finite limit to how accurate Bitmap Tracer can do its thing with not very much visual information.

7. Drag the Smoothing slider to about 78. You will get unwanted pixel edges in the trace of a low-resolution bitmap that has been artificially blown up unless you tell this utility to smooth the outlines.

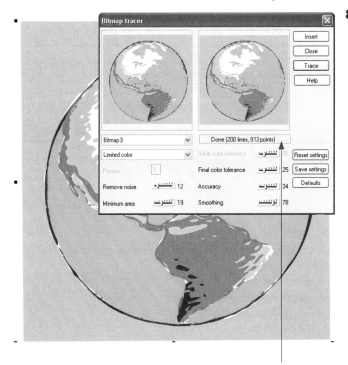

A good number of objects

8. Click the Trace button. If the preview looks good and the number of objects Bitmap Tracer proposes to generate is realistic, first click Save Settings; in case this trace doesn't work out, your current settings are close and you can backtrack later. If the utility reports that thousands of objects are going to be produced, try increasing the Remove Noise value and then the Minimum Area, and finally change the Final Color Tolerance, clicking Trace each time to see the preview and the object count. About 300 objects will be generated (most of them you'll discard as superfluous later); this is an acceptable value and few gaps appear between the objects. Click Insert and you now have the stock for the logo.

Reproducing the Logo

As mentioned in the previous section, Bitmap Tracer will generate more data than you'll need to reproduce most logos. The following steps take you through some object simplification, sifting, and refining. Use these steps in work of your own to quickly get to only the shapes you need to restore and improve on work you've copied:

1. Delete the original Bitmap copy (you no longer need it). The Tracer copy *should* already be grouped as one object—if it isn't, press CTRL-A to select all and then CTRL-G to group the selected objects.

2. With the Selector Tool, drag a corner control handle to scale the objects proportionately until the width is reported at about 280 pixels on the Infobar. Alternatively, type **280pix** in the Width field and then press ENTER.

3. Press CTRL-SHIFT-O to bring up Options. On the General page, set the Nudge Size to 300 pixels. Click Apply and then click OK.

4. Choose the Ellipse Tool. On the Infobar, click the Radius Creation button, and then drag a perfect circle that is about the same size as the globe. There's no reason to keep the scores of shapes that were traced to represent the globe's shape when a simple circle does the job.

5. With the Selector Tool, select the circle, press CTRL-B to put it to the back of all other objects on the page, and then press the LEFT ARROW on the keyboard to nudge the circle to the left of the grouped object. Use the Color Picker to fill the circle with an ocean-blue color; you'll come back to it later to add more elegant shading.

6. Select the grouped objects and press CTRL-U (Arrange | Ungroup).

7. Select one of the continents and nudge it with the LEFT ARROW key once. Do this with all the objects you want included in the finished illustration. Because the distance between the new composition and the trace is slightly greater than the width of the traced objects, you can quickly nudge only what you need out of the hundreds of shapes to a new location. Then do the obvious thing with the unwanted traced shapes.

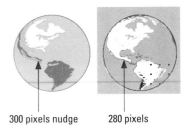

300 pixels nudge   280 pixels

As with all custom settings recommended in this book's tutorials—such as Nudge Size—don't forget to restore them for your own work.

Now that you have the globe shapes, it's time to refine a few edges, combine the shapes that should be connected as a single shape, and do a little elegant coloring. The original globe looked a little two-dimensional, and most of us no longer believe in a flat Earth.

1. It's unavoidable that certain areas traced from a bitmap that doesn't have a lot of visual information will result in some jaggy areas (representing the pixels themselves in the photo). Zoom into any problem areas first.

2. Choose the Freehand And Brush Tool. With an object selected, hover the cursor at the edge of the shape until the pencil cursor features an additional tilde symbol to the top left. This indicates that the tool will now edit instead of drawing a line. Drag from the beginning of the jaggy edge, moving inside of the shape and finishing your drag to the inside of the shape edge, where the path ceases to look so stair-steppy. This action removes and replaces this portion of the path with a smoother path. Conversely, if you want to smooth out a path area while adding to the shape, drag a segment to the outside of the shape. Dragging inside subtracts, dragging outside adds to the shape while changing the path segment itself.

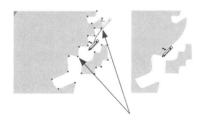

Start and finish to the inside of the shape's edge

3. If there are any shapes that *shouldn't* be shapes but instead empty areas carved out of a shape behind it (such as tiny water masses), select the top small shape, SHIFT-click the larger bottom shape, and then press CTRL-J to Join Shapes or CTRL-1 to Subtract Shapes.These operations will change the fill color in the resulting shape, but this is okay—you're not finished yet.

4. Load a copy of the original GIF image, crop it to just the globe, scale it to the same size, and set it next to your composition for sampling its colors.

5. Some areas in the new globe can be expressed as a gradient fill, smoothing the transition from a light to a dark color. Take South America, for example. Select this traced object, and then with the Fill Tool, drag from right to left.

6. Click the Start control point for the fill. Then drag the Color Picker (to the left of the Color Line) to the corresponding area in the GIF image. Click the End control point for the fill, and then use the Color Picker to sample the corresponding darker area in the GIF image.

7. Play with the exact colors to enhance them—your client approves of this action and the GIF's colors are not as strong as they could be to present a dynamic logo. Click the Start control point, and then display the Color Editor (the icon is right next to the Color Picker on the Color Line). Add saturation, decrease brightness, make the hue a little warmer. Repeat this for all the objects in your new composition.

8. Remove the outline of the back circle: with the circle selected, either choose None from the Outline Width field on the Standard Bar or SHIFT-click the Set 'No Color' box to the left of the Color Line.

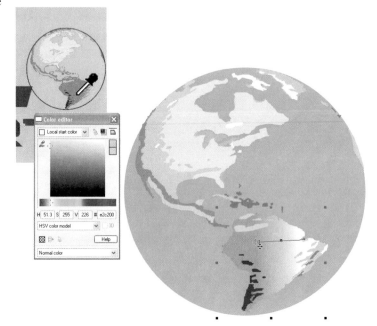

9. Let's turn the blue circle into something more illustrative now. With the Circle selected, choose the Fill Tool, choose Circular from the Fill Type drop-down list on the Infobar, and then move the Start point from the center of the circle to just over New York. Move the End point to an angle at about 4 o'clock.

10. Add transition colors to the circular fill to make the circle look like a sphere. The gradient fill control line should still be visible; double-click along the line to add two transition colors.

11. Open the Color Editor, select the newly added gradient control points one at a time, and then apply shades of blue. If the second-to-last color is deeper than the end color, you achieve a nice secondary lighting effect, making the globe look almost 3D.

To complete the logo for Mr. Globe and his partners, follow these steps:

1. Select all the globe objects and group them (CTRL-G).

2. For comparison and reference, open the Bitmap Gallery panel, press ESC so nothing is selected on the page (so you don't accidentally fill an object with a bitmap), and then drag the GIF logo thumbnail into the page. You can delete the cropped copy you still have on the page.

3. Create a rectangle for a background, and then press CTRL-B to send it to the back of the page order of objects. Put the grouped globe objects in position. Try doing some things in Xara with this logo that the original designer didn't consider. For example, give the background rectangle a linear gradient fill from dark at top to light at bottom for some drama.

4. Choose replacement fonts and add them to the composition. A very bold typeface for "GLOBE" will be in keeping with the original typeface, and you can use something such as Serpentine for the word "partners." Try adding a gradient to the word "Globe" to fancy it up.

See Chapter 8 for tips and tricks on creating effective logos, finding inexpensive typefaces, and choosing the ones that work best in a logo.

5. Add an ellipse (with the Bounds Creation button chosen on the Infobar) below the globe, fill it with black, and then drag the Feather slider on the Standard Bar to the right until the globe casts a nice soft shadow. Click the Transparency Tool and add a Flat transparency to the elipse and adjust the Transparency settings until they're visually appealing. Figure 12-2 shows a before and after, and the finished logo here is only one of scores of possible variations. Because they're vector shapes, you can arrange and rearrange elements to your liking—and your client's—in seconds with Xara.

Tracing a Photograph

If a photo features an object with sharp contrasting edges and relatively simple geometry—say, a potted plant or a candlestick (a human portrait is out of the question)—you can do some amazing stuff by auto-tracing it. The Bitmap Tracer truly excels at replicating photographs of objects, as the next sections will demonstrate. Remember: An object made of vector shapes can be scaled and distorted ad infinitum and never loses crisp edges when printed or exported as a bitmap.

FIGURE 12-2 With Xara, you can promise the world to a client. And deliver it.

Here is the concept: The Adirondack chair would be an interesting piece of geometry in a composition not once, but *several* times. The composition would be even more interesting if each chair had a unique variation on the original—a small one, a fat one, and so on. To pull this off, you need a vacant background of a lawn, provided in lawn.xar, and just a little time prepping Chair.jpg so Bitmap Tracer can easily create vectors of only the area of the bitmap you need.

 X marks the spot.xar is the finished tutorial file for your perusal.

Hand-Trace Diffuse, Unimportant Areas

The shadow the chair casts is visually important; however, you don't need to ask Bitmap Tracer to sketch it for you. There are scores of different-colored blades of grass, and you really don't need all those objects—you just need an approximation of the outline of the shadow. A key to illustrating photorealistically and at the same time quickly, is to remember that audiences don't make note of the accuracy of a shadow; they only detect something phony if a shadow isn't present but *should* be. Follow these steps to manually trace a serviceable shadow for the finished composition:

1. Import Chair.jpg to a new page.

2. Zoom into the shadow area and then choose the Freehand And Brush Tool. Set the outline width on the Standard Bar to 1 or 2 points and then SHIFT-click a contrasting color on the Color Line to set the outline color.

3. Set the Freehand Smoothing slider on the Infobar to a very low value such as 5, and then trace the shadow, making sure the outline is irregular—frequent coughing and sneezing helps here. It's not important that you match the outline of the blades of grass; just use them as a visual guide and concentrate on the shadow's shape.

4. Once you've closed the shape, move it out of the way so you can see the imported photo.

Prepping the Photo for Tracing

Although the chair photo has been cropped down to its essential geometry, an awful lot of distinctly shaded blades of grass remain, and therein lies a possible tracing problem. If you use the Limited Color setting, you won't get all the nice detail in the chair, but at the Photographic setting you'll wind up with thousands of small unwanted shapes. The solution is to create a solid mask around only the area you want Bitmap Tracer to evaluate, as follows:

1. Import Chair.jpg to a new page. Look at what the status line says about its resolution: it's 96 pixels/inch.

2. With the Pen or the Shape Editor Tool, trace a tight path around the chair, but leave some blades of grass at the base of the legs to make the chair easier to visually integrate into a new photo. Don't bother to trace in-between the gaps in the slats of wood: these areas contain muted greens and will integrate into just about any outdoorsy photograph, especially the lawn.xar document. Zoom in when necessary and use the Push Tool via the scroll wheel on your mouse by click-dragging with the wheel instead of using a scrolling motion.

3. Create a rectangle with a Flat fill (deep, rich green color, no outline) that covers the entire image, and then press CTRL-SHIFT-B to put the rectangle behind the shape you created in step 2.

4. Select both the chair shape outline and the rectangle shape. Subtract the shape from the rectangle by using the Subtract Shapes button on the Arrange menu or by pressing CTRL-2.

5. With the Selector Tool, drag a marquee around the entire image area to select the image green square and the chair and then press CTRL-SHIFT-C to make a bitmap copy of the entire composition. Save the copy to the same resolution as the original (96ppi) on the Bitmap Size tab, and do *not* save with an alpha channel—choose True Color from the Color Depth drop-down list on the Palette Options tab. Click Create to close the box and put the copy on the page.

Leave a few blades

6. Choose Utilities | Bitmap Tracer. Choose Bitmap from the first drop-down menu. Choose Photographic from the Tracer Mode drop-down list. Leave the number of passes at 1; you don't want to generate a lot of edge objects, the result of tiny color variations at the edge of the chair in the photo.

7. Drag the Remove Noise slider up to about 56: doing this helps eliminate very small blades of grass from the trace. Set Minimum Area to 22 to have the Bitmap Tracer ignore extremely small variations in the peeling wood.

8. Drag the Final Color Tolerance slider to about 12 and then click Trace. There is very little variation between similar colors in this photo; if you see any gaps in the preview image, drag the slider to a slightly lower (less tolerant) value and click Trace to preview again.

9. Set the Accuracy to 100 to trace all the detail in the chair. Then set the Smoothing to 0 (no smoothing). If the proposed objects these settings will yield is between 600 and 800 objects, go ahead and click Insert.

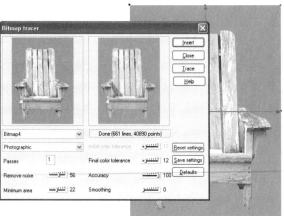

If gaps between objects prove to be a problem when you're creating a composition—if objects beneath the trace show through—try applying a small outline in a neutral color such as gray to the entire group by SHIFT-clicking a color swatch on the Color Line. You'll be surprised at how effective and easy this trick is to fill the gap between traced shapes.

Refining the Trace, Integrating Photo with Vectors

There is a trick in Xara for deleting unwanted objects in a group without ungrouping them, and you use this technique now because you *really* don't want to ungroup 600+ elegantly arranged objects that faithfully represent the photo. To remove the green from outside of the chair:

1. With the Selector Tool, CTRL-click on the green background, and then press DELETE. Because photos usually have anti-aliased edges, more than one background will be included in this group.

2. Repeat step 1 until there are no more background objects, leaving only the group of shapes that make up the chair.

3. Go get the shadow shape and put it in place below the chair. You created the chair trace last, so the previously drawn shape naturally is ordered behind the chair because objects go on a layer. Group the two shapes (press CTRL-G) for the moment.

4. Open lawn.xar from the location to which you saved it. Layer 2 is chosen by default in the document, and the photograph is on a locked layer beneath it. Press CTRL-TAB to toggle back to the chair drawing.

5. Copy the group (CTRL-C) and then press CTRL-TAB to toggle back to the lawn.xar document. Press CTRL-V to paste the group. You can save and close the trace of the chair at any time now.

6. Arrange the group so the chair is sitting on the lawn. Then press CTRL-U to ungroup the group. Because the chair is a group within the group you created, all 600+ objects are still grouped.

7. Select the shadow shape. Choose the Fill Tool and then drag to create a linear gradient from left to right (no outline). Select colors in the underlying photo of

the grass by clicking a gradient control handle and then using the Color Picker (Eyedropper) to sample a compatible color from the photo. Do this for the start and end control points for the gradient.

8. Choose the Transparency Tool. On the Infobar, set the Blending Mode to Stained Glass. Then drag from the bottom (fully opaque) to the top of the shadow shape (fully transparent), as shown on left in Figure 12-3, with the chair in position at right. It's hard to detect that the group of traced shapes isn't a bonafide part of a photo, isn't it? The trick all has to do with choosing a photo area that has crisp geometry and does not have complex shading. Group the shadow and chair again to make copies or to resize the chair if desired.

FIGURE 12-3 Stained Glass Transparency mode keeps lighter areas of a fill out of the composition, just as real-world shadows do.

Being Creative with the Freedom of Vector Traces

You probably don't need suggestions or even a tutorial to produce terrific and truly surreal compositions using the chair and this background photo. Because the chair is a vector, you can reposition, scale, flip, rotate, and apply the Mould Tool's functions to the chair, copies of the chair, you name it… and not one detail loses its focus.

Here are some suggestions anyway:

■ Make duplicates of the chair and then scale them to different sizes all over the lawn, party-style. Press CTRL-K to clone a chair, and then drag a corner control handle on the duplicate (using the Selector Tool) to proportionately scale the chair.

■ Disproportionately scale the chair. Make a fat, a skinny, even a tipsy chair by putting the chair into Rotate/Skew mode (click the group while it is selected) and then dragging a middle control handle.

■ Use the Blend Tool to blend the original with a duplicate chair. Put one chair at left and the duplicate at right and then drag with the Blend Tool from one to the other. Groups of objects can be blended

FIGURE 12-4 Buy a single piece of furniture and then create a complete dining room set by auto-tracing it.

exactly as single shapes can. Optionally, choose Arrange | Convert to Editable Shapes and then Ungroup. You now have multiple copies of the chair object to select separately and move around.

- Use the Mould Tool's Envelope Presets on the Infobar to create a version of the chair that looks plump or tapered. You're best off using the Mould Tool on only the chair and not grouped with the shadow to achieve predictable, bizarre results instead of unpredictable bizarre results.

- Consider using the Extrude Tool on a simple shape or a character you type, and then put the extruded shape in the chair. Figure 12-4 shows a number of possibilities.

Pop Art and Bitmap Tracing

Here's a quick set of steps that you can use with Bitmap Tracer to create *un*realistic tracings. For over half a century, pop artists (Andy Warhol in particular) have iconized common, everyday objects from comic strip panels to soup cans. In the twenty-first century, we still have icons: they're called *icons*. If you take a close look at a desktop icon, you'll see it's a miniature piece of artwork—an extremely limited number of pixels in an icon have to represent a complete artistic idea, and if you press PrintScreen and then paste the screen into Xara and zoom in, the structure of the color pixels becomes of more visual importance than the subject. A fly's-eye view of a small piece of artwork can become High Art when you auto-trace it and then apply some artistic touches of your own.

Sammy.png is an icon the author created so there is no legal encumbrance to using this file to trace commercially or for sport.

Follow these steps to create an accurate trace of this little icon that looks just like the icon from a distance, but close up (poster-sized) is a pixilated "super-graphic":

1. Import Sammy.png to a new page.

2. With the Selector Tool, scale the icon up until the status line tells you the bitmap is about 7 pixels per inch.

3. Press CTRL-SHIFT-C to make an enlarged copy of the image. In the Create Bitmap Options box, set the Color Depth to 256 from the drop-down list. The Dithering option should be set to None, Optimized Palette is fine.

4. Click the Bitmap Size tab. The default of 96 should be the current value; if the size reads 800 pixels or more in either Height or Width you're in good shape—click Create.

5. Choose Utilities | Bitmap Tracer. Set the Trace mode to Limited Color. Then set Remove Noise to about 80 (ignoring any trace of color variation), set the Minimum Area to 8 (the individual representations of the original pixels are quite large now), set the Final Color Tolerance to about 30 for good separation and high quality, and set the Accuracy to 100 and Smoothing to 0. Click Trace, check to see that about 800 objects will be produced, and then click Insert. You now have a seriously pixellated vector version of the icon.

If you'd like to try this with images and drawing of your own, try pressing PrintScreen while the Clipart Gallery is open in Xara, when you have a photo or drawing loaded. Xara builds terrific small thumbnails of your work.

6. Get creative and play with the hard rectangles against something such as a smooth gradient background. Delete the yellow background areas, create a rectangle, put it to back, and fill it with something cartoonish.

7. Ungroup the objects or CTRL-click on specific objects to rotate a few shapes. The audience will be a little startled to view what appears to be an enlarged bitmap icon with "rotated" pixels in it. Add drop shadows by using the Shadow Tool, making them a few pixels larger or smaller than the original.

You can examine get your head together.xar, the completed tutorial file. You can also name the file something more inspired!

13

Changing and Creating Photographic Elements

Like all content creators, designers choose the right tool for the right job. Naturally, one would think that to retouch an image, you need an image editor. But the correct answer is: Nope. Not always. Because Xara Xtreme handles bitmaps with the flexibility of vector shapes, and with Xara's precision and antialiasing, you can retouch even significant photo areas so the edits are photographically undetectable.

This chapter shows you how to replace a label on an image of a product and how to actually *create* a storefront sign in 3D. You'll soon see that some of the techniques the Xara GrandMasters use to create breathtaking photorealistic artwork can also be applied to photos—it's all about magic and hiding your work in plain view.

Replacing Signage

Signage loosely describes any identifying graphic, be it an outdoor billboard or the identifying graphic on packaging. These days, everything from automobiles (from surviving manufacturers) to canned goods are prototyped before an actual product can be manufactured and photographed. This means a designer is occasionally asked to *mock up* a product so it can be photographed. But you'll soon see that a less time-consuming alternative—one that doesn't require a glue gun—is to create the prototype picture in Xara Xtreme.

 Download and extract the contents of Chapter13.zip, which contains everything you need to work through this chapter's tutorial steps. Install the typefaces in this zip archive before working through the tutorials.

Chicken Soup.xar is a perfect example of food that looks appetizing in the bowl but whose appeal is totally offset by the packaging. Fortunately, this file has the beginning of a much better label here. It will be your charge to finish the label, distort it so it has the same curve and perspective as the generic label, and suggest lighting so the new label fits *into* the scene, not on top of it.

Finding a Font for a Logo

Although Chapter 8 is packed with creative steps for designing logos, this can label can be handsomely cobbled by simply using good taste in your choice of a few fonts. The Xara installation disk has scores of nice fonts, all arranged by category, and if you chose to install them when you installed Xara, you can quickly review and install a font from within Xara.

If you chose a custom Xara install, you can go back to the install disk and copy the typefaces to any hard disk folder you like, or reinstall Xara to include the Install Fonts option. To manually install a typeface, you drag its icon into the Fonts folder in Windows Control Panel—the typeface is then immediately available in every program that uses typefaces.

Let's go with the flow in this example: a certain brand of soup is highly recognizable for its script logo, brilliant warm color fields, and emblem above the type of soup. Imitation is the sincerest form of flattery, so you'll flatter (but not outright plagiarize) this iconic comestible. Here's how to install and begin the soup can label design:

1. With the Chicken Soup.xar document loaded in Xara, click the Fonts Gallery icon on the Standard Bar.

2. If you purchased the physical installation CD, proceed to step 4. If you installed the downloadable copy of Xtreme, click the Get Fonts button on the Fonts Gallery when you have an active Internet connection. In a moment, Xtreme will download the installation disk's typefaces to the gallery.

3. Navigate to the Script Fonts folder, double-click it to open it, and then scroll down to Biorst Regular, a fairly uncommon script font due to its heavy weight. Double-click its title to display a confirmation box: yes, click Install—Biorst is installed to your system and ready to use in Xara.

If you're running Windows Vista or Windows 7, before launching Xara, right-click its icon and choose to run the program as Administrator. Xara Xtreme itself needs Administrator permission to install a typeface to a Windows system folder. Alternatively, you can manually install typefaces in Win 7 and Vista by right-clicking a font icon, and then choosing Install from the shortcut menu.

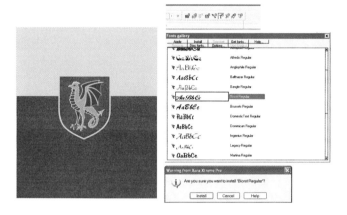

4. Choose the Text Tool, and then click an insertion point to the left and above the emblem.

5. Click on the Fonts drop-down list to make it the screen element in focus. Type the first few letters of Biorst. Typing **BIO** should bring up the typeface in the list window. This is the quick shortcut alternative to scrolling through a ponderously long installed font list. Click the name to select it in the box. Click in the Point Size box and type **60**; then press ENTER.

6. Type **Gryphon**—a fair description of the beast drawing inside the emblem. Your design should look similar to that shown in Figure 13-1.

7. Press CTRL-S to save your work up to this point; don't close the file.

Biorst was created (like most of the Xara typefaces) by FontBank, a design very similar to Elsner-Flake's Demi Bold Ballantines Script. Font names are protected by copyright, but not the design of the characters themselves. If you're looking for a bold script font for future use and don't want to constantly rely on Biorst (Ballantines), Krazy Kracks was designed by Nick Curtis. Engl(ish) Schreibschr from the Berthold Foundry is also very nice, as is Adobe's Citadel Script and Commercial Script, distributed by Bitstream, Letraset, and URW. Several popular typefaces are mastered by different foundries; your best bet is to shop for the least expensive one, because on paper and on the Web, the actual character differences are unnoticeable.

FIGURE 13-1 Use a bold but elegant typeface to denote a quality product, especially when a product isn't glamorous.

Use the Mould Tool for Customizing Text

Many good package designs integrate a graphic with the text: the Gryphon text is no exception and would look more appropriate if it wrapped around the emblem below it. There are two ways to go with text object distortion: using the Arrange | Fit Text to Curve command and using the Mould Tool. The Mould Tool's Envelope mode will provide a better graphical integration in this design, but before you use this tool, let's embellish the text a little. Default black is not an appetizing color for a food product label (hues around red are most frequently used), but a black outline around white text will do the trick, neatly providing separation from the yellow field behind it. Additionally, you'll manually add a drop shadow to the text in the steps to follow, to embellish the text and create a stronger visual association between the text and the emblem.

1. Press CTRL-K to clone the text, press CTRL-SHIFT-B to send it behind the original, and then use the DOWN ARROW key to nudge it down, about ¼ the height of the text.

2. Choose the Transparency Tool; drag the slider to about 40% on the Infobar. Done; with the Selector Tool, select the top text now.

3. To add an outline to the text without encroaching on the text as a regular outline width does, choose the Contour Tool. With the text selected, drag any of the control handles away from the shape until the Contour Width field on the Infobar reads about 2 to 2.5 pixels. Now, type **1** in the Number Of Steps field at left, and then press ENTER.

4. Click the Miter Join button to make the contour come to a point at its control points. Note that with text that has extreme curve handle angles, you're better off with round and bevel choices, to prevent the contour from overshooting at its edges.

5. By default, what your cursor is modifying is the text; the status line confirms this. You want to modify the contour now, not the text. Zoom in if necessary and click the contour shape, and then click the black color swatch on the Color Line.

6. Click the text to select it and then click White on the Color Line.

7. Press CTRL-SHIFT-S to convert the text and its contour to editable shapes. Doing this creates a group of two objects, and you can now distort the group by using the Mould Tool. Shapes with contours and bevels cannot be distorted with the Mould Tool, although blend objects and moulds can (a mould shape can be moulded a second time when in a group).

8. Select the group and the partially transparent bottom text and then choose the Mould Tool. Click the Banner Envelope button on the Infobar; although the top of the mould is wrong for this tutorial, this preset is a good quick way to get the top and bottom sides in an arc while leaving the left and right sides straight.

9. Choose the Shape Editor Tool. Click and drag the top of the envelope until it arcs a little upward, as shown in Figure 13-2. Then marquee-select the bottom two mould control points, hold CTRL (to constrain motion direction), and drag the points down about ¼ screen inches, exaggerating the curve of the text just a little more. Press CTRL-S, but don't close the document.

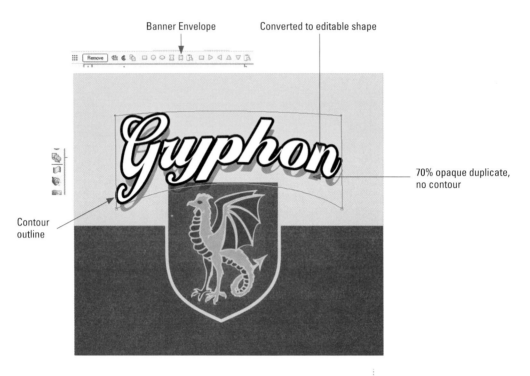

Banner Envelope

Converted to editable shape

70% opaque duplicate, no contour

Contour outline

FIGURE 13-2 Use the Mould Tool to artistically fit a group of shapes around other shapes.

Wrapping the Label Around the Can in a Photo

A few brief steps are in order to finish the label design; the phrase "Chicken Noodle" needs to be added to the design to let the customer know what type of soup is in the can. Also the word "soup" is a great clarifier when the product is on store shelves.

A nice typeface with some character is Megaton, MEGATON_.TTF (Megaton is based on the Metropolis typeface). It came with Xara in the TrueType folder and works for the word "SOUP." Type the text toward the bottom of the can (leaving space for "Chicken Noodle")—gold text with a black drop shadow helps separate the text from the red color field. Microbus, MICRO___.TTF, is based on Microgramma, and its squat characters make it easy to type "CHICKEN NOODLE" on two centered lines above "SOUP." Use white and use the CAPS LOCK key—Microbus has no lowercase characters.

When designing can labels, you can estimate the height and width by visualizing only the front *half* of a cylinder. For production, yes, you design the full wraparound, much wider than high, but for product previsualization, you only design for the height and width of the front face you see in the design.

Once you've completed the text, you need to do something seemingly redundant—you want to select the Gryphon text, which should include both moulded copies (text and shadow), and then right-click and choose Convert To Editable Shapes from the pop-up menu. Although in previous steps you'd converted the text objects to shapes, they're "special" again and need to be simplified before you apply a mould. The text shapes already have a mould on them, and applying a mould to the label design will produce unpredictable shifting of grouped elements as one mould effect contends with the other. Let's shake the mould off now and complete the dimensionalizing of this label to match the can in the picture:

1. You can group all the shapes now, and drop a copy—drag toward the soup can and then right-click before releasing the left mouse button. This gives you a spare of your label.

2. Select the copy you intend to use, and then press CTRL-SHIFT-S, or choose Convert To Editable Shapes from the right-click pop-up menu.

3. If necessary, with the Selector Tool, relocate the label so it sits approximately over the generic label in the image.

4. Choose the Mould Tool, and then click the Banner Envelope button on the Infobar.

5. Choose the Shape Editor Tool. Begin by dragging the upper-right mould corner point to the exact upper-right point of the generic label in the image.

6. Drag the upper-left mould corner to meet the upper-left corner of the generic label.

7. Drag the top mould line to shape it and move it until it matches the curve of the upper lip of the generic label. Then select, one at a time, the top two mould control points, and click and drag the control handles of these points to steer the top curve and perfect the match of the mould to the top curve of the original generic label.

Megaton
(AKA Metropolis)

Microbus
(AKA Microgramma,
Eurostyle)

Shape Editor Tool

8. Repeat steps 6 and 7 with the bottom mould control points. Because the bottom mould line arcs upward and you need it going in the opposite direction, you can click and drag the curve as you did in step 7 as a partial adjustment. Then you need to rely on the mould control handles to match the arc perfectly to the bottom lip of the original label. Figure 13-3 shows these steps nearing completion.

One of the more important points in faithfully reproducing photographic areas is that a camera tends to flatten surfaces by showing far less of the perspective sides than the front of an object or person. This is why portraits occasionally make a person look heavier than in real life, especially when flat or flash lighting is used. Therefore, the new label on the can might not look photographic. To simulate this effect—making something artistically wrong into something photorealistically right—follow these short steps:

1. Click the upper-left mould control point with the Shape Editor to reveal its control handle.

2. Drag the handle horizontally toward the control point.

3. Perform steps 1 and 2 with the upper-left mould control point handle, and then move on to the bottom control handles until all four control handles are a shorter distance from their control points, as shown in Figure 13-4. What you've done is bulge the center of the label design and compress the design at its outer edges.

Drag handles outward to bulge label at center

Lighting the Label

The perspective of the new label is fine now, but it shows none of the lighting you see on the other objects in the scene and, as such, it looks phony. This is where a shape with transparency shades the label so this design is not obvious photo-trickery. Follow these steps to shade the label and then you'll add a touch of highlight (the complement of shading) to complete the assignment.

1. Move the label until you can see the original shading on the soup label for reference.

2. In this example, it's simplest to choose the Pen Tool, click a point at the top right of the label, a point at the bottom right, and then two more points at the vertical center of the label to create a polygon shape. Fill the shape with a rich brown and apply no outline width or color.

3. With the Shape Editor Tool, drag on the top edge to convert it to a curve and then continue editing the line directly. Drag the point control handle of the top edge until it matches the curve of the label.

4. Perform step 3 on the bottom of the polygon so it matches the bottom curve of the label.

5. Choose the Transparency Tool. Drag from right to left (hold CTRL to constrain your drag to a perfectly horizontal line) to make the right side opaque, fading to transparent at left, exactly like the shading of the spoon and bowl in the scene.

6. Set the Transparency type to Stained Glass on the Infobar.

7. Click the far right transparency control point to select it. On the Infobar, drag the Transparency slider to about 80%.

8. Click the left control point and then set the slider to 100%, complete transparency.

9. Double-click three-quarters to the right on the transparency control line to create a new transparency intermediate value, sometimes called a *stop* or a *pin* on gradients. The default value of transparency is weighted between the left and right existing points, and not what you need, however. You'll create a bounce lighting effect to emphasize the curvature of the can, suggesting a little light at the right of the can, more light at the left, and then lighting falloff toward the right. Set the value by dragging the slider to about 60%.

10. Repeat step 9, double-clicking a new point to the left of the point you created in step 9 and using the same 60% value. What you've done is make a wide, consistent area of shading, tapering to transparency at left and right, as shown in Figure 13-5.

Double-click line to add
a new transparency value

FIGURE 13-5 Create intricate shading by building a linear transparency with multiple values.

A very subtle highlight running the height of the label at left completes the retouching assignment, and the steps you use are very similar to the shading steps.

1. With the Pen Tool, create a tall, narrow shape that's the height of the label and about as wide as to cover the *Gr* in "Gryphon." Use the Shape Editor Tool to curve the top and bottom edges as needed to fit the label. Fill the object with white (no outline) and then put it over the letters. Leave it selected on the page.

2. Choose the Transparency Tool. Choose the Bleach Transparency type on the Infobar, and then drag from left to right, with your drag angled to match the perspective of the label.

3. Set the right transparency control point to 100% (completely transparent) and the left to about 10%.

4. Double-click the middle of the control line to add a transparency intermediate point. Set this point to about 40%. Figure 13-6 shows the completed composition, with the transparent object duplicated at left against black so the effect is obvious in this example.

FIGURE 13-6 Bleach transparency is good for highlights, while Stained Glass works well for shadows and shading.

Just keep in mind when you're retouching over a photo that you have several clues in plain view for what a shape and its color should look like. Shadows indicate a light source in a scene that will be in the opposing direction as highlights. Make use of the Color Picker (Eyedropper) next to the Color Line also. It's much better to sample a color in a photo than to guess the right color for retouching. Colors in photos are usually duller—containing less saturation—than you imagine.

Creating Signage

Signs on commercial buildings are usually put up last, just before a store opens—sometimes done to thwart neighborhood groups from protesting a fast-food chain moving in. Regardless of why, this just-in-time sign-posting stuff is good news for the artist who serves as both a designer and prototyper, because you can easily sneak a snapshot of a building and add the store logo you designed by using Xara. The tutorials in the following sections make heavy use of Xara's Extrude Tool— you'll learn how to make a 3D sign within a scene that looks photographically correct and practically undetectable from an actual photographed sign.

Open Add signage.xar. The Object Gallery shows that the bottom layer with the photograph is locked and you have a new layer on top for the sign construction work. This is going to be both fun and educational.

The photo has been significantly tricked-up to remove signage and put autos on the street. This has no effect on the tutorial, but books almost never tell the reader when they're working on a pre-edited piece of artwork.

Sign Design and Extruding Text

In reality, you *could* put up a "painted" sign in the Add signage .xar file, but it wouldn't have the impact and drama of building a 3D extruded sign above the windows. Dimensional creations are simply the most appropriate for photographic retouching, because there are subliminal clues all over the place in most photographs that buildings and other objects have height, width, and depth. Also, a three-quarter view of a building, such as this one, is often the most flattering; when you see one- and two-plane perspectives in photographs, they don't provide viewers with as complete visual detail about the scene as when all possible sides of an object are revealed and presented.

The fonts you'll use in this adventure are knock-offs of Rundfunk and Carbaga Cursive; they do not contain the complete character set nor are they intended as replacements for these fine commercial typefaces. They simply work well in sign design, they're fresh, and investigating commercial typefaces is a good idea before you begin a paying gig.

 Windows and the Mac OS natively support OpenType fonts. To install typefaces in Windows, go to Control Panel, open the Fonts panel, and drag the files into the folder. In OS X, drag and drop the fonts into the Fonts folder in the Library folder.

Let's say the store's name is "Fresh Antiques." In the following steps you'll use Runymede, all caps and wide spacing, to create the base upon which the 3D "Fresh" lettering will rest. Let's pay attention to lighting and compatible colors for the sign.

1. Zoom into the top area of the building where one expects signage.

2. Choose the Type Tool, and then click an insertion point at the left of the area for the sign.

3. Click in the Font list on the Infobar. Type **RUN** to get Runymede in the box, and then click the name of the font in the list below the box to select it.

4. Type **ANTIQUES**. Highlight the text and increase the font size to 48 pts; then click the Increase Tracking button until the field reads about 180 (alternatively, type the number in the field and then press ENTER). Wide *tracking* (sometimes called *kerning*, though not exactly the same thing) is a novel design trick, and extruded text needs a little air between characters for legibility.

5. With the Selector Tool, scale the text larger or smaller until it just fits in the area for the sign. The text will be extruded and rotated to match the angle of the building so it's okay if the text is a little on the large side.

6. Choose a tropical pink color for the fill.

7. With the Fill Tool, drag from just outside the left of the text to a point around the Q. You do this for a lighting effect; the sun is casting from about 10 o'clock and actual extruded text on the face of the building would have a little more illumination at its left than its right.

8. Choose the Extrude Tool, and then click the Apply Extrusion button on the Infobar (the same icon design as the "3D" Extrude Tool icon) to set an initial extrusion.

9. Showtime: Although you can drag on the face of an extruded shape to change its angle of rotation, precision is required here to match the perspective of the building front. For that, you'll use the angle settings on the Infobar instead of manual adjustment. First, choose Angle 1 from the Extrusion Parameter drop-down list to the right of the 3D button on the Infobar. Angle 1 (unless a 2D shape has been rotated) controls the top-to-bottom rotation, called Y axis rotation in most 3D modeling programs. Set this to **20**—type in the value and then press ENTER or drag on the slider until your view shows just a little of the bottom facets of the lettering.

10. Choose None as the Bevel Type from the drop-down list. The fancier the text looks, the more illustrative and less photorealistic it will appear in the composition. Less is more in the art of misdirection in magic.

11. Choose Angle 2 from the drop-down list; this controls the left-to-right rotation, called X axis rotation in modeling programs. Set the Angle 2 value to about 20 so the text is facing left a little. Angle values are interdependent, and adjusting one value occasionally requires that you go back and re-tune another value.

12. Place your cursor over the side, not the face of the 3D text. When your cursor changes to a two-headed arrow (not the four-headed one that controls object rotation), you can drag to increase the depth of the extruded text.

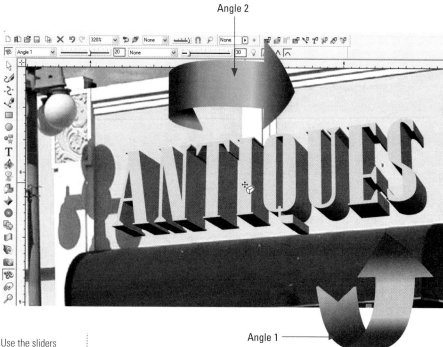

Angle 2

Angle 1

FIGURE 13-7 Use the sliders to precisely angle the text to match the camera angle in the photograph.

Use your artistic judgment as to how deep the text should look, or enter **20** in the field on the Infobar after choosing Extrude Depth from the drop-down list. See Figure 13-7; the lighting isn't perfect but the angle works very well for this previsualization. You'll work on lighting in the following section.

A quick way to rotate an 3D object along the clockwise-counterclockwise axis—the Z axis—is to simply rotate the extruded shape *as a regular object*. Use the Selector Tool in Rotate/Skew mode to rotate the extruded shape to the angle you need.

Working with Extrude's Lighting Features

Three lights are available for every 3D object you create in Xara, and the lights are unique to an extrude so you can have three different extruded objects all with different lighting setups in one document. The lighting effect can be seen on extruded objects, but the lights themselves are hidden from view. When the Extrude Tool is selecting an object, the Infobar displays a lightbulb icon—click the button to show the light icons and click the button again to toggle the icons off.

Work through the following steps to get the illumination of the 3D sign matching the lighting in the photograph as closely as possible:

1. With the 3D text selected (using the Extrude Tool), click the Show Lights button on the Infobar.

2. The position and the color (about 90% white) of Light 1 is fine for this scene. Come back to this light last and adjust the positioning only if needed. Light 3, the lavender icon, is casting down and to the left from an angle that really doesn't contribute to visible illumination on the sign, so it's okay and you can leave this light as is. However, Light 2, a dull green, is the wrong color for the pink sign on a sunny day, and it's not catching the edge of the sign to provide tone separation from the building. Click on Light 2's icon in the scene to select it.

3. Make sure that the Gloss/Matte button is toggled off. This gives the 3D extruded object a shiny appearance, and in reality, few objects have the sort of specular highlights one sees on website buttons.

4. Click the Color Editor icon at the bottom of the interface (or press CTRL-E). Drop the list down at top and choose Light 2. The Color Editor is how you set both the intensity and the color of a selected light.

5. Use the Color Picker on the Color Editor to sample a dull warm brown in the image itself. The building trim to the left of the blue awning is fine, as you can see in Figure 13-8. Now drag the light icon around a little until the pink sides of the extruded shape show some variation in color. Secondary light is common in outdoor scenes, as light bounces off objects to illuminate other objects. This scattering effect is called *diffuse* lighting; it's most visible on matte, not glossy objects, and this small artistic touch helps the scene's plausibility through adding visual detail to a digital object.

FIGURE 13-8 Use the Color Editor to change light color; drag light icons on the page to change light direction.

Gloss/Matte toggled off

Create a Sharp Outdoor Shadow

All of the shadows in the photo are crisp, unlike the drop
shadow the Shadow Tool produces by default. However, you
can easily change this. You'll have the 3D sign casting a proper
shadow on the building in no time, by following these steps:

1. With the 3D lettering selected, choose the Shadow Tool
   from the Toolbar, and then drag down and to the right on
   the face of the lettering to set the direction (the same as
   the real shadows in the photo).

2. On the Infobar, drag the Shadow Transparency slider left
   and right until the tone of the shadow looks the same as
   the actual shadows in the photograph. Anywhere from
   35 to 65% looks about right.

3. Drag the Shadow Blur almost to zero; a tenth of an
   inch is good—not perfectly sharp because nothing is
   perfectly sharp in a photo, but *about* as crisp as the real
   shadows. See Figure 13-9.

You could change the color of the shadow ever so slightly in this example to suggest that
ambient lighting from the sky is coloring the shading. You click the shadow (not the extruded
text), use the Color Picker on the Color Editor to sample a shadow color from the photo, and
then change the shadow color to a slightly darker, desaturated blue.

FIGURE 13-9 Make a quick and
photorealistic shadow with the
Shadow Tool and its options on the
Infobar.

Visually Integrating the Fake Sign

A highly trained eye will note that the bulbs on the lamppost directly to the left of the 3D text cast a shadow on the building but not on the 3D text at the moment. This is visually wrong, but easy to correct. Follow these steps to manually add the required shading on the 3D text:

1. With either the Shape Editor Tool or the Pen Tool, trace the shape of the lamp and a little of the post attached to it. Move the text to get a better view of the shadow, if necessary.

2. Here's a trick: Photographically, if the text were really in the scene, it would protrude from the building face. This means it's marginally closer to the sun casting into the scene; the shadow shape you've drawn needs to be a little higher and slightly to the right of the original shadow to be optically correct. With the Selector Tool, first move the object over the original lamp shadow and distort it as needed to approximate the necessary distortion as the shadow information already provided in the photo. Then move or nudge, using the ARROW keyboard keys, while the shape is selected.

3. Use the Pen Tool to create a new shape, tracing the straight lines of the letter *A* and just enough straight lines of the letter that are outside the shadow that still fall on the inside of the letter *A*.

4. With the Selector Tool, select both this new shape and the shadow shape. Click the Intersect Shapes button on the Toolbar (or Arrange | Combine Shapes | Intersect Shapes). This produces a shadow shape that conforms to the outer shape of the letter *A*.

5. Fill the shape with black and then choose the Transparency Tool.

6. Choose the Stained Glass Transparency Type on the Infobar, and then drag the Opacity slider left and right until the density of the shadow looks copasetic with the photo's actual shadows. Figure 13-10 has an outline around the shadow object that's purely for your reference and should not be on your own shadow.

FIGURE 13-10 Create an offset of the original shadow shape to suggest that the extruded text is extending toward the viewer.

Create a Sign by Editing a Copy of the Original

This leaves the word "Fresh" to be stacked above the word "Antiques" on the storefront. Matching the perspective will be easier than you think: You can make a duplicate of the word "ANTIQUES," un-extrude it, edit the text, recolor the text and use a different font, and then re-extrude the text. Xara remembers your last saved extrude settings, making it easy to toggle an extrude on and off for editing.

1. With the 3D "ANTIQUES" shape selected, press CTRL-K to clone it and then move it above the original.

2. With the Extrude Tool selecting the duplicate, click the 3D button on the Infobar to remove the extrude.

3. Highlight the text by using the Text Tool, and then choose Embargo Cursive from the Fonts drop-down list. Click the font name in the list below the box to apply the font to the highlighted text. While the text is still highlighted, reduce the tracking to 0.

4. Click away from the text to un-highlight it. Then click the Text Tool in the line of text so there is an I-beam there. Backspace and then type **Fresh**.

5. Choose a pale green color for the new text.

6. With the text selected, choose the Extrude Tool, and then click the 3D button on the Infobar. Your text is now in exactly the same perspective as it was before step 2.

7. Press CTRL-SHIFT-B to put the text behind the word "ANTIQUES."

8. Use the Selector Tool to move the text into position and, if necessary, scale the text to fit (design-wise) into the composition. Figure 13-11 shows the result of these steps, and the fellow in the window looks pleased with them.

Adding a Little 2D Signage

FIGURE 13-11 Edit an extruded shape by first un-extruding it.

The awning was retouched; a simple Xara feathered shape in matching blue covered the original awning signage, and the image and object were then exported to JPEG file format. However, the Fresh Antiques store looks a little too clean with a pristine awning, so the following steps show you how to put text into perspective; in 2D, no extruding this time, because the weight of extruded text would collapse the awning.

1. With the Text Tool, type **SELL** and press TAB twice to move the insertion beam over significantly. Type **BUY** and add two more tabs, and then type **SELL**… because the owner doesn't want to trade anything.

2. Highlight the text and then choose Arial from the Font drop-down list, a serviceable sign font. Make the text about 10% black so it is not glaring at the viewer. Pure white signage in photos is uncommon and looks like retouching took place; almost no colors in photos are absolute or pure.

3. Position the text so it sits roughly over the bottom part of the awning, where the viewer expects vinyl lettering to be affixed to a commercial awning.

4. Choose the Mould Tool, and then click the Default Perspective button on the Infobar.

5. SHIFT-click to select two control points at a time (first the left side and then the right side), and move the points by using either the Mould Tool or the Shape Editor Tool until the lettering appears to be slanting down toward the left of the composition. Select the top two points, hold CTRL, and drag to the right for a slight italicized effect (for better matching of the three-quarter view perspective in the scene). Finally, add a 37%

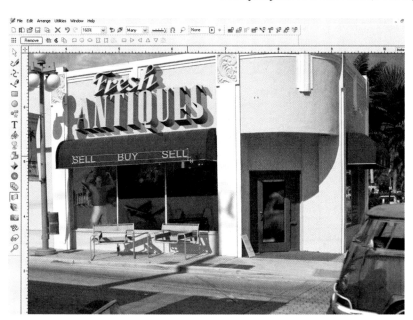

Transparency to allow the color of the awning to mix slightly with the lettering. You're done; save the file and consider exporting the composition by pressing CTRL-A to select all and then pressing CTRL-SHIFT-E to export to a bitmap file format such as JPEG or PNG so your client can see the piece as an e-mail attachment.

When you use your eyes to scope out a photo for details you need to match in Xara with signage or other editing, don't mentally jump to conclusions. Art is not the same discipline as photography, and photographs are both more complex and less detailed than illustrations. Don't add too much detail or your photo-editing will look fake. Use the Color Picker (Eyedropper) to sample colors in the photo for the shapes you add. A "boring," under-detailed Xara drawing often fits into a photographic composition better than an exciting, over-illustrated piece of work. Let your illustrations be illustrations; photographs deserve a treatment that is photographic.

GrandMaster Gallery

The following pages show the art of the **Xara GrandMaster Competition**,
which ran in *The Xara Outsider* in the spring of 2009. All entries can be viewed online at
http://outsider.xara.com/competitions/july09/winners.html
Congratulations to all; thank you for showing the power of Xara Xtreme and helping us to
celebrate the wonderful depth and variety of talent of the artists who work with Xara.

"Helix Manus"
Derek Cooper–U.K.
A designer by trade, Derek has been drawing with traditional tools for 30 years
or so and has been using a PC and Xara since Xara Studio, 1995-ish.
masque@blueyonder.co.uk

"My Beautiful Princess"
José Campoy–Mexico

Originally José wanted to become a software engineer. Today graphic design is José's passion. Initially, he began with Xara X in 2004; his first drawing was a Lamborghini Murciélago. Sometimes using it up to 13 hours a day, the artist has been known to fall asleep with the mouse in his hand.

"Moulay Ismail Mausoleum"
A doorway leading to the inner courtyard of the mausoleum of Moulay Ismail in Meknes, Morocco.
John Swann–Australia

John is a graphic designer and illustrator in Melbourne. The artist uses Xara Xtreme exclusively for magazine advertising for its speed and the mission-critical need for print-ready files.

http://groups.melbpc.org.au/~graphics/

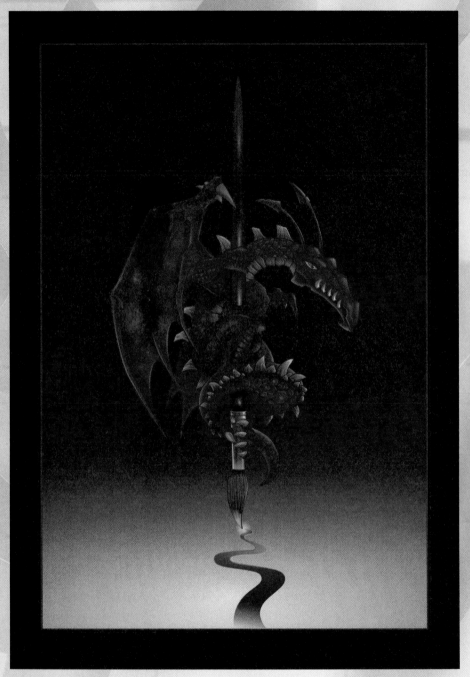

"Dragon with Brush"
Laszlo Mayer–Hungary

A professional illustrator, Laszlo has been working in this field since 1993 with traditional tools. The artist has been experimenting with digital painting since 2006 and using Xara since 2008.

"B17A"
Ragnar Kullenberg–Sweden

A technical writer and illustrator, Ragnar has used traditional tools since the 1970s and PC since the 1980s. Xara Xtreme has been the author's preferred tool since 2007.

"This way, sorry—that way (a tribute to Escher)"
Emanuel Brito–Portugal

Creative director, copywriter, and designer, Emanuel Brito has been a digital artist for over a decade.
He discovered Xara Studio in the 1990s as an offer to readers of *PC Plus Magazine*.
www.homographicus.com

"Golfist"
Derek Cooper—U.K.

Derek has become a member of the Xara GrandMasters with his *"Helix Manus"* composition. We felt our readers might like to see Derek's artistic alter ego, that of a skilled cartoonist and caricaturist. And golfist.

"Dancer"
Valery Kouleshov–Russia

A Xara GrandMaster for more than a decade, Valery is a commercial artist living near Moscow. The artist has been using Xara since 1996, when he was Grand Prize winner in the Corel World Design Contest... by using CorelXARA.

Index